Anthropology of organizations

Edited by Susan Wright

London and New York

First published 1994
by Routledge
11 New Fetter Lane, London EC4P 4EE

Simultaneously published in the USA and Canada
by Routledge
29 West 35th Street, New York, NY 10001

Transferred to Digital Printing 2002

Routledge is an imprint of the Taylor & Francis Group

Typeset in Times by LaserScript, Mitcham, Surrey
Printed and bound in Great Britain by
Antony Rowe

British Library Cataloguing in Publication Data
A catalogue record for this book is available from the British
Library

Library of Congress Cataloging in Publication Data
A catalog record for this book has been requested

ISBN 0–415–08748–1 (hbk)
ISBN 0–415–08747–3 (pbk)

Printed and bound by Antony Rowe Ltd, Eastbourne

Contents

Contributors

Cynthia Cockburn is senior research fellow in sociology at the Centre for Research in Gender, Ethnicity and Social Change, The City University, London. She is the author of several books on local government, gender and technology, and sex inequalities in youth training. The complete study from which this article is drawn is *In the Way of Women: Men's Resistance to Sex Equality in Organizations*, Macmillan Education, 1991.

Jean Collins worked in social services for ten years before embarking on a career in social anthropology. She was awarded her doctorate at the University of Sussex in 1990, after conducting research into social support systems in an English town. She is currently engaged on research into the resettlement of people from long-stay hospitals. She has contributed extensively to the community care debate and is particularly interested in the interplay of language and power.

Sandra Cullen has a PhD in social anthropology from the University of Cambridge. This investigates policy implementation and organizational culture from an ethnographic perspective, with specific reference to Job Centres and Unemployment Benefit offices. She is currently employed by the Employment Department working on personnel policy. Her research interests include anthropological perspectives on state institutions and policy formulation and implementation. She also teaches social policy for the Open University.

Donald Curtis has sustained an interest in organizational design and development since he worked in voluntary sector organizations in both Birmingham and Botswana. Most of his professional career has been based at the Development Administration Group at the University of Birmingham where he is now Director. In this setting, issues to do with the organization of government can be studied and discussed along with forms of non-governmental and informal organization.

Jeanette Edwards is the Leach/RAI Fellow at the Department of Social Anthropology, University of Manchester. She gained her PhD in social anthropology in 1990 for a thesis entitled '"Ordinary People": a study of factors affecting communication in the provision of services'. Since then she has researched first the social and cultural implications of new reproductive technologies and, second, the work of community health and social service providers with families deemed to be 'in need'. She is co-author of *Technologies of Procreation: Kinship in the Age of Assisted Conception* (Manchester University Press, 1993) and is currently working on a project within the ESCR's Management of Personal Welfare Initiative.

Deborah Kerfoot has recently completed a doctorate at UMIST, and is now lecturer in organizational behaviour in the management division of the School of Business and Economics at the University of Leeds. She also holds a visiting fellowship at the School of Management, UMIST, and is part of a research team undertaking a two-year project on the links between human resource management and quality management in financial services companies funded by an ESRC award. Her research interests and publications are primarily in the critical study of management and organization, employment practices in UK financial services, and in gender and sexuality in organizations.

David Knights is Professor of organizational analysis at the Manchester School of Management at UMIST, where he is also Director of the Financial Services Research Centre (FSRC) and Deputy Director of the Programme on Information and Communication Technology (PICT). He holds an MA and a doctorate in management from Manchester University and has published in the fields of equal opportunity, labour process, organization theory, information technology and financial services. His most recent books are *Labour Process Theory* (Macmillan, 1990); *Managing to Discriminate* (Routledge, 1990); and *Markets, Managers and Technology* (Wiley, 1994).

Christine McCourt Perring's PhD in social anthropology was a study of the closure of psychiatric hospitals and transfer of long-stay patients to community group homes. She has recently completed a Department of Health sponsored development project on residential care based at Brunel University where she continues to teach part time. Her latest publications are *The Experience of Psychiatric Hospital Closure: An Anthropological Study* (Avebury, 1993); and she co-authored with P.J. Youll *Changing Practices in Residential Care: An Evaluation of the Caring Homes Initiative* (HMSO, 1993).

David Marsden is a social anthropologist attached to the Centre for Development Studies at University College Swansea undertaking consultancy work in social development. His recent publications include a co-edited book with Peter Oakley, *The Evaluation of Social Development Projects*, published by Oxfam in 1991. His current interests are in the field of local level organizational development and the monitoring and evaluation of social development projects.

Trish Nicholson is field director in the Philippines for Voluntary Service Overseas. She is an anthropologist and worked previously for the West Sepik Provincial Development Project, Papua New Guinea. She is concerned in the Asia-Pacific region with participative and gender-fair development, project evaluation and appraisal, and human resources development. She is also involved in photo-documentation and freelance writing.

Rosemary Pringle teaches sociology and women's studies at Macquarie University in Sydney. She is the author of *Secretaries Talk: Sexuality, Power and Work* (Verso, 1989) and co-author of *Gender at Work* (Allen & Unwin, 1983). She is currently working on a comparative English/Australian study of gender and medicine, focusing on women doctors who, she feels, have been given an unnecessarily hard time by many feminists.

Michael Roper is a lecturer in the Sociology Department at the University of Essex. He is a social historian by background, but has increasingly become interested in contemporary issues concerning masculinity and emotion in organizations. He recently published *Masculinity and the British Organization Man Since 1945* (Oxford University Press, 1994), and now hopes to research the rise of management education in Britain, focusing on the application of business principles to higher education.

Susan Wright is lecturer in social anthropology at Sussex University. After studying people's relations with the state in Iran and Britain, she became involved in doing participant observation in state organizations themselves. Drawing on research on rural decision making and on community development, she was recently attached to a county council to evaluate their corporate strategy for empowerment. Her most recent publications are on organizational change for empowerment, the politics and practice of participatory development, and community arts.

Preface and acknowledgements

The starting point for this book was a series of meetings organized by Mark O'Sullivan and myself for GAPP, the Group for Anthropology in Policy and Practice. GAPP was formed in 1981 as a national organization to bridge the gap between anthropologists working inside and outside the academy; to create a network among anthropologists using their discipline in policy and practice; to make their experience available to students and to help with training students in the additional skills needed for such employment. By the late 1980s meetings and conferences were held on a number of fields, raising theoretical issues of mainstream relevance to the discipline, and of importance to practitioners. GAPP has now become part of a wider organization with the same aims called Anthropology in Action.

The meetings held in 1990 brought together anthropologists working on or in organizations in both the Third World and the West. The aim was to explore how anthropological concepts were being used by researchers and practitioners in the context of rapid organizational change. These meetings culminated in a GAPP conference held at University College Swansea in January 1991. The conference was organized by Mark O'Sullivan, David Marsden and myself, with sessions also organized by Michael Roper and Ed Young. The organizers are grateful to the Overseas Development Administration for a grant towards the conference and to the Centre for Development Studies, University College Swansea for providing financial and practical support.

Turning conference papers into a volume, when contributors are not only the usual hard-pressed academics, but contract researchers and practitioners, especially when they are fax-less in far flung places, takes time. I took overall responsibility for editing and producing the volume and am grateful for the contributors' continuing commitment and enthusiasm. Each of the three sections in the book is introduced by a specialist in the field and many thanks are due to David Marsden and Michael Roper for their contributions. In addition, Michael Roper was generous with his time and provided very helpful comments on the chapters in the section on Gender and organizational change.

In editing the volume and writing the introduction, I am very grateful for stimulating and sustaining discussions about organizational culture with Michael Roper. Earlier versions of the introduction were also read with great care by colleagues at Sussex University, Hilary Standing and Brian Street. They offered quite different but invaluable advice and I am very grateful for their support and suggestions. The Introduction also benefitted from very helpful conversations with Jennifer Platt and Liz Stanley about the early history of organization studies.

Special thanks are due to Delphine Houlton for excellent 'sub-editing' of the Introduction and to Rahnuma Ahmed for her help and efficiency in the last stages of turning chapters and corrections, stacked in heaps across the study floor, into a neat and final manuscript.

Susan Wright

1 'Culture' in anthropology and organizational studies

Susan Wright

This book concerns the contribution of anthropology to the study of government, non-government (voluntary), and private sector organizations in the Third World and the West. The 1980s and 1990s have been a time of change for organizations in all sectors. The discrediting of modernization as a western domestic policy and as the basis for Third World development has been accelerated by the international reorganization of capital.[1] Production has become organized on an international division of labour with competition between First and Third World sites and the introduction of new management systems. Structural adjustment in the Third World and New Right policies in the West have reduced the role of the state, moving functions over to the private sector and relying more heavily on voluntary and non-government organizations. These changes have been accompanied by questions about different styles of organizing. The western model of bureaucracy is seen to have shortcomings: it is asked in the Third World, but not yet in the West, whether it is possible to build upon indigenous methods of organizing? Despite such widespread institutional change, some aspects of organizations have proved recalcitrant to alteration. Notably this concerns gender. Initially public sector organizations, and now more private sector companies have been concerned to improve opportunities for disadvantaged categories of people, especially women, and to maximize their potential in the labour market: but why have organizations proved so difficult to change? And who is benefitting? One theme running through these programmes is 'empowerment'. But who is empowered by empowerment? Is it principally the intended beneficiaries, people in the Third World, women and customers or clients? These questions about changing ways of organizing through indigenous management, addressing gender inequalities and empowerment of clients are the focus of the three parts of this book.

In the search for new ways to manage organizations in these changing contexts, 'the culture concept' has become prominent. Organizational studies literature attributes the culture concept to anthropological sources (Geertz 1973, Turner 1974, Bateson 1972 and Douglas 1987). For an anthropologist reading this literature there are moments of recognition closely followed by the discovery of familiar ideas being used in disconcertingly unrecognizable ways. It is the aim of this introduction to explore the reasons for this and to clarify some of the ways the concept 'culture' is being used both in the organization studies literature and by anthropologists in the chapters of this book.

In organizational studies 'the culture concept' is used in four ways. First, it refers to problems of managing companies with production processes or service outlets distributed across the globe, each located in a different 'national culture'. Second, it is used when management is trying to integrate people with different ethnicities into a workforce in one plant. Third, it can mean the informal 'concepts, attitudes and values' of a workforce; or, fourth, 'company culture' can refer to the formal organizational values and practices imposed by management as a 'glue' to hold the workforce together and to make it capable of responding as a body to fast changing and global competition (Deal and Kennedy 1982: 178, 193).

A 'strong company culture' has been deemed the *sine qua non* of success in the private sector and now no public or voluntary organization can be without its mission statement. Even these company cultures are of different kinds: one is strengthened Fordism while the other is a turning away from that idea. In the first case, an organization's 'culture' is converted from a mission statement into detailed practices, dividing each task into tiny details and specifying how each should be done. These are imposed on the workforce through training and disciplined supervision. This strengthens the Fordist management style of the modernization era whereby management was separate from the workforce which was divided according to clearly demarcated repetitive tasks. Some companies with international operations have used this system to institute a standardized way of performing tasks (the most quoted example is McDonald's). In opposite cases a 'culture' of flexible organization has been introduced. The Fordist division between management and workers has been revised, the role of middle management reduced, and the workforce organized in teams, with each member able to take on a full range of tasks. Instead of being adjuncts to a machine or to a predetermined sequence of paper movements, workers are 'empowered' to take initiatives and ensure operations are continually improved by communicating ideas directly to management. In this way workers' knowledge is to be harnessed in a flexible response to fast changing environments and to new or high standard demands from clients. Already it can been seen that 'culture' refers to diverse problems, ideas and styles of organizing.

How do these ideas connect with anthropological approaches to culture? One reason for introducing anthropological ideas about culture into organizational studies was methodological. Organizational studies from its inception has had a close relationship to the thinking of practising managers, such that, as Calas and Smircich have pointed out (1992: 223), organization researchers have played a central role in 'making' organizations.[2] The institutional changes outlined above inspired a search for new methods. In place of the modernist paradigm of organizations as rational and replete with objective facts which had dominated organizational studies, anthropological studies of culture offered a more interpretive approach through which to understand organizations as sites for constructing meaning.

However the paradigm shift does not seem to have been fully achieved. For example, Schein (1991) holds both an interpretive and a positivist approach to organizations in a way that appears contradictory to an anthropologist. He takes the anthropological argument that culture resides in conceptual categories and mental models. Therefore, he argues rightly, it cannot be researched through 'thin' description of its surface features which miss the holistic and systematic aspect of culture, or through questionnaires with their *a priori* assumptions and reliance on attitudes expressed out of context. But he also hankers for a 'real' positivist hold on a world of slippery intangibles, constructing culture as an object capable of standing free of its context: 'We cannot build a useful concept if we cannot agree on how to define it, "measure" it, study it, and apply it in the real world of organizations' (Schein 1991: 243).

Schein returns to an interpretive approach when he explains that culture is 'deeper' than its symbolic manifestations, the rites, rituals and stories of origin on which Deal and Kennedy (1982) focused. Schein's 'deeper' level of culture is recognizable: it is systematic, permeating all aspects of daily life, persisting over time, and shared. However, his concluding definition of culture provokes further realization that what seemed like anthropological ideas of culture have been twisted into a different form:

> If there is no consensus or if there is conflict or if things are ambiguous, then, by definition, that group does not have a culture in regard to those things . . . the concept of sharing or consensus is core to the definition, not something about which we have an empirical choice.
>
> (Schein 1991: 248)

'Culture' has become the property of a 'group' (both conceptualized as bounded and unitary), which 'persists over time' in the sense of being unchanging, and is 'shared' in the sense that there is consensus and no ambiguity.

This focus on consensus seems to be a key point of difference between organizational studies and anthropology. Initially, as will be explained below, the two disciplines shared a concern with consensus. But its weakness was identified; it led the Hawthorne Bank Wiring study (see below), for example, to conclude that only management had 'rationality'. Subsequently, the Manchester shop floor studies focused on conflict. Now, to an anthropologist influenced by Geertz's ideas, 'sharedness' is more likely to imply a common repertoire of ideas which are reworked continually in imaginative ways that are systematic, explainable, but not predictable. Not only is ambiguity essential, as it provides the space for this reworking, but the process is political: meanings of concepts and symbols are not just not fixed, they are actively contested. In organizational studies literature which also uses Geertz, often only one, supposedly consensual definition of the situation is given. Culture has turned from being something an organization *is* into something an organization *has*, and from being a process embedded in context to an objectified tool of management control. The use of the term culture itself becomes ideological.

This literature provokes an anthropologist into realizing that culture has become one of the discipline's own 'taken for granted' categories or working assumptions.[3] In order to explore its meaning it is essential to understand the methodological processes by which we arrive at culture as an analytical concept. Anthropology is best known for its fieldwork by participant observation, yet this is only part of the methodology. The distinctive anthropological process of 'problematizing' relies on continually testing the ability of existing ideas or theories about society to explain the detail of what is experienced in the field. Out of this interplay analytical concepts like culture are generated and progressively refined. Some of the chapters in this book look to anthropology more for its fieldwork methods (indeed a few of the authors might not call themselves anthropologists) while others develop the distinctive problematizing process of anthropology in their analyses.

All of the authors contributed papers to the conference organized by GAPP (Group for Anthropology in Policy and Practice) on the anthropology of organizations held at University College Swansea in January 1991. The aim was to bring together researchers and practitioners engaging with anthropology whilst involved in the extensive contemporary organizational changes in the Third World and the West. Their work clustered around indigenous management, gender and organizational change, and empowerment of clients, the issues represented in the three parts of this book. It was found that all used various concepts of culture in their research and analysis. Anthropologists treated this in a 'taken for granted' fashion, but practitioners and participants from other disciplines encouraged us to subject this analytical concept to far more scrutiny. The book is therefore designed to be approached in two ways. Firstly, specialists in any of the three substantive issues covered by this book will find each part has an introduction which sets out current thinking in that field, followed by chapters taking different approaches to the central issues. Secondly, the book is to be read for anthropological analyses of culture in organizations. The introduction is written with this in mind. By providing an historical account of the development of anthropological studies of organizations, and of the research and analytical methods used, it contextualizes the approaches to culture to be found in subsequent chapters. These historical studies of organizations are largely missing from accounts of the development of the discipline and one aim of discussing them in detail is to give this work on organizations more visibility within anthropology itself. There have however been a number of interchanges of ideas between anthropology and organization studies during their parallel histories, and the second aim is to show how anthropological approaches to culture can contribute to current developments in organization studies.

EARLY ANTHROPOLOGICAL STUDIES OF ORGANIZATIONS – THE HAWTHORNE EXPERIMENTS

There were three periods when anthropologists made particular contributions to organizational studies. These were the 1920s, when both disciplines were in their early stages of development; the 1950s and 1960s; and the present. Each period of interaction reflected the development of the discipline's methodology and of ideas about social organization and culture. Each raised a number of issues about participant observation, analysis of context and meaning, and refinement of analytical concepts, which continue to be relevant.

The history of organizational studies often starts with 'Scientific Management' (also called Taylorism, following Taylor's paper of 1911, incorporated into his 1947 text). This took a manager-centred or top-down view of how to get right the production system within an organization. Production processes were divided into strictly demarcated tasks. The details of each task were investigated, and if physical conditions for the work were correct, the appropriate human behaviour and performance were meant to follow automatically. Between 1927 and 1932 a study of the Western Electric Hawthorne Plant in western Chicago and in Cicero, Illinois, was to test these scientific management principles. But, the story goes, with the help of anthropologists, they discredited these principles by discovering the social organization of the workplace and establishing the Human Relations school which was to dominate organizational studies for the next twenty-five years.

At first the research methods were 'experiments' dislocated from everyday working conditions. The Hawthorne management was testing the impact of changing physical conditions on output. They called on Harvard

University for help, where a Committee on Industrial Psychology had been set up with funding from the Rockefeller Foundation. Elton Mayo, a psychologist, with a team of researchers from the university and the company, tested the effect of ten physical and incentive changes on fatigue levels of six women workers. They discovered the now disputed Hawthorne effect: the women's output increased whatever changes were made and even when the women were returned to their original working conditions. The researchers attributed this to the effect of the experimental conditions. The women were in a special Relay Assembly Test Room which did not replicate their usual working conditions. They formed a tightly knit friendship group, with much less 'apprehension of authority' (Roethlisberger and Dickson 1939: 189) and took much more initiative in their relations with their supervisor than usual (Chapple 1953). In particular, the researchers took on a supervisory role and paid a great deal of sympathetic attention to the workers. The conclusion of the experimental work was that psychological factors were more important than physical conditions in achieving changes in output.

The second stage of the research adopted another method. To explore further the link between morale and supervision, and to provide materials for training supervisors, a large-scale interviewing programme was embarked upon. Between 1928 and 1930 a new Industrial Research Division in the company interviewed 21,126 workers (Roethlisberger and Dickson 1939: 204). This programme ended with the lay-offs of the Depression. Whilst the Industrial Research Division waited for an upturn, they compared the results of this large-scale programme of single interviews with individuals, which had proved difficult to analyse, with repeated interviews of a small group. This produced a finding which had escaped them before: social groups on shop floors were capable of very strong control over the work behaviour of individuals (1939: 379).

To study the social organization of work groups, the team entered a third stage and introduced a further method: anthropological direct observation study. Mayo, who was a friend of leading anthropologists Malinowski and Radcliffe-Brown, brought in one of the latter's students, Lloyd Warner. He had just returned from studying Aborigines in Australia and was keen to use anthropology in 'modern' societies. He helped the research team apply anthropological fieldwork techniques to the workplace (1939: 389). The aim was to treat a shop floor as a small society in which every aspect of life was interconnected in a social system. However, because most shop floors consisted of more than a hundred workers they were too large and complex to study if 'technical, administrative, supervisory and personal problems are all mixed up into one interacting whole' (1939: 385). Therefore three teams of three men who wired banks of switches for telephone offices, the three solderers who worked to them, and two inspectors (fifteen in all) were moved into a separate room. In this Bank Wiring Observation Room the layout, the conditions of work, and the supervision replicated that on the shop floor. To test the impact of the experiment a base line study of output had been made in the preceding eighteen weeks.

The research was carried out by two staff from November 1931 to May 1932, although the later months were disrupted by lay-offs occasioned by the Depression. One researcher, the interviewer, remained an outsider to the group, believing this would enable the employees to talk about their attitudes. The other, the observer, stayed as unobtrusively as possible in the workroom and detailed the formal organization of the work process and the workers' informal organization, that is, their interactions, each individual's participation in groups, and expressions of solidarity. The aims were to treat the shop floor as a small society and to understand the function of the informal organization for the workers and its relation to the formal organization of the work.

Results of this research were analysed using Radcliffe-Brown's idea of a social system; that is, actual interactions between people form a systematic whole. The three work units formed two cliques which organized spontaneous games whenever there was a lull: bets and games of chance, group candy purchases and binges. Friendships and antagonism were also sited within and between these groups, although helping each other with work (against the formal rules) was not confined to work groups or cliques and integrated all the men. Variations and discrepancies in the workers' output were explained in terms of individual workers' positions within the informal social organization (1939: 520). All elements of the social organization had a function in a coherent informal system.

The informal system contrasted with the company's formal system of rules and incentives which was designed to make it to the workers' advantage to strive continually to increase output. Company records showed instead that most workers maintained 'straight line' output curves.[4] Moreover, company records were at variance with the actual output recorded by the researchers. The workers went to great lengths to keep an even record of output, whilst carrying in their heads complicated yet accurate accounts of their under- and over-reporting. The workers had a shared idea of a standard day's work, and thought it to their advantage to maintain a constant daily and weekly output. If the workers had a shared idea which was opposed to the assumptions of management, how did the researchers deal with the expectation, embedded in their methodology, that there would be consensus between workers and management?

In Third World societies anthropologists were concerned to demonstrate that a social system was informed by shared ideas which were logical, even if based on different premises to those of western middle-class observers. This idea was not transferred to the study. Roethlisberger and Dickson showed that the workers had a shared idea about constant output underpinning their social organization, but they called this idea 'sentiment', and denied that it was rational and logical. They reported that the workers refused to respond to the company's incentive scheme and kept to their constant output norms 'in case something happened'. Roethlisberger and Dickson called this irrational: the workers were 'non-logical' and 'not acting in accordance with their own economic interests' (1939: 533–4). Yet, from their report, it is possible to discern a logical position on the part of the workers. They were worried about short-time working and job cuts in the Depression. They feared that if they attained a higher output rate it might be set as the new target, with pay rates reduced, so they would have to work harder for the same income. This they took as further subordination by management. By resisting the company's incentive scheme they were, as far as possible, 'controlling' the actions of management (1939: 534). However, Roethlisberger and Dickson refer to this as non-rational 'sentiments': rationality remained the sole preserve of managers and researchers, reflecting the top-down stance of the analysis.

The interpretation was further confused when a social explanation of the workers' behaviour was supplanted by an individually-based psychological one. Mayo claimed the workers' irrational noncooperation with management was because of a frustrated urge to collaborate (Schwartzman 1993:14). Mayo concluded that the managers' role was to create the conditions for spontaneous cooperation between workers through which their commitment to the achievements of the organization could be secured. In Hawthorne this was sought through a 'non-directive counselling programme' which tried to reproduce the cathartic effect of the previous mass interview programme. This blocked any further Hawthorne research into the workplace as a social system (Chapple 1953; Whyte 1991: 187–8).

After the Bank Wiring Observation Room experiment there was a ten-year gap before anthropologists resumed attempts to combine analysis of workplaces as social systems with the devising of practical solutions to organizational problems. In 1943 two anthropologists, Lloyd Warner and Burleigh Gardner, established the Committee on Human Relations in Industry at Chicago University. They were joined by Whyte in 1944 and by colleagues from other departments (Whyte 1991: 89). The programme was funded by six industrial companies (at the small sum of $3,600 each), later joined by Sears, Roebuck and Co (1991: 89). The network of anthropologists spread. In 1946 Warner and Gardner set up a consulting company called Social Research Incorporated (Gardner 1977: 172). Whyte went to the School of Industrial Relations at Cornell University. Warner's students,

Arensberg and Chapple, further developed industrial research at Harvard. In 1941 they established a professional Society for Applied Anthropology which received reports on industrial research. In the 1940s and 1950s there were ethnographies of technological change, incentive systems and social organization of shop floor productivity. For example, Richardson and Walker (1948) identified changes to the 'social framework' of factory life and how these affected productivity when International Business Machines Corporation (IBM) introduced technological changes and doubled in size. Whyte (1948a) studied the restaurant industry; an attempt to increase productivity in Bundy Tubing Company (1948b); and concentrated on collective bargaining and industrial relations, including a study of a long strike (1951). This work is summarized in Baba 1986, Chapple 1953, Gardner 1977, and Holzberg and Giovannini 1981.

One of the great strengths of this Human Relations research was the application of anthropological fieldwork methods to make fine-grained ethnographies of factory units. The Bank Wiring Observation Room study remains a classic in the use of observation and interview methods. In later studies anthropologists developed other methods systematically to record the flows of interaction and communication within the spatial layout of organizations (Chapple 1953). These methods were applied with a standard of rigorousness which some feel we can learn from today.

One of the weaknesses of the Human Relations school was that the studies were top-down. That is, the agenda was derived from senior managers for whom 'problems' existed on the shop floor. The results were presented as a consensus, and in ways which were more suitable for managers to act upon than workers. Managers were not problematized in the same way. The studies did not examine the irrationality of managers' ideas and actions from the point of view of workers, and did not produce results that workers could use to their advantage.

A further criticism is that the studies of social organization on the shop floor were not placed in a wider framework of social, political and economic systems. Whyte admits that they treated technology and ownership as constants rather than as capable of change (1991: 90). In the modernization era, technological change and new management techniques in expanding industrial plants introduced contradictions and conflicts with which the prevailing equilibrium model of organizations could not cope. The studies did not speak to or critique these wider social processes. Both the top-down approach and the problem of conceptualizing small-scale studies in wider systems were treated differently by another school which started in Britain once Human Relations was well under way.

PROBLEMATIZING CONTEXT: THE MANCHESTER SHOP FLOOR STUDIES

In a series of studies by Manchester anthropologists in the 1950s and 1960s, fieldwork methods for studying shop floors were developed into full participant observation. Equally importantly, anthropology was not only associated with a method for creating ethnographic description; it was also a way of analysing detailed social situations so that they contributed to an understanding and theorizing of wider aspects of social organization. This was consciously critical and radical. The focus was on conflict and the problems of analysing context, two issues which remain relevant in current studies of culture. Gluckman, Professor of anthropology at Manchester University, was keen to try out social theories developed in Africa on diverse contexts, including industrial Britain. In 1953–4 Homans, Professor of sociology at Harvard, was visiting professor at the Manchester department. He suggested carrying on the Hawthorne work. In the transfer across the Atlantic, neither Mayo's ideas of an essential harmony of interests between workers and management, nor psychological individualism were imported (Emmett and Morgan 1982: 140).[5]

Industrial sociology was already practised in Britain (Stansfield 1981). The Second World War had proved the value of Operational Research; Liverpool University's department of social science was studying Merseyside firms and the docks; the National Institute of Industrial Psychology was very active; and the Tavistock Institute, which had many connections in the United States, was developing Human Relations and 'socio-technical systems' approaches to industry. With the need to revive industry after the war, funding came via Marshall Aid through the government's Department of Scientific and Industrial Research. The Manchester department of anthropology and sociology gained funding for a series of five workshop studies to explain 'output norms' and their relation to informal group structure.

Tom Lupton (who later became the head of Manchester Business School) joined the department to direct the project and studied Wye's modernized waterproof garment factory which employed mainly women, and Jay's which employed men in the production of heavy electrical transformers. Sheila Cunnison studied Dee's, a small, traditional manufactory of waterproof garments, and Kay's multiple tailoring, both of which employed men and women. Shirley Wilson studied Avalco which employed women in valve assembly. In a second phase in the 1960s a further team studied the Citroën works from three different vantage points: Isobel Emmett studied the managers, David Morgan the assembly shop and Michael Walker the machine shop (Emmett and Morgan 1982).

In each of the five studies in the first phase, the researcher spent at least six months carrying out full-time factory work on the shop floor. This they called open participant observation. It was open because their fellow workers knew they were doing a study. In the Hawthorne experiments, 'participation' had been kept to the minimum needed to approach the objects of study sufficiently closely to observe them (that is, to listen to their conversations as well as to watch their interactions). Care had been taken to be unobtrusive and to interfere as little as possible with their 'normal' activities in the observation room. Observation was the main research method employed. Now in the Manchester studies, participation meant full involvement on the shop floor and required researchers to learn how to do the work, to learn the language and concepts workers used, and to understand their perspectives. Experiential learning was combined with observing and listening so that out of the evening note-taking about people's different versions of myriad incidents and interactions, the field-worker gradually unravelled the social processes of the workplace and the relations within groups and between categories of workers over time. While 'participant' meant becoming as much as possible an insider, 'observer' took on the additional meaning of not only watching and recording systematically but of being an outsider with a theoretical understanding of society, against which the detail of the field was being constantly held up (Emmett and Morgan 1982:161). The two roles of participant and observer were therefore held in tension.

Emmett and Morgan (1982: 142) describe very well how out of this tension between the two perspectives of an insider and an outsider, as participant and observer, anthropological analysis commences through the discovery of 'problems'. These are not *a priori* hypotheses. They arise from the interaction between the anthropologist's wider understanding of social organization and the perspectives of workers learned in the field.

The 'problems' developed in the first Manchester studies took a very different line from the conclusions of the Hawthorne experiments. Tom Lupton from the start dropped the phrase 'workers "restricted" output', as such language carried a pro-management bias. He had no difficulty understanding how men at Jay's organized levels of output and earnings, and their rationality in combining to try and attain some control of their working lives. He had more difficulty in explaining why women at Wye's did not have this solidarity and 'will to control' their working lives. At Dee's, Cunnison found that whereas workers performing all the different production tasks operated as teams around a table, they did not keep up a steady flow of work for each other but engaged in 'militant individualism'. At Kay's, the women appeared to acquiesce individually to the output demands of management until they suddenly acted collectively in a crisis.

In each of the five studies there was a range of informal organization among the workers, and different relations with management – from acquiesence through to attempts to control their own work rates.

This was a 'problem'. What wider theories of social organization could be used or refined to explain this variation of patterns of accommodation between workers and managers? At Manchester there were many debates about how to relate the detail of a social situation to wider issues in society. Gluckman (1940) had established a model for this in a famous account of a social situation in Zululand. He began by first describing the ritual opening of a bridge in Zululand; second, by setting out a historical framework of social structure, and then by moving between the two to show how the detail of the bridge opening spoke to wider issues of Black–White relations in South Africa. The Manchester researchers saw the workshop as an analytically-central social situation on which similarly to focus social analysis of Britain (Cunnison 1982: 135). The problem was what to take as the context.

Lupton's initial context was the economic and organizational structure of industries. He tried to argue that in sectors with large, heavily capitalized firms which had collusive rather than competitive relations over pricing, where there was a low ratio of labour costs to production costs and strong trade unions, workers would organize collective control over output. In sectors with the opposite features, workers would acquiesce to management output norms (Cunnison 1982: 100). Based on deductive reasoning, this mechanical linkage between detailed workshop situations and macro industrial structures provided no space for unevenness. Most importantly it failed the anthropologcal test: it lost sight of the interaction between theory and field material and it did not hold true against other examples.

A second approach was to analyse the varied patterns of accommodation between workers and managers within the context of class in Britain. To relate the fieldwork detail to the social theory, the researchers drew on ideas of conflict which had been especially developed in Manchester anthropology. This replaced the Human Relations idea – that the 'natural' relation between workers and management is 'spontaneous cooperation' – only impeded by lack of communication. However, they did not replace this with workers and capitalists standing on either side of an unbridgeable cleavage (Frankenberg 1982: 12). Within an unequal system, the researchers were interested in the 'cross-cutting ties', the paradoxes and unexpected alliances which maintained both the system and its inherent conflict over time, in what Gluckman called successive moments of 'equilibrium'. Rejecting this word for its connotations of functionalism, Cunnison (1982) analysed the first five studies in terms of the different styles of 'accommodation', with tentative and temporary overtones, between workers and management. Emmett and Morgan (1982), writing defensively in the light of the attack on early industrial sociology by later Marxist writers, said that whereas international capitalism, national government, banks, and the structure of firms and trade unions in each industry set the limits for any struggle on the shop floor, that struggle was continuous, with a balance constantly changing in a 'daily running outcome'. They claimed that this rarely took the form of overt class struggle, but saw conflict instead in daily diverse and less obvious 'acts' of struggle, in singing, trying to extend tea-breaks, or in maintaining silence. Thus they would not call even the apparently acquiescent workers 'non-militant'.

A third way was to treat the workshop as a point of articulation of wider social structures in the surrounding community. Cunnison discerned variations in patterns of accommodation between workers and managers according to differences in the social context of each workplace. She argued against treating the factory as a closed system and brought 'external' factors into the analysis. The production system on the shop floor was only one of the structures in which workers had roles. Individuals held positions in a number of structures and systems of categories in 'wider society'. These included social class; whether the local community was close knit (that is, whether or not workers and managers were linked in a number of social relations outside the factory); sexual divisions in the family; age and ethnicity. It was assumed that the roles a person had in all these structures influenced their behaviour in the workplace. This model of ever-inclusive multiple roles from overlapping social structures was somewhat unwieldy.

One important outcome of this analysis of social context was in terms of what was then called 'sexual divisions'. Where a work group was made up of women subject to male managers, their interaction might be in terms of 'sex roles' imported into the work situation from their families. This was thought not to be the case with male workers and male managers. Perhaps the best example is Wilson's 'mock courtship'. In a crisis at Avalco two girls were resisting new standards of output until they engaged in a mock courtship with a new male trainee manager. Through explicitly phrasing the relationship in sex roles rather than roles in the system of production, they accepted the highly authoritative and pressured situation of unequal power (Cunnison 1982: 117).

This search for a way of analysing the context in which workplaces were embedded began to identify limitations in the idea that society is made up of face-to-face contact between people in different roles in a social structure. The early work on sexual divisions, although still about sex roles, touched on the ways people work with ideological concepts. Towards the end of the series of five studies the emphasis on social structure was reduced. Cunnison says they were still interested in the interrelation between sex, class, and the productive system but emphasized 'how the meanings people brought into the work situation were expressed, how these meanings were drawn into the work situation and integrated into the productive process' (Cunnison 1982: 135). Emmett, Morgan and Walker tried to refine Cunnison and Wilson's approach further by using Goffman's idea of a 'semi permeable membrane'. In any workshop situation, or any encounter within it, not all the characteristics of all the individuals from all aspects of their lives are treated as relevant. Some are ruled irrelevant. Others are given prominence, regardless of their salience to the individual or group outside. Even those characteristics which are drawn into the workshop situation are not 'raw'; they are transformed in the process. It is as if the factory walls are a semi-permeable membrane through which this selection and transformation takes place. Thus 'some aspects of family life of women workers were brought in through the factory walls, but selectively and transformed in the process, to serve purposes peculiar to the workplace and interaction in it' (Emmett and Morgan 1982: 156).

The Manchester shop floor studies had moved from the Harvard model of a factory as a closed system. They tried to situate the detail of the social situation of a workshop in wider social structures. Finally, in keeping with developments in anthropology at the time, they moved away from conceptualizing workshops and society as made up of structures, and towards an analysis of the way people make meaning in a particular situation out of an available cultural repertoire.

STUDYING UP

Anthropological methods in the 1960s, as has been shown in the above account, had changed from participation in order to observe, to full 'insider' participation, held in tension with 'outsider' observation in the light of current conceptualizations of society. Anthropologists were beginning to slough off scientism's pretence of being value-free. They were moving away from functionalism and the idea of society organized in terms of structures made up of social roles. They were moving towards an interest in symbolism and the construction of meaning in social events (parallel to what in sociology is called 'interpretative'). Organizational studies was moving in the opposite direction. Czarniawska-Joerges (1992) dates the parting of the ways between anthropology and organizational studies to Waldo's 1961 review of literature from both fields. Waldo said the future for organizational theory was to espouse the positivist paradigm: to think of organizations as objectively existing, capable of being studied by value-free science, and explained by analysing their constituent parts as elements of a functioning whole. He considered anthropologists to be neither scientific nor value free because they became part of a society in order to study it (Czarniawska-Joerges 1992: 77).

However very few anthropologists continued to work on western organizations. There was no anthropological follow-up to the Manchester shop floor studies and they, like other aspects of British urban anthropology, have been written out of the discipline's history. British anthropologists concentrated on Third World societies and those with an applied bent developed critical analyses of the process of modernization with studies of technological transfer, entrepreneurship, dual economies and the ways tribalism and ethnicity were ordering devices in the development of classes and trade unions. To a lesser extent they studied the formation of state bureaucracies which were also essential to the process (e.g. Cohen 1980; Fallers 1974). There were no anthropological studies of equivalent modernization processes in Britain – the growth of major industrial and public sector organizations and the restructuring of communities and urban spaces.

In the late 1960s national and world systems came to be viewed as the context within which to analyse ethnographies. There was a cry for anthropologists to study the institutions which controlled so much of everyday life both in western and Third World societies (Berreman 1968; Gough 1968). To include such world systems in the fieldwork and analysis required changing the unit of research. The functionalist paradigm was no longer adequate wherein a face-to-face 'society' (whether a tribe or a western factory) was treated as a bounded entity in which every aspect of social, political and economic organization had a function for the maintenance of the whole. 'Holism' could no longer mean studying a community or industry in isolation from national bureaucracies and international firms and agencies, which although invisible, influenced the local economy and politics. For example, in the Third World, Wolfe (1977) analysed Congo mining operations within world systems; Nash (1979) studied the cultural constructs and material conditions of Bolivian tin mining in the context of national and international political and economic processes; while Mintz (1985) traced different facets of the sugar industry. Traditional anthropological methods also came under attack for producing documents which might be used by those in power, but were not usable by those subordinated and governed. Participatory methods were advocated whereby those traditionally studied should help define research issues, collect and analyse data, and own the results, so that they could use them in negotiations with those in power over them (Huizer 1979).

An important influence on the methodological and conceptual issues was Nader's (1972) suggestion that anthropologists should 'study up' as well as down – including both powerful institutions and state bureaucracies in the idea of 'holism'. In 1980 she developed the idea of a 'vertical slice'.

Looking at children in the United States, instead of emphasizing families as the sites of child development, she suggested looking at hidden hierarchies of industrial and government organizations which shape their food, health and housing:

> corporations feed our children, clothe our children, and help determine their genetic legacy. The important link is between the child and General Foods, Gerber, and Beech Nut, as well as the Food and Drugs Administration. These are but facets of the hidden hierarchies.
>
> (Nader 1980: 37)

Such research had an avowedly political agenda: how could a democracy work if people in the First World knew so little about the organizations which affected their daily lives and if they had so little ability to cope with their manipulation (Nader 1972: 294)? This kind of research rarely focused on the social organization of face-to-face communities. It involved studying 'the culture of power' (1972: 289), the ways these hierarchies remain hidden, their distancing mechanisms, the cultural constraints members of the organizations feel in dealing with the public and the ways clients are manipulated.

Twenty years later most ethnography has remained single locale, and there are still problems about how to contextualize it in wider systems. Marcus (1986: 173), suggests the most successful strategy is 'inventing a representation of the larger order', by using the ethnography to explore one of the key concepts of Marxist theory – as Willis (1981) does for the cultural meaning of the production of labour. Otherwise the larger system is painted in as a background which externally impinges on but is not integral to the highlighted foreground. Such an analytical framework presents the effects of large-scale systems on daily life but does not have the ability to explain linkages between the macro and micro.

Pettigrew (1985) has gone further in trying to explain the influence of local and large-scale contexts on each other. He argues against treating context 'either just as descriptive background or as an eclectic list of antecendents which somehow shape the process [of organizational change]' (1985: 36–7). He sees organizations as systems of political action (1985: 26) and change as the legacy of struggles for power emerging through time (1985: 24). The struggle involves both interest groups in the firm and their mobilization of aspects of the wider economic and political structure which they seek to adjust to obtain their ends. The key to his analysis is to track interactions between what is happening in the firm and in the wider context in a complex, dynamic and untidy mixture of processes occurring at various rates. He tries to introduce a causal or explanatory link between micro- and macro-contexts which is not mechanical and which leaves room for uneveness.

Nader and Pettigrew in different ways have interlaced levels or contexts in their analysis of organizations. In doing so both use the concept of culture. In Pettigrew's case, culture is the frame of reference by which individuals and groups attach meaning to their daily work and make sense of intra-organization and external trends which they try to manage. However he does not regard culture as a unitary system of shared meanings. He acquires more purchase in his analysis from regarding culture 'as the source of a family of concepts' which are used in political processes through symbolism, language and myth to create practical effects (Pettigrew 1985: 44). Both authors have moved the meaning of 'culture' beyond earlier descriptions of the routines, physical layouts, methods of keeping records, and other material aspects of interaction that underpinned social interaction (Chapple 1953). 'Culture' has become more associated with language and power, with systems of ideas and the ways they are manipulated in performance of interactions.

ORGANIZATIONAL CULTURE

It is around the idea of culture that anthropology and organization studies have just begun to resume a dialogue. However, culture has acquired multifarious meanings in the literature on organizations, and this section will unravel a few of them.

From the Hawthorne experiment's 'discovery' of informal systems onwards, most models in organizational studies have divided organizations into three components: formal system, informal system, and environment. This is also found in anthropology, for example in Britan and Cohen's (1980) review of anthropological studies of bureaucracy. The formal system is the map of the organizational structure, job descriptions, the hierarchy of decision making, the goals, rules and policies. The informal system is the way individuals and groups in the organization relate to each other, which might influence the formal system and achievement of the organization's aims. Where the formal system is associated with Weberian criteria for rational organizations (achievement of efficiency through an explicit hierarchical system, clear division of work into specified roles, separation of bureaucrats' working and personal lives, appointment on the basis of technical qualifications and promotion through regularized systems based on merit), it may be considered to be influenced by the informal system. Cullen (1992 and this volume) points out that when Third World bureaucracies are measured against Weberian criteria they are found to be 'corrupted' by nepotism or tribalism whereas when informal systems in western bureaucracies deviate from formal ones this is 'initiative' to improve the organization's ability to achieve its aim. In either case, the informal system is connected to members' lives outside the organization and is influenced by the 'environment'. Culture is therefore seen to reside both in the informal system and in the environment, but not in the – supposedly neutral – formal system.

Morgan (1986) argues that the formal systems of organizations are not immune from culture. He shows that formal systems have been based on three models of organization, each resting on a 'root metaphor'. Each of these – organization as machine, as organism and as culture – enable people to understand organizations in distinctive yet partial ways, closing off other ways of seeing. Whereas in academic theory these metaphors form a historical progression (Burrell and Morgan 1979), in management practice they are all still current, informing the rules of organizations and the practice of managers. 'Organization as machine' framed the way organizations were set up and managed under classical or scientific management. Organizations in this sense are thought of as closed systems, with a segmental structure dividing up the overall goal of the organization into smaller and smaller tasks in a hierarchy of departments. The departments all have clearly defined relationships, with every part functioning in the smooth running of the whole. All are held together by managers' central control with workers expected to behave like parts or adjuncts of the machine. Morgan publishes a fast food company's checklist of the pre-planned actions involved in counter staff serving a customer. For example there are three components to 'greeting the customer': smile, sincere greeting, eye contact. This checklist is for managers to evaluate staffs' standardized performance of even personal interactions. They are to behave with mechanical repetition and precision.

The metaphor 'organization as organism' derives from Human Relations and subsequent Systems and Contingency Theory. Borrowed images from biology and ecology inform the formal system of organizations and the language of management. The Hawthorne experiments recognized that workers had needs which had to be satisfied in order for the organization to perform effectively. Gradually the idea of needs was extended to envisage an organization as an open system depending on a satisfactory relationship with its wider environment to survive, satisfy its needs and develop. Organizations as organisms are broken down into subsystems (strategic, technological, managerial, 'human resources') each of which might have a different relationship with its environment but all also need to be interrelated. A successful organization is still thought of as seeking a 'healthy' state of equilibrium (in anthropology) or homeostasis (in organizational studies). The means to do this is not only through rigid hierarchies but also a matrix of cross-departmental teams to integrate the subsystems, especially when their environments are 'turbulent'.

A third metaphor, 'organization as culture', takes many forms. As was pointed out at the beginning of this chapter, the culture of an organization is sometimes taken to be a list of attributes or shared values which glue a delineated group into a static state of uniformity and consensus. A variation on this concept is to think of a company as having one culture and the workforce as having another culture, or subculture (Turner 1971). Nicholson (this volume) contests the idea that cultures interact as monolithic, bounded units with fixed attributes. She examines the interaction between western models of bureaucracy and indigenous systems of organizing in Papua New Guinea. These cannot be considered as two 'cultures', since the same bureaucrats were continually deciding when indigenous concepts should be incorporated to protect bureaucratic procedures and budgets (as when a staff member died on duty) and when they could appeal to western bureaucratic values to resist claims on resources (including their salaries) made in terms of indigenous forms of organizing. Instead of 'the culture of an organization' it is more useful to consider 'organization as culture'.

Organization as culture is used to question assumptions in both the scientific management and organism schools that organizations have an existence which is objective, material and unproblematic. For these writers, organization as culture problematizes the very concept of organization:

> When culture is a root metaphor, the researcher's attention shifts from concerns about what do organizations accomplish and how may they accomplish it more efficiently, to how is organization accomplished and what does it mean to be organized.
>
> (Smircich 1983: 353)

Instead of presuming a thing called an organization with a boundary against its environment, the emphasis is on a continuous process of organizing (Pondy and Mitroff 1979). It suggests that even the most material aspects of organizations are only made real by being given meaning. This meaning-making is seen as a continuous process; they try to dispel the idea of an organization as static, in homeostasis or equilibrium. An examination of how people negotiate the meaning of their everyday routines is involved, and of the way they generate symbols through which organized activity is mobilized – including the construction of boundaries (Young 1989). Cullen (this volume) shows how aspects of daily routines, ideas of professionalism, gender identities and dress were combined and recombined in different ways to create identities within and boundaries between different units of the benefits services as they underwent repeated restructuring in Britain. As Smircich (1983) argues, culture is a process – it cannot be fixed into a checklist of attributes of a delineated group: that would be to treat culture as a thing. Smircich says that once theorists adopt this root metaphor for 'organizations as culture', 'they leave behind the view that culture is something an organization *has*, in favour of the view that a culture is something an organization *is*' (1983: 347).

But 'organization as culture' is itself a metaphor, just as much as organization as 'machine' and 'organism'. All three are ways in which people conceptualize organizations and are therefore cultural. Although both organization studies and anthropology refer to culture as a process of meaning-making through symbols, there is a difference between their approaches. As referred to above and explored further below, in analysing these processes of negotiating meaning, anthropologists focus more centrally on issues of power.

CULTURE AS PROCESS AND IDEOLOGY

If organization is based on metaphors which inform the way people have structured the organization, the type of hierarchy, and the style of management, how has this cultural process of meaning-making, negotiating and organizing through the minutiae of daily life in specific social, economic and historical contexts been analysed?

An early attempt to conceptualize organizations as a continuous process of organizing and negotiating meaning was Strauss *et al.*'s (1963) treatment of a hospital as a 'negotiated order'. They show the aim of the hospital, to 'turn patients out in better shape', was adhered to by all, but masked discrepancies on how to achieve it. Formal rules were minimal and not widely known. A sense of order was achieved by the different professionals, lay staff and patients daily negotiating agreements over individual patient care. These became patterned understandings between staff who worked together for any length of time but were continually susceptible to change. When these negotiations broke down a crisis was solved by a committee making a formal decision which became a 'rule' until it was forgotten. Similarly, informal ward rules would be forgotten 'until another crisis elicited their innovation all over again' (1963: 306). Both formal and informal spheres were part of a daily round of negotiating order. This action-oriented or transactional analysis locates 'culture' – the process of continuously organizing and negotiating order – in the surface of everyday activities.

Others see such rules and decisions as symbols and take culture to be a 'deeper' system of meaning 'underlying' and 'informing' these surface interactions. For example, Morgan argues that

> the slogans, evocative language, symbols, stories, myths, ceremonies, rituals, and patterns of ritual behaviour that decorate the surfaces of organizational life merely give clues to the existence of a much deeper and all pervasive system of meaning.
>
> (1986: 133)

The phrases 'system of meaning' and 'shared beliefs' occur widely in organization literature. Weiss and Miller's critical review reveals that they are used interchangeably with 'cognitive maps', 'perceptions and norms', 'values' and 'ideology' (1987: 111). They find such phrases used to denote something which binds people together and maintains what an organization is (1987: 107). These usages lose sight of the processual, negotiated idea of culture and reassert the static, uniform and consensual concept of organization, though located at a 'deeper' level. How to conceptualize and analyse 'deep seated' metaphors or systems of thinking has been the subject of debate in anthropology. Two anthropologists with very different arguments, Douglas and Geertz, are often cited in organization texts but the full implications of their different approaches do not seem to have been taken up in organization studies.

Douglas (1987) is concerned with the ways 'institutions think'. Insti- tution, in Douglas' sense, is a much broader concept than organization (see McCourt Perring this volume). Douglas speculates that social solidarity evolves through cognitive processes or 'thought worlds' on which institutions are built.[5] That is, social groupings develop their own view of the world, a distinctive 'thought style' which sustains their patterns of interaction. This thought style is encoded in institutions through which major decisions are taken. Institutions then make classifications for us, they put uncertainty under control, and channel memory and perceptions into forms compatible with the relations they authorize, so that other things become unthinkable. An individual's cognitive processes become shaped by social institutions.

Asad (1979) criticizes anthropologists, including Douglas, who base their constructions of society on 'authentic culture', that is, an underlying system of essential shared meanings to which the researcher connects all actions and discourse in an integrated totality which self-reproduces through changing political and economic conditions. He argues that this makes individual experience, social interaction and collective discourse parasitic on the set of shared concepts. All are so tightly held together that transformation is impossible. For Douglas

> a system of human meanings . . . has the function of rendering the structure of cultural experience and of political action isomorphic . . . the cultural and political preconditions for saying and doing things, as well as the meaningful statements and actions produced in those conditions, are neatly fused together. Nothing can be said or done with meaning if it does not fit into an *a priori* system, the 'authentic' culture which defines the essential social being of the people concerned.
>
> (Asad 1979: 618)

As will be discussed further below, Asad argues that instead of trying to devise an essential, authentic culture, the problem to be explained is how certain 'essential meanings' become authoritative in specific historical circumstances.

A more interesting part of Douglas' argument is that institutions are based on systems which classify types of people and the relations between them. Douglas points out that the great growth in collecting statistics and ordering them into labelled categories in the nineteenth century resulted in new kinds of people coming forward to accept the labels and live accordingly. These classification systems are legitimized by analogy with the way the natural or supernatural world is classified, for example metaphors drawn from parts of the body, head/hands or left/right are used. These are formal structures of equivalence which are loaded with patterns of hierarchy and dominance that fit the prevailing political order. Institutional stability relies upon natural-ization of social classifications, so that the institution is seen to be founded on rightness in reason and in nature. Young (1991) has found the ideas of analogy and naturalization useful to reveal the metaphors, classifications and symbolic systems that he calls the 'deep structures' of the police as an institution of power and control in Britain. Fairclough (1985) uses 'naturalization' as a key concept while rejecting the idea of an organization as an authentic culture of essential meanings. He argues that within organizations there are several competing 'ideological discursive formations'. One becomes dominant when its ideology – with its associated classifications and behaviours – becomes 'taken for granted' and treated as real, normal and natural. He argues that new or minority ideological discursive formations have to de-naturalize the dominant one in order to contest it and accomplish any change. Douglas' approach, however, is limited by its emphasis on stability and assumption of consensus, so that there is no differentiation of people's relative power to resist or change institutions.

Whereas Douglas only has one deep-seated conceptual system for an institution, for Geertz there is a multiplicity in any organizational setting. He argues that it is the researcher's aim to interpret through cultural categories what is going on in a field situation. To establish his inter-pretive position he clears away alternatives. He argues against treating culture as if it is a thing with forces and purposes of its own; nor is it a coherent and impeccable formal system, reducible to a pattern in an identi-fiable community. Nor can culture be treated as a symbolic system

> by isolating its elements, specifying the internal relationships among those elements, and then characterizing the whole system in some general way – according to the core symbols around which it is organized, the underlying structures of which it is a surface expression, or the ideological principles on which it is based.
>
> (Geertz 1973: 17)

To Geertz, what must be attended to is the flow of behaviour and social action, and this can only be described and perused to interpret the constructions we imagine people to place on what they live through 'in the informal logic of actual life' (1973: 17). He describes a sheep raid in Morocco to show the different constructions placed on a sequence of events by a Jew, Berber tribesmen and French colonialists. The reader can discern the different conceptual structures involved in this interaction, and their systematic misunderstandings. He describes the process of analysis as using small facts from a fine-comb field study to think creatively with large concepts like legitimacy, modernization, colonialism, conflict. The aim is to sort out the structures of significance, their social ground and import. Put another way, once human behaviour is seen as symbolic action, the important question is, what is being said by the different people involved, and why? This is the background to the oft-quoted introduction to the article:

> The concept of culture I espouse . . . is essentially a semiotic one. Believing, with Max Weber, that man [sic] is an animal suspended in webs of significance he himself has spun, I take culture to be those webs, and the analysis of it to be therefore not an experimental science in search of law but an interpretive one in search of meaning. It is explication I am after, construing social expressions on their surface enigmatical.
>
> (Geertz 1973: 5)

This quotation has a different meaning for anthropologists than is often found in organizational studies. Geertz is not suggesting all people are caught in the same way in one web. He did not use his example of the sheep raid to produce '*the* Moroccan culture', either surface or deep. He described three people with different understandings of a sequence of actions. The argument can be taken further than it is by Geertz: the three people had different structural power and personal ability to impose their meanings on events so as to make their interpretation definitive and thereby accrue very material outcomes. It is this political process, a contest to assert definitive interpretations which produce material outcomes, that is the key to anthropological understandings of culture, of relevance to organization studies.

Geertz' notion of culture has been taken up by, but given very different significance within organization studies. After the discovery of 'corporate culture' (Deal and Kennedy 1982) and the claim that excellence derived from 'stong culture' (Peters and Waterman 1986), the above quotation has appeared in much organizational studies literature. The 'web of meaning' seems to be equated with a vision statement, implemented from the top of the organization with the aim of drawing into it the informal structures of different departments and levels. Techniques are developed to self-identify these informal cultures and reflect on their difference from the corporate culture with a view to bringing them into line. 'Strength' is equated with 'coherence', the new word for consensus.

Curtis (this volume) contests this equation of strength with coherence. Provocatively, he uses Peters and Waterman's chapter headings to describe the organization of a major irrigation system in Nepal. This organization has all their characteristics of success, despite the 'incoherence' of its egalitarian principles in a highly stratified society. Interpretive anthropologists would argue that 'coherence' within an organization is impossible. The organization's equivalents of the Moroccan Jew, Berber tribesman and French colonialist will immediately begin to signify their own meanings of corporate culture through the way they act in a sequence of events. The process is essentially political, with people situated differently in any sequence of events trying to impose their definition and garner the outcome.

In organization studies, Linstead and Grafton-Small (1992) treat organizational culture as a political process but in a slightly different way. They distinguish between Corporate Culture and organization culture. The former they attribute to management – who devise it and impose it on the organization through rites, rituals and values. Organization culture they associate with workers, and unfortunately describe as 'organic' (1992: 332). Their aim is to explain that workers are not just passive consumers of Corporate Culture. In a way reminiscent of the Manchester shop floor studies' 'daily running outcome' between workers and managers (described above), they argue that workers engage in a creative process of producing culture from mundane details of their work and through innumerable and infinitesimal transformations of the dominant culture, adapting it to their interests. This approach accepts *a priori* that there is a dominant culture and that a category of managers acts as a dominant group. It is just this that is being problematized in anthropological concepts of culture which question the conditions under which, and the ways in which people situated differently in any sequence of events, try to make their definition 'stick', and to assert their dominance.

The need for this is recognized by Linstead and Grafton-Small when they conclude that

> Researchers have inadequately considered the contours of the field of power relations against which symbolic determinations are played out in particular historical moments and which shape the coding possibilities which prefer particular meanings without limiting them.
>
> (Linstead and Grafton-Small 1992: 340)

To analyse this process of contestation and transformation, Asad (1979) opens up analytical space that has been closed down by both 'authentic culture' and determinism. As described above, the former seeks a unitary system of 'underlying' shared values to which all actions and discourses are connected in a self-reproducing totality. Determinists argue that ideologies are produced directly by elements of the class system to maintain their interests. To Asad, this is tautological, a point exemplified in organization literature by Weiss and Miller's claim that ideologies are 'sets of ideas that are predicted by social structure, and that promote the interests of those who promote them' (Weiss and Miller 1987: 113). Asad is seeking to provide an analysis of historically specific processes of contestation, transformation and domination that is not made possible by either of these approaches. He did not, however go to the other extreme of some later postmodern writers whose accounts of people's multiple, open-ended and infinitely imaginative interpretations of a fractured reality, offer a spurious equality to disenfranchised voices (Marcus 1990). Asad asks how in particular social and economic conditions, certain forms of discourse become 'authoritative' (Asad 1979: 619).

In the sense that control of discoursal practices is integral to the reproduction of inequalities in class and gender relations, discourses are materially founded but not determined. It requires constant discoursal effort continually to reassert the status of a discourse as 'true', objective, neutral or normal and to displace other emergent discourses, labelling them as abnormal, disordering or political. As Asad says, an authoritative discourse 'seeks continually to preempt the space of radically opposed utterances and so to prevent them from being uttered' (Asad 1979: 621).

Yet, he adds

> Even when action is authorised, it is as discourse that such action establishes its authority. The action is read as being authorised, but the reading and the action are not identical – that is why it is always logically possible to have an alternative reading.
>
> (1979: 621)

This is an approach to ideology which tries to combine ideas which break down totalizing views of 'reality', with a sense of material conditions and outcomes, much as Cockburn (this volume) does in her gendered critique of 'power'. It is an approach which is material in the sense that Collins (this volume) demonstrates for divorce court proceedings. Tinkering with 'surface' symbols of wigs and seating arrangements in no way increased the power of clients *vis à vis* legal professionals; nor did legal power derive from discourse alone: it was their triangle of legal knowledge, command of procedures and discursive practices which gave authority to their definitions of a client's situation.

Ideology can be defined as systematic knowledge made up of materially-founded and related discourses that are claims to truth, believed, taken as self-evident or considered 'natural' – making alternative possibilities unthinkable, but rooted in historical conditions and subject to challenge. Pringle (this volume) identifies three discourses about secretaries, each founded in particular historical conditions. They describe boss–secretary relations in terms of sexuality and desire, relations of domination she calls hegemonic, in that they are so taken for granted that they are not enforced through coercion but maintained by consent and experienced as pleasurable.

Reinhold (1993), in a policy analysis revealing the way New Right ideology is constructed in Britain, shows how the terms of five connected discourses were transformed. She demonstrates the need for discourses to be uttered in institutional settings of the state in order to be asserted as authoritative. In this volume, in the radical restructuring of two very different British organizations – a community home for former patients of a psychiatric hospital and an insurance company – both McCourt Perring and Kerfoot and Knights identify that discourses about the 'family' were very important in the promulgation of new corporate identities. Family is a concept with multiple and contradictory meanings, for example, caring versus control; equal sharing versus hierarchies based on gender and age. It was the latter meaning from both of those pairs that was asserted in the corporate discourse, and contemporaneously in the discourse of the ruling 'party of the family'. Asserting these meanings of 'family' as authoritative has had very material outcomes for the women's wages and careers in the insurance company and for former patients and carers in the community homes. Yet ambiguities, contradictions and alternative meanings remain available for contestation of the authoritative discourse. Edwards' analysis (this volume) is of an organization whose identity rested on resistance to authoritative discourses within the state. She shows how the housing aid organization tried to assert a meaning for 'ordinary people' in opposition to 'bureaucrats' not only as a discourse about their ideal practice in individual case work, but also as a way of locating their work overall in a discourse about class inequalities and social transformation in Britain.

Culture as a process places emphasis on language and power, showing how the terms of discourses are constructed and contested and why, with what outcomes. Discourses are rarely made authoritative within one organization but are uttered and contested in several settings simultaneously. Treating culture as political process provides a theoretical approach to the problems identified in this chapter: it helps avoid conceptualizing organizations as bounded units, and deals with the problem of context by placing organizational settings within national and international systems of relations which are ideological, as well as material.

CONCLUSION

Anthropologists are critical of their discipline's previous conceptualizations of culture – either as a checklist of surface characteristics of a bounded group, or as a 'deeper' set of shared authentic meanings. Both rely on an idea of 'shared meaning' without asking 'is it actually shared? to what extent? by whom? how does it come to be shared?' (Cowan 1990: 11). A consensual notion is unhelpful. To answer these questions an individualistic model, or one based on unsituated multiple voices, loses sight of social relations. Relations and processes of domination are central to an explanation of how people – differently positioned – contest the meaning of a situation, use economic and institutional resources available to them at that historical moment to try and make their definition of the situation 'stick', and try to garner the material outcome. It has to be shown how a discourse which defines words, ideas, things, or groups becomes authoritative. This is culture as process. As Street says 'culture is an active process of meaning-making and contestation over definition, including of itself' (Street 1993: 25).

At a time of capital restructuring and institutional reorganization, the claim to 'culture' in organizations is itself ideological. The meaning of culture is being negotiated: is organization culture to be defined as a set of fixed corporate attributes or a political process, contesting such definitions and relations of domination? The objects of social research such as those in this volume contribute to the process. In organization studies, according to Alvesson (1991), some writers implicitly share managerial, top-down perspectives and agendas, similar to that identified above in the Hawthorne experiments. Others, like Cockburn in this volume, seek to develop a concept of power to assist women in explaining and struggling against processes which reproduce inequality in organizations. The chapters in this book suggest that corporate definitions of culture have not yet become authoritative to the extent of being naturalized and taken for granted. Contesting the meaning and the ambiguities and contradictions in the terms of related discourses about 'family', gendered ideas of 'power', new formulations like 'indigenous knowledge' and the meanings of 'client', 'customer', 'citizen' and 'consumer' will have material outcomes for all concerned. Culture is double faceted. Culture is an analytical concept for problematizing the field of organizations; in that field, culture is an ideological claim, rooted in historical conditions and subject to challenge.

NOTES

1 Berman (1982) characterized modernization as continuous attempts to create order and control on a progressively larger scale, accompanied by wiping out

preceding 'traditions' and by fending off fears that new concrete forms and social order may disintegrate. These ideas underpinned the expansion of industrial capital and development of support services through the state in both the West and the Third World.

2 I am indebted to Michael Roper for this point.

3 Cultural anthropology has always been an important element of the discipline in the United States. In Britain the emphasis was on social anthropology and on actual social relations. Until recently culture referred to material artefacts and dramatic performances. In the 1990s however, British anthropologists working on issues that cannot be contained by face to face relations like ideology, state policies and organization, and especially those who have made links with a parallel tradition of British cultural studies, have used culture rather than social as the embracing term for their work.

4 This disproved the Hawthorne effect. In the Relay Assembly Test Room the women's increased output was put down to the effect of researchers, taking a sympathetic interest in them. In the Bank Wiring Observation Room the men's output remained constant, and at the same level as before the experiment started, despite the presence of a sympathic observer. Mills (1988: 353) points out the gender blindness of not asking why the women organized themselves to increase output continually whereas the men organized themselves to limit it.

5 Douglas is contesting the position of rational individualists who argue that society can only be based on the unlikely altruistic relinquishing of self interest and independent action.

REFERENCES

Alvesson, M. (1991) 'Organizational symbolism and ideology', *Journal of Management Studies* 38 (3): 207–25.

Asad, T. (1973) *Anthropology and the Colonial Encounter*, London: Ithaca Press.

Asad, T. (1979) 'Anthropology and the analysis of ideology', *Man* (N.S.) 14: 607–27.

Baba, M. L. (1986) *Business and Industrial Anthropology: An Overview*, NAPA Bulletin No. 2, Washington DC: National Association for the Practice of Anthropology.

Bateson, G. (1972) *Steps to an Ecology of Mind*, New York: Chandler Publishing Company.

Berman, M. (1982) *All That is Solid Melts into Air. The Experience of Modernity*, London: Verso.

Berreman, G. D. (1968) 'Is anthropology alive? Social responsibility in social anthropology', *Current Anthropology* 9 (5): 391–6.

Britan, G. M. and Cohen, R. (1980) 'Towards an anthropology of formal organizations', in G. M. Britan and R. Cohen (eds) *Hierarchy and Society. Anthropological Perspectives on Bureaucracy*, Philadelphia: Institute for the Study of Human Issues.

Burrell, G. and Morgan, G. (1979) *Sociological Paradigms and Organizational Analysis*, London: Heinemann.

Calas, M.B. and Smircich, L. (1992) 'Using the "F" word: feminist theories and the social consequences of organizational research', in A. J. Mills and P. Tancred (eds) *Gendering Organizational Analysis*, London: Sage.

Chapple, E. D. (1953) 'Applied anthropology in industry', in A. L. Kroeber (ed.) *Anthropology Today*, Chicago: Chicago University Press.
Cohen, R. (1980) 'The blessed job in Nigeria', in G. M. Britan and R. Cohen (eds) *Hierarchy and Society. Anthropological Perspectives on Bureaucracy*, Philadelphia: Institute for the Study of Human Issues.
Cowan, J. (1990) *Dance and the Body Politic in Greece*, Princeton, Princeton University Press.
Cullen, S. (1992) Anthropology, State Bureaucracy and the Community. Unpublished PhD thesis, Cambridge University.
Cunnison, S. (1982) 'The Manchester factory studies, the social context, bureaucratic organization, sexual divisions and their influence on patterns of accommodation between workers and management', in R. Frankenberg (ed.) *Custom and Conflict in British Society*, Manchester; Manchester University Press.
Czarniawska-Joerges, B. (1992) *Exploring Complex Organizations. A Cultural Perspective*, London: Sage.
Deal, T. and Kennedy, A. (1982) *Corporate Cultures. The Rites and Rituals of Corporate Life*, Harmondsworth: Penguin.
Douglas, M. (1987) *How Institutions Think*, London: Routledge & Kegan Paul.
Emmett, I. and Morgan, D. (1982) 'Max Gluckman and the Manchester shop-floor ethnographies', in R. Frankenberg (ed.) *Custom and Conflict in British Society*, Manchester: Manchester University Press.
Fairclough, N. (1985) 'Critical and descriptive goals in discourse analysis', *Journal of Pragmatics* 9: 739–763.
Fallers, L. A. (1974) *The Social Anthropology of the Nation State*, Chicago: Aldine.
Frankenberg, R. (ed.) (1982) *Custom and Conflict in British Society*, Manchester: Manchester University Press.
Gardner, B. (1977) 'The anthropologist in business and industry', *Anthropological Quarterly* 50: 171–3.
Geertz, C. (1973) *The Interpretation of Cultures*, New York: Basic Books.
Gluckman, M. (1940) *Analysis of a Social Situation in Zululand*, Manchester: Manchester University Press,
Gough, K. (1968) 'New proposals for anthropologists', *Current Anthropology* 9 (5): 403–7.
Holzberg, C. S. and Giovannini, M. J. (1981) 'Anthropology and industry: reappraisal and new directions', *Annual Review of Anthropology* 10: 317–60.
Huizer, G. (1979) 'Research-through-action: some practical experiences with peasant organization', in G. Huizer and B. Mannheim (eds) *The Politics of Anthropology: From Colonialism and Sexism to a View from Below*, The Hague: Mouton.
Linstead, S. and Grafton-Small, R. (1992) 'On reading organizational culture', *Organization Studies* 13 (3): 331–55.
Marcus, G. E. (1986) 'Contemporary problems of ethnography in the modern world system', in J. Clifford and G. E. Marcus (eds) *Writing Culture*, Berkeley: University of California Press.
Marcus, J. (ed.) 1990 *Writing Australian Culture, Social Analysis* Special Issues Series 27.
Mills, A. J. (1988) 'Organization, gender and culture', *Organization Studies* 9 (3): 351–69.
Mintz, S. W. (1985) *Sweetness and Power. The Place of Sugar in Modern History*, Harmondsworth: Penguin.

Morgan, G. (1986) *Images of Organization*, London: Sage.

Nader, L. (1972) 'Up the anthropologist – perspectives gained from studying up', in D. Hymes (ed.) *Reinventing Anthropology*, New York: Random House.

—— (1980) 'The vertical slice: hierarchies and children', in G. M. Britan and R. Cohen (eds) *Hierarchy and Society. Anthropological Perspectives on Bureaucracy*, Philadelphia: Institute for the Study of Human Issues.

Nash, J. (1979) *We Eat the Mines and the Mines Eat Us: Dependency and Exploitation in Bolivian Tin Mines*, New York: Columbia University P. ess.

Peters, T. J. and Waterman, R. H. (1986) *In Search of Excellence. Lessons from America's Best-Run Companies*, New York: Harper & Row.

Pettigrew, A. M. (1985) *The Awakening Giant. Continuity and Change in Imperial Chemical Industries*, Oxford: Basil Blackwell.

Pondy, L. R. and Mitroff, I. I. (1979) 'Beyond open system models of organization', in L. L. Cummings and B. M. Staw (eds) *Research in Organizational Behaviour*, 1: 3–39, Greenwich CT: JAI Press.

Reinhold, S. (1993) Local Conflict and Ideological Struggle: 'Positive Images' and Section 28. Unpublished D.Phil. thesis, University of Sussex.

Richardson, F. L. W. and Walker, C. R. (1948) *Human Relations in an Expanding Company: A Study of the Manufacturing Departments in the Endicott Plant of the International Business Machines Corporation*, New Haven: Yale University, Labour Management Centre.

Roethlisberger, F. J. and Dickson, W. J. (1939) *Management and the Worker*, Cambridge: Harvard University Press. (All references in the text are from the thirteenth edition, 1964).

Schein, E. H. (1991) 'What is culture?', in P. Frost, L. F. Moore, M. R. Louis, C. Lundberg and J. Martin (eds) *Reframing Organizational Culture*, London: Sage.

Schwartzman, H. B. (1993) *Ethnography of Organizations*, London: Sage.

Smircich, L. (1983) 'Concepts of culture and organizational analysis', *Administrative Science Quarterly* 28 (3): 339–58.

Stansfield, R. G. (1981) 'Operational research and sociology: a case-study of cross-fertilizations in the growth of a useful science', *Science and Public Policy* 8 (4): 262–80.

Strauss, A., Schatzman, L., Ehrlich, D., Bucher, R. and Sabshin, M. (1963) 'The hospital and its negotiated order', in E. Friedson (ed.) *The Hospital in Modern Society*, New York: Macmillan.

Street, B. (1993) 'Culture is a verb: anthropological aspects of language and cultural process', in D. Graddol, L. Thompson and M. Byram (eds) *Language and Culture*, Clevedon, Avon: British Association for Applied Linguistics in Association with Multilingual Matters.

Taylor, F. W. (1947) *Scientific Management*, New York and London: Harper.

Turner, B. A. (1971) *The Industrial Subculture*, London: Macmillan.

Turner, V. (1974) *Dramas, Fields and Metaphors*, Ithaca, NY: Cornell University Press.

Waldo, D. (1961) 'Organization theory: an elephantine problem', *Public Administration Review* 21: 210–25.

Weiss, R. and Miller, L. (1987) 'The concept of ideology in organizational analysis: the sociology of knowledge or the social psychology of beliefs?', *Academy of Management Review* 12 (1): 104–16.

Whyte, W. F. (1948a) *Human Relations in the Restaurant Industry*, New York: McGraw Hill.

—— (1948b) 'Incentive for productivity: the case of the Bundy Tubing Company', *Applied Anthropology* 7 (2): 1–16.

—— (1951) *Pattern for Industrial Peace*, New York: Harper & Row.

—— (1991) *Social Theory for Action. How Individuals and Organizations Learn to Change*, London: Sage.

Willis, P. (1981) *Learning to Labour*, New York: Columbia University Press.

Wolfe A. W. (1977) 'The supranational organization of production: an evolutionary perspective', *Current Anthropology* 18 (4): 615–35.

Young, E. (1989) 'On the naming of the rose: interests and multiple meanings as elements of organizational culture', *Organization Studies* 10 (2): 187–206.

Young, M. (1991) *An Inside Job. Policing and British Culture in Britain*, Oxford: Clarendon Press.

Part I

Indigenous management

Introduction

David Marsden

In the Third World, as in the West, there has been a restructuring of capital and of the role of the state. In both contexts there has been a 'contracting out' of services formerly dealt with by the public sector and an increased reliance on voluntary or non-governmental organizations and on 'local initiative' (on the assumption that greater efficiency and effectiveness of programmes will follow). In the Third World there is an additional concern to enhance the use of indigenous management styles and of local understandings of 'organization' and 'development' as appropriate foundations for intervention efforts. So far this concern seems not to have been raised in contexts of development in the West, perhaps because it is assumed that differences between 'professional' and 'indigenous' ideas about organization and management are not so great. However, there may be lessons to be learned from the much more advanced Third World development debates about the establishment of trans-cultural measurements of quality and of evaluations of the performance of individuals, organizations and development projects, as against the recognition of particular cultural traditions as the basis for development strategies.

The current aims of many development agencies are, *inter alia*, to build more effective partnerships between 'donors' and 'beneficiaries' and between government and people, and thereby to enhance the possibilities for successful interventions made in the name of 'development'. The emphasis is on appropriateness and sustainability. But appropriate to whom and sustainable in what contexts?

Central to these issues is a fundamental concern with the problem of cultural relativity and the 'space' to be given to the elaboration of local development strategies, in the face of trans-cultural preoccupations which suggest that certain sets of values are not negotiable – for example, the values that underpin conditions for structural adjustment, environmental sustainability, enhancement of the role of women, participation, and 'good governance'.

The global restructuring of capital necessitates a changing relationship between the North and the South and between the centre and the periphery. The emphasis on new partnerships through which development programmes and projects might be more effectively implemented introduces a search for new forms of alignment between governments of the North, governments of the South, non-government organizations and local communities. This involves not only new relationships between donors and beneficiaries, but also new forms of organization to administer the transfer of resources from bilateral and multi-lateral donors. Non-government organizations in particular are being given a more central role in this process.

Anthropologists are increasingly drawn into this changing reality, in particular to evaluate the performance of local level development projects which aim at qualitative change in people's lives. There is, first, a recognition that many projects have failed to meet their objectives because they have not taken the 'human factor' into account. Second it is also recognized that if sufficient attention is not given to the development of appropriate organizational forms on which sustainability might be built, projects are likely to fail. A search for the most appropriate organizational forms embedded in particular cultural milieux implies the renegotiation of the aid relationship itself.

As more development aid is channelled through non-government organizations, questions about their effectiveness and efficiency and their organizational appropriateness to deal with new issues of 'quality management' are raised. What sorts of partnerships should be developed? What sorts of organizational forms are most appropriate for the delivery of sustainable development strategies? What sorts of aid initiatives can ensure that the development effort is demand-led rather than supply-driven – responding to the needs and priorities of the 'beneficiaries' rather than 'donor' agencies?

These issues raise further questions about whether 'indigenous' institutions can take a more central role in development initiatives, and about the appropriateness of northern solutions. Such discussions underpin the work of the International Institute for Environment and Development and the Institute of Development Studies at the University of Sussex, for example, in their search for ways of 'putting farmers first' and in elaborating methodologies for the participatory appraisal and evaluation of development projects (Chambers 1993; IIED/IDS 1992). The search for the most appropriate organizations on which sustainable development strategies can be built is to be seen in the current stress on 'institution' or 'capacity' building. The assumption is that without strong organizational foundations, little of lasting value will emerge. Rather than building new 'synthetic' organizations derived from western experience, such as 'co-operatives' and 'development committees', much more attention should be given to those 'organic' institutions which have served local populations well in adjusting over time to changing circumstances and environments.

Different objectives, enshrined in different value systems, will lead to the development of different sorts of organizational forms. Such objectives may not be 'developmental' in the sense in which development agencies define that term. Fowler *et al.* (1993) in his analysis of institutional development draws a distinction between three different sorts of organization based on three different types of objectives – the profit-oriented private organization, the public sector organization, and the not-for-profit (or charitable) organization. Each type will require a different configuration of personnel and will thus develop a different style and organizational form. The cement that binds the different members of the organization together will vary according to the different motivations of members and the understandings of the costs and benefits to be derived from membership. The same is true of 'indigenous' organizations where kinship relationships may be of more importance. If allegiance and motivation are to be ensured, then the legitimacy of the organizational cement must be recognized by members. In programmes to develop institutional capacity, the parameters of allegiance must be clearly understood.

Charles Handy, in his attempts to understand voluntary organizations and how they might deal with change and development, distinguishes between four different organizational types (Handy 1988). He identifies organizations as 'communities' each with their own 'cultures'. He discusses the organizational styles associated with i) 'club culture' whose patron deity is Zeus, a very personal ruler; ii) 'role culture' whose patron deity is Apollo, god of harmony, rules and order; iii) 'task culture' with Athena, goddess of war and patron of the commando leader Odysseus as its deity; and iv) 'person culture' with Dionysus as its deity. Each 'culture' provides different opportunities for and constraints on improvement. This set of classical analogies is reminiscent of Ruth Benedict's (1935) attempts to separate out Apollonian from Dionysian cultures in her analysis of native Americans. This is a type of analysis that Robert Pirsig (1992), in his account of the 'metaphysics of quality', has revisited in a stimulating way.

Handy (1988) and Fowler *et al.* (1993) illustrate a convergence of the work of those involved in the development of management and organizational effectiveness with that of anthropologists working in the field of organizational studies. It points to a rethinking of the relationships between organizational forms and cultural values. The need to look at the cultures of organizations in order to understand whether or not they are appropriate for achieving the objectives of that organization is increasingly recognized. The objective is to focus on those elements which provide opportunities for positive change, and to develop more effective partnerships in the process of development.

The expansion and elaboration of management systems derived from northern models of bureaucracy are increasingly questioned, as are the value premises of such models. If more appropriate systems of management can be derived from indigenous organizational systems, then appropriate development strategies might be more easily attainable. The emphasis is on appropriate building blocks rather than on the preservation of old and inappropriate cultural forms. In the North, the search for 'excellence' has included an examination of Confucian ethics as one of the keys to successful Japanese industrial practices. Are there other such 'keys' embedded in different cultural traditions?

Curtis takes the issue of 'excellence' as his starting point for a discussion of 'common good' and the workings of a farmer-managed irrigation system in Nepal (Chapter 3). He makes extensive use of Peters and Waterman's (1982) classic management study. In doing so he addresses the questions of commitment and ownership which are at the heart of concerns to develop motivation, loyalty and allegiance in modern organizations. The managed irrigation system is successful, he argues, because it is driven by the needs of the customers, the farmers themselves (i.e. it is demand-led rather than supply-driven).

Where governments have lost, forsaken, or never realized their ability to command allegiance and motivate supporters, except through patronage networks, there is a search for alternative means whereby the benefits of development might be more equitably distributed and the legitimacy of elected governments enhanced. The lack of fit between models derived from 'western/northern' experience and those which have characterized 'southern' realities is blamed for the lack of success of many development efforts. If a narrow and unreflexive view of those 'southern' realities is taken, then the fault is attributed to southern patronage networks, institutionalized corruption and extended kinship connections. These are said to inhibit the rational development of effective and efficient organizational forms. If we shift our focus to the values which underpin those 'southern' realities in the eyes of the people themselves, then we might be able to build from where people actually are rather than where we think they are, or where we would like them to be. Nicholson, in her analysis of Papua New Guinean public administration (Chapter 4), gives us a useful example of the ways in which the mores of indigenous systems of obligation, and perceived responsibilities and attitudes towards time, affect the work of civil servants. This points to the possible elaboration of more appropriate organizational forms.

Nicholson argues that to take into account not only the views of local people, but also the bases on which authority and thus legitimacy are constructed, implies a much more participatory approach to development planning. She cites the work of Rondinelli (1983) and Korten (1990), who, among others, have called for greater flexibility in achieving a fit between the objectives of development projects and programmes and the needs of the recipients. This requires a rethinking of 'top-down' development planning in favour of more 'grass-roots' processes. While this inevitably involves less predictability, the chances of achieving success are greater. Such approaches are now enshrined in strategies aimed at 'empowering' local populations to take control of their own development. These strategies shift the onus of responsibility for development on to local populations with development efforts 'facilitating' rather than directing the process.

But the issue of 'empowerment' has to engage with the issue of 'value'. If development efforts are to be context-specific and driven by the norms and values of local cultures, what happens to the development 'mission' with its western or northern values? How does one *evaluate* success and measure risk when there are multiple interpretations of what is important? For example, how does one operationalize a population policy of 'children by choice' in circumstances where great value is attached to having more children in order to ensure security? Or how does one develop an environmental policy for range management in marginal climatic conditions when cattle holders measure wealth in terms of the numbers of animals owned? The question of power and power relationships can never be far from the analysis. In this volume Marsden (Chapter 2) argues that management is inherently about control and that current concerns with more appropriate management styles may be merely another way of extending a cultural hegemony through the cooption of local value systems. If, on the other hand, control is vested in the local organization itself, how can one ensure accountability to a wider support network which facilitates such local organizational development?

Issues of accountability and 'conditionality' and the associated values underlying policies which suggest, for example, that 'structural adjustment' is a necessary process, and that 'value for money' is an unproblematic concept, enshrine values of the 'free market'. In a multi-cultural and multi-vocal world we are witness to the rapid development of a 'world system' which eschews diversity. Do we insist on the development of a set of universal values, or do we engage in a struggle to resist the monopoly over explanations that such a set of values enshrines?

In both the Third World and the West the ethics and morality surrounding interventions in the name of 'development' are subordinated to the demands for objective measurement and the development of more rigorous instruments to evaluate success. But little attention is given to the values that inform the evaluation process, or to the culturally specific contexts in which costs, benefits and risks are assessed. How do we introduce qualitative and participatory analyses into project and programme formulation, implementation and evaluation in ways which enhance partnership and break down distinctions between 'us' and 'them'? Is this 'harmony of interest' already emerging in a United Nations derived consensus or in agreements about what 'value for money' actually means?

The problems of dealing with notions of excellence, quality and the evaluation of performance when different cultural environments have to be taken into account is indeed a formidable one for the anthropologist. The three chapters in Part I suggest that issues of value and quality are culturally determined, and that if development efforts are to be truly sustainable and partnership-based much more negotiation about the harmonization of values will have to be undertaken.

REFERENCES

Benedict, R. (1935) *Patterns of Culture*, Boston: Houghton Mifflin.
Chambers, R. (1993) *Challenging the Professions; Frontiers for Rural Development*, London: Intermediate Technology Publications.
Fowler, A., with Campbell, P. and Pratt, B. (1993) *Institutional Development and NGOs in Africa: Policy Perspectives for European Development Agencies*, Oxford: International NGO Training and Research Centre (INTRAC)/ Netherlands Organization for International Development Cooperation (NOVIB).
Handy, C. (1988) *Understanding Voluntary Organizations*, Harmondsworth: Penguin Books.
International Institute for Environment and Development/Institute of Development Studies (IIED/IDS) (1992) Proceedings of Conference entitled *Beyond Farmer First*, held at the University of Sussex, October.
Korten, D.C. (1990) *Getting to the Twenty First Century: Voluntary Action and the Global Agenda*, West Hartford: Kumarian Press.
Peters, R. and Waterman, R. (1982) *In Search of Excellence*, New York: Harper & Row.
Pirsig, R. (1992) *Lila: The Metaphysics of Quality*, London: Vantage Press.
Rondinelli, D.A. (1983) *Development Projects as Policy Experiments: An Adaptive Approach to Development Administration*, London: Methuen.

2 Indigenous management and the management of indigenous knowledge

David Marsden

INTRODUCTION

Current development efforts focus on building institutional capacity through the encouragement of local self-reliance. These are aimed at empowering the hitherto excluded and at encouraging individual entrepreneurial activity. Different understandings of the purposes of development converge on the assumption that if progress is to be achieved it cannot be imposed from the outside and has to be built on small locally-based initiatives. It is now commonplace to hear that there are many paths to development, each built on a different cultural base and using different tools, techniques and organizations. The assumptions underlying the view that it would be sufficient to transfer western technology and expertise no longer hold. It is not the 'native' who is backward, nor is it a failure to incorporate the 'human factor' which is at fault, but the essential inappropriateness of the western package that was on offer.

In this chapter I want to try to uncover some of the complexities that lie behind the concept of 'indigenous management' which is seen as a possible way forward in the task of institution building and developing sustainable capacity. There are many threads to this analysis which need to be pulled together – differing interpretations of reality and thus of the development task.

The dominant discourse of development is imbued with the supposedly neutral vocabulary of management. This has replaced, or is rapidly replacing the vocabulary of economics. Efforts are directed at increasing efficiency, economy, and effectiveness and providing opportunities for the encouragement of private entrepreneurial activity. A radical renegotiation of the limits to government is taking place. Policies for privatization are aimed at sectors that have traditionally been defined as part of the public domain. This is not, of course, peculiar to the Third World.

Failures of 'top-down', externally conceived projects and programmes have led to the elaboration of locally based, indigenous strategies and to the development of more flexible management approaches. The assumption in both the First and the Third Worlds is that people will be more responsive if they are central to the design and implementation of programmes that affect them and if they have made some investment or commitment to them. In these attempts to get the state off the backs of people, attention is paid to the development of local institutions which are small enough to command authority and foster participation. The complexities of micro-level intervention move centre stage and analyses of local cultures gain increased importance. A recognition that there is more to development than just economic productivity leads to a focus on processes as well as on products – on building institutional capacity and more effective dialogue between donors and recipients through the elaboration of methodologies such as participatory appraisal and evaluation.

In pursuit of these aims the appeal of indigenous management is self-evident – the elaboration of local strategies by local people for the control and use of their own resources in the struggle for self-reliant development. But two major conceptual problems immediately arise when we begin to reflect on what is meant by the terms 'indigenous' and 'management'. These are key terms in current development discourse and the different ways in which they are used and the meanings attached to them need to be unpackaged before we are in a position to assess the appropriateness of further encouraging this kind of development.

PROBLEMS OF DEFINITION: INDIGENOUS PEOPLES

The analysis of terms like 'indigenous people' takes us to the centre of current discussions in the social sciences about how we are to understand other cultures. *The Oxford English Dictionary* defines 'indigenous' as 'born or produced naturally in a land or region; of, pertaining to, or intended for the natives; "native", "vernacular"'. This definition raises more questions than it answers. What is meant by 'native'? What does 'naturally' mean? Is the term equivalent to 'traditional'? An additional meaning is also perhaps implied which refers to 'authenticity' and local 'legitimacy', derived from claims for originality, not in terms of unique-ness so much as in terms of connections with an unbroken historical association with a place. As Illich has pointed out in his analysis of vernacular culture: 'Each village does its own dance to the tune of its own regional music' (1982: 108). In development discourse at least three distinct uses of the term 'indigenous' can be isolated. First, there is that use which refers to 'indigenous peoples'. Second, there is that use which refers to the process of 'indigenization'; and third, there is that use which refers more generally to 'insider' knowledge and its use.

Indigenous peoples are marginal peoples, dispossessed or threatened minorities, such as native Americans, Australian Aborigines, and Brazilian Indians. Current interest in these people focuses on the vulnerability that such groups exhibit in their relationships to neighbouring dominant cultures which threaten to overwhelm them. These groups are in danger of extinction as a result of the homogenizing processes of modernization and the expansion of populations into more marginal areas which make up their 'homelands'. Their plight is linked to similar concerns about environmental destruction and maintaining species diversity, in a world-wide concern to adopt 'greener' development paths.

Diversity and pluralism are hallmarks of the western liberal democratic tradition and these 'indigenous peoples' provide vivid examples of the rich diversity that characterizes the 'Family of Man'. In the face of the overwhelming power of external forces their struggle to retain their separate identity highlights the plight of the underdog and the rights to which these hitherto invisible and ignored groups are entitled. In this discourse indigenous peoples are 'entitled' to practise a style of life which is seen to be in harmony with nature and to have evolved over many years. Their use of natural resources has been assumed to be judicious, and the tools and techniques that they employ have apparently ensured a sustainability which should be emulated rather than destroyed.

One particular expression of concern for 'indigenous peoples' focuses on preservation and conservation. (This is paralleled in the natural world by movements which attempt to draw boundaries around 'wilderness areas' and 'game reserves'.) Indigenous peoples are put in 'native reservations' which are devoted to the exclusive use of particular groups, and also (in more complex terms) in 'tribal homelands' governed by separate development strategies that acknowledge the 'rights' of different groups to pursue different ends, according to their 'traditions'. Here we enter dangerous ground. Are we not in danger of advocating apartheid and denying the essential unity of humankind? Who can we really identify as 'indigenous peoples'? Are we dealing only with those people who occupy marginal areas – a very small proportion of the human population? Or do we include groups like the Mennonites in the US? How do we deal with the many others who claim rights to separate identity by virtue of their continuous (and original) occupancy of particular tracts of land – the Bretons, the Armenians, the Kurds, the Palestinians? Where can calls for separate identity end? 'Indigenous' begins to refer to an attitude of mind and assumes a struggle for rights somehow abrogated or ignored by a colonizing power. It may also refer to those types of organization that emphasize communal use of resources, untainted with the selfish individualism associated with the expansion of private property.

Where can calls for separate identity end, or should the 'Balkanization' process be allowed to proceed unfettered, in pursuit of infinite diversity and in the interests of pluralism, but with the severe genocidal consequences we witness in former Yugoslavia? Conservatives might argue that we are witnessing the breakup of what was called society by the atomization of cultures and the dissolution of communities. If we adopt a position which acknowledges the uniqueness of individual cultures, based on the assumption that local adaptations are the results of a long history of fine tuning responses to the environment and thus are 'best fits', then we are pushed into a position which denies the possibility of meta-interpretations, and which precludes the use of any overarching value system through which a unifying morality might be established.

While demands for separate cultural and perhaps political identity might be made by 'natives' of particular places, and acceded to in a process reminiscent of decolonization, but now labelled decentralization, it is quite clear that at another level a process of centralization is at work and the overarching values associated with individual capitalist accumulation are spreading even further. Populations are becoming more rather than less integrated in terms of common aspirations, common goals and common needs, expressed in a mutually intelligible language: the language of the market. Any understanding of how indigenous peoples come to be isolated for separate treatment must take account of this wider context. Indigenous peoples are central to the arguments of those who would resist the imposition of a narrow, uni-dimensional view of the world and the direction that development should take. They are also important for those advocates of diversity who would wish to divest themselves of responsibility for the welfare of traditional or minority groups, who might inhibit their progress. Separate development, under the guise of self-reliant development, is advocated in the breakup of large public-sector conglomerates in the North as well as in the South, in the encouragement of regional autonomy, of small-scale enterprises, and in the legitimacy afforded to activities within the 'informal sector'. Participation, from this point of view, is the right to pursue an individual course of action unfettered by the constraints of centralized bureaucracy, but also unbolstered by the security of collective welfare provision.

INDIGENIZATION OF MANAGEMENT

The second way in which the term 'indigenous' is used is encapsulated in the term 'indigenization', and illustrated by the concept of 'Africanization' (Adedeji 1981). The process here referred to is characterized by a bid to get rid of expatriates and is a product of nationalism in the post-colonial era. It means the transfer of ownership, control, manpower and technology from foreigners or aliens, who formerly dominated the economy, to citizens of the newly independent states.

It is this process of indigenization that has given rise to many of the demands for indigenous management. The large exodus of skilled manpower after independence meant that the human resources needed to fill the many vacant positions were not available. There was little question that replacements needed to be found and the emphasis of much development aid in this period (and arguably continuing to the present) was on human resource development and on crash programmes to train people so that they could fill the gap. Business schools modelled on their western counterparts, and usually linked with them in one form or another, rapidly expanded, as did the numbers of graduates from western institutions of higher learning. Products of these various institutions replicated views of management promoted in the United States, where management was seen as being based on a general set of principles and analytical techniques which could be applied to organizational problems in a universalistic way. The local context and culture were deemed to be unimportant. And in any case, too much of a preoccupation with local colour would inhibit trainees from being incorporated into the international community which was the natural orientation of management and business studies (Davies *et al.* 1989).

Can we really term this 'indigenization' when the same techniques were employed and the underlying presumptions of this western practice were not questioned? Only the personnel were changed.

WHOSE KNOWLEDGE COUNTS?

If management is not to be based on western practice but on indigenous cultural forms, this leads to a greater interest in non-Western knowledge systems. This coincides with an increased reflexivity within western social sciences which draws attention to the partiality of knowledge. Until relatively recently the dominant paradigm which stressed the superiority of western objective, scientific rationality consigned 'other' forms of knowledge to positions of inferiority. 'Traditional' was synonymous with 'primitive' and with 'simple' as this dominant world view impressed an image of unilinear evolutionary development on scientists and the general public alike. It was expressed in one way through the separation of the 'great' from the 'little' traditions and in the distinctions between 'high' and 'folk' cultures.

A major programme of the United Nations University challenges this particular interpretation of events through a focus on indigenous intellectual creativity and an examination of the importance of the great cultural traditions of the East – notably those of India and China. It seems that the scientific tradition itself is the one that is 'traditional', endowed with magic, religion and superstition, as its tenets turn into dogma and as intellectual creativity is thereby stifled. With the recognition that development strategies must be altered if sustainable benefits are to be gained, if destruction of the environment is to be avoided, and if the tension resulting from increased differentiation within and between populations is to be reduced, comes the search for paths which are more appropriate, more flexible and more local. 'Participation', 'self-reliance', 'dialogue', 'grassroots', become key words in this search, in association with calls for 'deconcentration' and 'devolution' in attempts to break away from the suffocating effects of large-scale monopolies, whether these be private or public, urban or international.

Into this quest comes a renewed interest in indigenous knowledge systems, in the belief that they may be the bases for building more sustainable development strategies, because they begin from where the people are, rather than from where we would like them to be. It is commonly maintained that these indigenous technical knowledge systems if articulated properly will provide the bases for increasing productivity, for creating more viable livelihood strategies and for encouraging alternative living arrangements. The assumption is that because peasants, nomads, natives and women have survived for centuries in harmony with nature they have obviously developed highly attuned adaptive strategies which need to be recuperated and used as a basis for planning for the future. Indigenous technical knowledge is to be 'harnessed' for the purposes of development. The assumption is that peasants and poor people, the usual objects of development aid, are well-informed decision makers who know what will and will not work. They are not the irresponsive, conservative traditionalists that the architects of modernization theory would have us believe.

'Local', 'traditional' or 'folk' knowledge is no longer the irrelevant vestige of 'backward' people who have not yet made the transition to modernity, but the vital well springs and resource bank from which alternative futures might be built. The arrogance with which policy makers and planners assumed that they were writing on a *tabula rasa* as they intervened in the Third World in the name of development, is being replaced by a reflexive understanding of the partiality of their own knowledge and a heightened appreciation of the value of other ways of perceiving the development task. This is highlighted by, but not confined to, current attempts to focus on processes rather than products of development, to incorporate the traditional objects of development (women, the urban and rural poor) much more centrally into planning and implementation, to institutionalize reversals in decision making, and to understand the complexities associated with micro-environmental and contextual changes.

But the current prominence of other world views in the search for more effective development strategies should not lead us into assuming that this is a new form of enquiry. An interest in other cultures and the ways in which they interpret and explain the world is as old as civilization itself; as long as cultures have been in contact with each other there have been attempts at interpretation. So why the current concern? When development writers speak of indigenous technical knowledge they are not usually referring to the 'great traditions' of Buddhism, Taoism, Hinduism or Islam. Their focus is much more on that knowledge which plays a role in the everyday existence of local people – what Illich refers to as 'vernacular' knowledge. The ingenuity of local coping mechanisms in technical and agricultural activities is a constant theme. A rich literature now exists which bears testimony to this ingenuity. This legacy provides a basis on which promises of alternative development strategies might draw and which might provide the foundations for more sustainable strategies.

CONSERVATION AND PRESERVATION

A dominant theme in this discussion is that of 'conservation' of resources both natural and intellectual in the interests of 'preserving' heterogeneity. The monolithic forces that apparently guide modern development strategies and lead to the homogenization of world cultures in a process of convergent development are responsible for the destruction of our environment and the disappearance of worlds of understanding. This 'declining base' inhibits opportunities for expansion and for cultural and natural adaptation in the future.

Strategies for 'conservation' and 'preservation', as noted earlier, are informed by a world view which assumes that somehow the earth offers a finite number of opportunities. This world view informs many attitudes to education and the acquisition of knowledge generally. It ignores the ways in which knowledge is created and also the dynamism and imminence of culture and resources. As Raymond Williams (1974) and others have demonstrated, techniques, technologies and cultural forms (organizations and institutions) do not stand alone. They are tools that can be used in a variety of ways. It is important to understand how and why they are used in particular circumstances as well as to understand who uses them and under what conditions. Knowledge, like technology, is never neutral. It can never be completely packaged. Its history and its context must be uncovered if we are to approach its meaning and not be mystified by its current form.

This is the essence of the 'process' approach to development which seeks not to impose a preconceived understanding of the most efficient, effective and economic ways forward but rather to build, through increased trust and mutuality, sustainable strategies that create room for manoeuvre by building on where people are rather than where we would like them to be, and by constantly creating their own texts rather than reading the texts of others prepared with little understanding of the constant realignment required of such a process approach.

COMPETING THEORETICAL PERSPECTIVES

The project, as the predominant organizing concept for intervention in the name of development, remains only partially articulated to the realities of everyday life. Indigenous management is an attempt to further this articulation. This process can be viewed from competing theoretical perspectives. Both of these would concur that the issue of control is central to the managerial task. Some perceive management as a neutral activity: 'the process of control is broken down into an inter-related set of mechanisms or procedures through which [it] can restructure . . . to meet more effectively the demands and threats posed by its environment' (Reed 1989: 34). For these people the issue is finding the mechanisms that can produce a neater fit between those doing the managing and those being managed. For those who perceive management in more Machiavellian terms, the problem of control is 'one of simultaneously securing and mystifying the exploitative relationship between a dominant and a subordinate class whose interests are placed in a position of structured antagonism because of the conflicting priorities embedded in such a relationship' (1989: 34). As Bourdieu has argued, the instruments of control are enshrined in 'good faith' relationships which disguise the actual ways in which unequal relationships are maintained and through which surplus value is extracted (Bourdieu 1977).

It is obvious that there are many ways of understanding, perceiving, experiencing and defining reality. In addition to conflicting interpretations generated within the western scientific tradition, there are very different interpretations within local groups – the knowledge of elites is different from that of peasants, the knowledge that women have is different from that which men have. If indigenous management is about utilizing local, folk, or vernacular knowledge and organizational methods in the service of more appropriate development strategies, then it is important to investigate how that knowledge is gained and interpreted, what that knowledge is and how it might be most effectively used. Knowledge is a key asset in securing control and thus any discussions about it must necessarily recognize the political dimensions of its use.

But how is it produced, and what is the distinction between indigenous knowledge and exogenous knowledge? Who creates the distinction between the two sorts of knowledge, bearing in mind that many of the scientific bases of western knowledge are derived from non-western (indigenous?) sources? What sorts of knowledge count and who decides when they count? To answer such questions it is necessary to analyse the ways in which knowledge is generated, exchanged, transformed, consolidated, stored, retrieved, disseminated and utilized (cf. Rolings and Engel 1989). 'Indigenous management' in this initial understanding is then an understanding of so-called indigenous institutions and organizations in order to harness them for the wider development effort whose objectives have already been set. Management here means control and the subordination of indigenous institutions to achieve externally set objectives.

TEXT AND DISCOURSE

When conceptualizing indigenous knowledge systems we are essentially thinking of 'other cultures' and the technical and non-technical features of such cultures. Such knowledge is supposed to be based on unique epistemologies, philosophies, institutions and principles which are often seen as tied to mystical or religious beliefs (Rhoades 1984). All knowledge is culture-based whether it is classified as indigenous or not. The danger is that we perceive cultures as discrete, bounded systems in a functional way and, through certain forms of representation, present them as undynamic and unchanging. Current research on the production of ethnographies cautions against such a view and eloquently and forcibly proposes a much more sensitive approach to modes of cultural representation. The activity of cross-cultural representation is distinctly problematic. As Clifford points out, 'an ambiguous multi-vocal world makes it increasingly hard to conceive of human diversity as inscribed in bounded, independent cultures' (1988: 23).

In the analysis of cultural identity it is necessary to examine how histories and ethnographies are produced. A distinction needs to be made between 'text' and 'discourse'. A commonly asserted dichotomy distinguishes between the written and the oral tradition. 'Indigenous' is associated with 'oral' – information is not written down and thus remains outside recorded history. One temptation is to consign this oral knowledge to a position of inferiority, as Farrington and Martin (1988) seem to do – it is slower and less dependable. The old divisions between 'traditional' and 'modern' are thereby resurrected in a new way. Another temptation is to romanticize and idealize local knowledge in a new reverence for the 'noble savage', thereby implying a functional separation between two sorts of knowledge, assessed through different and mutually exclusive criteria for validation.

SPECIALISTS AND GENERALISTS

Can we therefore recast the distinction between indigenous knowledge and exogenous knowledge in terms of distinctions between 'professionals' and 'generalists', or 'amateurs'? Those employed as 'experts' in development projects bring specialist knowledge to the task, as distinct from the lay-person who brings practical knowledge of everyday existence and who has until recently been ignored. But this distinction is attacked by those who would encourage reversals in development thinking – by putting the farmer first, and seeing her too as a 'professional'.

Niamir, in a literature review of indigenous knowledge and natural resource management, points out that 'traditional decision making is flexible and fluid' (1989: 3) – just the attributes that modern management theory is attempting to inculcate. Similarly, she argues that indigenous knowledge systems contain mechanisms which promote relatively equitable access to resources by weaker and poorer members of society. These are features which have not been prominent in many 'top-down' approaches and which are now seen as central to effective, sustainable development.

Thus modern management principles based on contingency theories would themselves appear to be conflating the roles of professionals and generalists. As Blunt has noted, 'the tidy picture is nearly always clouded by informal considerations' (1990: 14). Reed points out that 'Managers' interest in participation strategies springs directly from [the] problem of consent and coordination that is at the heart of the "management" job' (1989: 117–18) and, although referring to industrial enterprises, 'the search for flexibility has become something of a catch-all concept for everything and anything employers find desirable to increase operational efficiency and company profitability' (1989: 155). Davies *et al.* also point out that 'in the UK and the USA much of the interest has shifted away from management as a science, towards understanding the values and belief systems in an organization that can lead to excellent performances' (1989: 3).

This shift in management principles reflects a wider shift in social values, as consumers struggle to gain more control over the things they purchase and to use their power and influence to reshape the environment and the direction of development. The progressive division of labour, seen as the foundations of industrial urban societies, produces counter-productive specializations which provide some with the resources and the legitimacy to maintain inegalitarian monopolies, others with inappropriate technical qualifications which consign them to unemployment, and still others who are increasingly dependent on external inputs for goods and services.

Generalist (or indigenous?) knowledge is then focused on breaking the hierarchical control of those with specialist access, through the development of generic competence. Part of this interest is driven by the high costs of professional advice and service, and the inability or reluctance of governments to finance escalating costs, but another part is driven by the need to incorporate this knowledge more effectively into systems of managerial control – to 'capture' this knowledge on the assumption that it is wild and needs to be tamed!

The development of more effective managerial systems requires, then, more and more general, informal, indigenous information. The pursuit of effectiveness in this case is founded on attempts to increase productivity in areas hitherto neglected, ignored or excluded from interventions in the name of development. Attention is focused on the informal sector and on women's work. As Illich notes, 'The economic formalization of the informal sector, and its bureaucratic policing by professional agencies promoting self care will, during the last quarter of the twentieth century take on a function analogous to colonialism in earlier decades' (1982: 37). Attention is also focused on organizational culture – gaining more understanding of how organizations function and thereby creating environments more conducive to meeting organizational objectives. Indigenous management is associated with enhancing these internal objectives as well as with articulating more closely with them by manipulating the external environment. This is a process which is, indeed, very reminiscent of colonialism and 'indirect rule', as long as the objectives are not made public and subject to participatory debate.

In a recent collection on management for development (Ndegwa 1986), there is a clear association between management and general political competence. Recognition of 'the crucial role of political leaders as managers' (1986: 18) and a 'more socially responsible and managerially oriented political leadership' (1986: 17) are called for. Are we to assume that there is a growing convergence between managers and politicians, and that the state is little more than a managed enterprise whose tentacles reach into the farthest recesses of citizens' lives, as the minutiae of daily existence are brought under the critical purview of a centralizing vision? This extension of administration from being re-active to pro-active smacks of social engineering on a large scale and of totalitarian control.

If this is the case, then the 'crisis of management' so often alluded to is indeed real, and the objectives of its specialist attention will decompose in the pursuit of 'generalist', 'generic' principles. Indigenous knowledge teaches us to respect that 'generalist' knowledge which our grandparents or 'other cultures' have, as the bases for constructing more humane and wholesome development strategies. To assert, as do Shanti-Sadiq and Gupta, that 'the basic objective of management is to achieve perfection by removing deficiencies in man [sic] and his environment' (1989: 57) displays a profound hubris which unfortunately seems to underpin much thinking in information technology and management science generally.

Generalist perspectives are often incorporated in 'texts' which are assumed to have no place in the rational–scientific tasks of managers. As indicated in a recent collection of papers on management for development in Africa:

> we discard those old thoughts of people who are just romantics, who want to talk to us about the good old African way of life which is disappearing and must be restored. They glorify their own perception of traditional African societies and write in a romantic manner. This should be left to novelists and poets who write about the village life and how it must be restored, and how everything else there must remain as things used to be.
>
> (Ndegwa 1986: 10)

Unfortunately many of those 'romantics' end up in exile or in prison because they dare to criticize the dominant regime. Their ideas and perceptions are ridiculed and consigned to inferiority. But as Illich perceptively comments,

> the researcher who wants to avoid the bias implicit in a central perspective ought to identify himself closely as one engaged in research that is disciplined, critical, well documented and public, but emphatically non-scientific. Only non-scientific research that uses analogy, metaphor and poetry can reach for gendered reality.
>
> (1982: 62, n. 46)

So the trend in modern management is towards increased generalization within a professional context which attempts to secure control over more and more areas of knowledge. It is interesting to note that in current discussions of non-government organizations, they are being advised to move in the opposite direction by casting off their amateur second generation image and developing 'third' and 'fourth' generation characteristics of increased professionalism rooted in modern management practice.

COMMUNAL VERSUS INDIVIDUAL/PERSONAL VERSUS PUBLIC

If we have difficulties dealing with indigenous knowledge in terms of distinctions between specialist and generalist knowledge, can we focus on distinctions between personal and public knowledge? Only with caution. It is undoubtedly public or communal knowledge which is displayed, at least initially, when strangers confront each other: they adopt non-threatening public faces which provide room for accommodation and negotiation.

Unfortunately the history of this contact as written in the annals of colonialism and of the post-independence era has been asymmetrical. It is the development experts who probe into the inner workings of rural households, who wish to 'mine' the rich seams of local knowledge whereby indigenous populations make sense of and act on their local environments. When interpreters of other cultures pass a threshold of involvement, when they become 'insiders', but not through being honorary members on whom public title is bestowed, then a reflexive awareness of the asymmetry displays itself in a spirited defence of the 'oppressed'. Dialogue has replaced extension in an attempt to make sense of the 'multi-vocal' world that Clifford identifies. Only in such instances does the private world of the expert enter into the negotiated field.

There are then at least two circuits of knowledge – the private and the public – which interact in very complex ways. In addition to this crude characterization there are different types of public knowledge. It is in the nature of interactions within and between 'knowledge systems' to make manifest certain sorts of information and to keep other sorts hidden. The essence of all communities resides in sacred places, symbolically represented by cultural objects: the Ashanti stool, the Muslim *ka'aba*, the sacred grove, the American flag, the war memorial. These are, at the same time, both public and private, where the symbol of communal solidarity is displayed in rituals of public affirmation, and where legitimacy and authority is conferred on particular people.

At such rituals the public rhetoric of solidarity often disguises jockeying for position, or is accompanied by less formal opportunities to exchange 'secret' information or to gossip. It also disguises the fact that such rituals serve to confer probity on dubious individuals. The sacredness of such rituals is defended with much vigour because they are the symbols through which the old order defends its privileges. In materialist terms they serve to disguise or veil the processes whereby surplus value is appropriated, and people are consigned to inferior or subordinate positions in the household, the organization, the nation, or the world order.

An interpretative social science, committed to uncovering the hitherto hidden, excluded, or ignored agenda of social action brings with it the tools to violate these 'sacred groves' as well as the pre-conditions for effective dialogue based on mutual trust and informed by greater understanding. Such an analysis provides the prerequisites for an examination of the sorts of indigenous knowledge that are currently at the centre of discussions about indigenous management. In collecting that knowledge one has already changed its essential nature, through the ways in which it has been appropriated.

To conclude then. While current rhetoric focuses on building self-reliance and sustainable development strategies through strengthening local institutions, we are in danger of overlooking the cultural and historical contexts in which such rhetoric has emerged. This chapter has attempted to point out some of the obstacles associated with the appropriation of 'insider' knowledge, and to highlight the essentially political nature of knowledge acquisition. It has attempted to raise questions about the development process itself and the current efforts to focus on participatory development which call for people being put first. It has also called into question the attempts to develop more appropriate management tools and cautions against the imposition of externally conceived and defined understandings. It raises questions about the development of cross-cultural understanding and thus about building partnerships in pursuit of more equitable development strategies.

REFERENCES

Adedeji, A. (ed.) (1981) *The Indigenization of African Economies*, New York: Africana.

Blunt, P. (1990) 'Strategies for enhancing organizational effectiveness in the Third World', *Public Administration and Development*, 10 (3): 299–313.

Bourdieu, P. (1977) *Outline of a Theory of Practice*, Cambridge: Cambridge University Press.

Chambers, R. (1983) *Rural Development: Putting the Last First*, London: Longman.

Chipeta (1982) *Economics of Indigenous Labour*, New York: Vantage Press.

Clifford, J. (1988) *The Predicament of Culture: Twentieth Century Ethnography, Literature and Art*, Cambridge, MA: Harvard University Press.

Davies, J., Easterby-Smith, M. and Mann, S. (eds) (1989) *The Challenge to Western Management Development*, London: Routledge.

Farrington, J. and Martin, A. (1988) *Farmer Participation in Agricultural Research: A Review of Concepts and Practices*, London: Overseas Development Institute.

Illich, I. (1982) *Gender*, London: Marion Boyars.

Ndegwa, P. (1986) *African Challenge: In Search of Appropriate Development Strategies*, Nairobi: Heinemann.

Niamir, N. (1989) 'Local knowledge and systems of natural resource management in arid and semi-arid Africa', in D. M. Warren, L. Van Slikeveer and T. Titilola (eds), *Indigenous Knowledge Systems: Implications for Agriculture and International Development*, Studies in Technology and Social Change, Ames, Iowa: Iowa State University Press.

Reed, M. I. (1989) *The Sociology of Management*, Hemel Hempstead: Harvester Wheatsheaf.

Rhoades, R. E. (1984) *Breaking New Ground: Agricultural Anthropology*, Lima: International Potato Center.

Rolings, N. and Engel, P. (1989) 'IKS and knowledge management: utilizing indigenous knowledge in institutional knowledge systems', in D. M. Warren, L. Van Slikeveer and T. Titilola, (eds), *Indigenous Knowledge Systems: Implications for Agriculture and International Development*, Studies in Technology and Social Change, Ames, Iowa: Iowa State University Press.

Shanti-Sadiq, A. and Gupta, A. (eds) (1987) *Africa: Dimensions of the Economic Crisis. An Analysis of the Problems and Constraints of Development*, New Delhi: Stirling.

Williams, R. (1974) Television, *Technology and Cultural Form*, London: Fontana.

3 'Owning' without owners, managing with few managers
Lessons from Third World irrigators

Donald Curtis

This chapter is about organizations and about understandings of organizations through anthropology, through management science, through formal economic analysis, and the applicability of these things in a cross-cultural context. There is also a conscious reversal of the notion, still powerful, that advanced industrial society always provides lessons for the less industrial.

The title of the chapter points to two sets of ideas in management science, each backed in theory, that management consultants commonly attempt to sell to their customers. The first suggests that managers and other workers, to be effective, need to have a sense of 'ownership' of their jobs. Ownership has to be in inverted commas, because we are not talking about actual ownership but about a management style that gives people a sense of responsibility and commitment. The second, which will be explored in greater depth, concerns structures, processes and relationships expressed through what management scientists are now inclined to call organizational culture as, for example, when they discuss the 'new enterprise culture'.

The chapter is based upon the finding that Third World farmers who manage their own irrigation systems seem to have come to similar conclusions about structure and culture to those drawn by management scientists about the desirable features of responsive organizations in northern industrial societies. It presents some evidence for this assertion and asks why this should be the case, particularly when so much of the management literature that applies to the Third World cautions against any assumption that management theory derived from the industrial world is relevant in the non-industrial world.

The short answer is that, in looking at farmer managed irrigation, one sees effective organization through which a complex task is managed in an uncertain environment in the interests of the customers; all characteristics that are shared by effective modern firms. The focus of the analysis is on task, environment, responsiveness to key interests and a value system reflective of this orientation. It would follow that the reason for failures of management theory in the Third World lies not in differences in economic location but in its application to organizations that are *not* driven to carry out complex tasks, or to be responsive to customers, as is still the case with much of the public sector.

The assertion that effective farmer managed irrigation shares characteristics with effective modern firms needs further exploration.

FARMER MANAGED IRRIGATION

Farmer managed irrigation has received considerable attention from social analysts. There is much careful empirical study (Martin and Yoder 1987) and several authors, including Edmund Leach in his classic study of Pul Eliya (1961), have sought to locate their observations in a broader theoretical framework. Some more recent studies have attempted to draw out practical insights into how 'modern', government-run irrigation should be managed (ODI 1984). One or two use our knowledge of farmer managed systems to seek general principles for the development of self-reliant local organizations (Ostrom 1992). But let us start with simple explanation.

What is farmer managed irrigation? An early challenge to my sociological imagination occurred on a drive with my in-laws through the Punjab and up into Kashmir. As the plains gave way to the hills the terrain became radiated with purposefully constructed rivulets, each hunting along a contour and opening into fields that reflected sunlight through a haze of green. Having messed around with water in my youth I wanted to know, 'How was this done; village panchayats, local government or what?' A dismissive 'Clever fellows these farmers' was the best that I could get out of my middle-class in-laws for whom the watering of the paddy-fields was so much part of the landscape that it could be taken for granted.

Twenty years later the complexity of the task has been acknowledged. Irrigation is about taking water from a source or a collection point and reticulating it across a cultivatable command area that lies below the source. Headworks, main canals, secondary and sometimes tertiary canals are required, besides the levelling and terracing of the fields that are to be cultivated. Downstream drainage may also be necessary. All this represents massive capital development even when the hardware appears to be unsophisticated. Many farmer managed systems are small, some single farm-sized, but others span hundreds of acres and several villages. It is of course the latter which face problems of social articulation that can be analysed in terms of structure and management system.

Studies indicate that the organizational structures of farmer managed irrigation systems tend to reflect the physical structures, all irrigators being involved in the parts of the system that serve the system as a whole, but dividing into groups and subgroups as canals divide to serve different sectors of the command area. Each cultivator contributes labour for system construction and maintenance as required and for this receives an entitlement to water. This way individuals can see themselves as serving a personal interest that is a part of the collective interest. The relationships involved can be seen as a complex form of reciprocation, in which there is a proportionality of commitment and benefit, obligation and entitlement (Coward 1979). Usually certain leadership roles are differentiated.

My first chance to study such systems came when I conducted fieldwork in Nepal. My associate in that study, Tarak Bhadur KC, of the Nepalese Administrative Staff College, had personal knowledge of the Bansbote system in Dang Valley and we made this one of our case studies (Bhadur 1986; Curtis 1991). The Bansbote system has a command area that serves three villages and is one of three adjacent systems on the left bank of the Sewar river, a small river that flows into the valley from the North. The logic of the system in Bansbote conformed to the norm described in the above paragraph but a notable feature was the fact that the detail of the management system had apparently been changed over the years as the power of the landlord class, the Zamindar tax farmers, had been abolished, leaving other elements of the social structure to manage their own affairs. What one could see in this system, as in others that we studied, was a structure subject to constant popular debate amongst the cultivators. Important distinctions remained between landowners and tenants or sharecroppers, all men, differing in wealth and status, but alike in the need to respond to demand for labour for system maintenance.

Is it possible to study management within this cultural context with the tools and concepts of a management science applied in modern firms?

MODERN MANAGEMENT

Much modern management theory finds its roots in practice. For instance, Peters and Waterman's splendidly pragmatic study of excellence in American industry (1982) rejects the theorizing of the Weberian tradition and looks instead for what makes for success. They are captivated by the smile of the hotel receptionist who remembers them after a long interval, and look for what motivates her to represent her firm so well. They are full of anecdotes about hamburgers, jet planes and micro-computers. They disguise any semblance of psychology (or indeed any other 'ology) with catch-phrases or colloquialisms. And indeed they have become a part of what they were looking for – the management culture that works for American industry. There are many advantages to the approach. The stuff is readable. But more important, they leave the errors to others. While management consultants throughout the world trade on Peters and Waterman chapter headings – 'A Bias for Action', etc. – as I do below, the authors themselves make no claims to the universal applicability of their findings.

Empiricism has the limitation that, while one may be able to distinguish between better or worse according to some valued criterion (innovative ability, profitability, happiness or whatever), it is not possible to consider whether some other form of organization might not have been equally effective in the circumstances. Peters and Waterman do not develop a comparative framework through which to analyse the institutions of late capitalism – as compared with early capitalism, or perhaps developing country capitalism. However, many more methodologically sophisticated formal studies, like some of those about Japanese industrial practices, still run into problems of comparison. In many such cases we are left thinking: yes it works for the Japanese, but isn't there something unexplained about the circumstances of that country that makes a difference?

The Peters and Waterman empiricism and pragmatism made refreshing reading after the laborious formalism of much organization theory to that date. But it has to be noted that it was the more acceptable because so many of the observations were generally confirming the arguments of the formal, theory based studies – particularly the early studies of innovative firms such as that of Burns and Stalker (1961). This kind of theory, as well as economic analysis that I use here, could provide the link that enables comparison between organizations in such different settings as hill irrigation and modern industrial production.

Properly speaking, therefore, I should not use Peters and Waterman's findings to illustrate the excellence of farmer managed irrigation, because that was not their chosen problem. Instead we should look to formal studies of some kind. In the latter part of this chapter I shall do just that, with an attempt to apply some neo-classical economic logic to the behaviour of the farmers.

But an improper application of Peters and Waterman will serve to show the fit between the generalizations that they find useful in searching for excellence in industrial America and the endeavours of farmers in mountainous Nepal.

MANAGING AMBIGUITY AND PARADOX

The first focus of attention of Peters and Waterman is upon 'Managing Ambiguity and Paradox'. Under this heading Peters and Waterman discuss the post-1970s view of the world of modern enterprise. At first glance this is the least likely feature of modern management to have any relevance for the analysis of excellence in farmer managed irrigation. Farmers are not in the business of constant modification of products for fashion-conscious markets and may be less exposed than are computer manufacturers or fast food chains to the booms and slumps of the world market. But, as we are coming to appreciate across the range of rural development studies, it is never safe to assume that static models of behaviour or environment will fit.

Peters and Waterman make some radical assumptions about how one is to understand the behaviour of people in business.

> The rational actor is superseded by the complex social actor, a human being with inbuilt strengths, weaknesses, limitations, contradictions, and irrationalities. The business insulated from the outside world is superseded by the business buffeted by a fast paced, ever-changing array of external forces. In the view of today's leading theoretists, everything is in flux – ends, means, and the storms of external change.
>
> (Peters and Waterman 1982: 100)

As a methodological statement, the first sentence of this quote indicates a fairly extreme departure from the kinds of assumption that are required in formal analysis. I would want to replace this sentence with cautions about whose rationality one is seeking to understand in interpreting action or institutions. As the latter part of this chapter illustrates, I do not give up on rational models. But it is certainly true in farmer managed irrigation systems as in business that conflicts of interest are to be expected, and much of my own study in Nepal consisted of an attempt to see how farmer managers were responding to the buffeting demands of politics, institutional change and the vagaries of the aid process. The short answer was that they survived because their individual and collective interest in water far outweighed any interest that different parties could have in the fruits of office or other temptations of development.

Farmers are also engaged in a constant battle against nature. Landslides destroy capital structures, floods alter the course of rivers washing away some farmers' fields while leaving others, water shortages or cold spells alter growing season patterns, all of which contingencies have to be accommodated through changing the management of resources.

Farmer irrigators in Nepal not only face the uncertainties of their environment but also a major social paradox. This is the contrast between the premise of inequality which pervades the caste structures and racial divisions of rural society and the principles of fair shares of work and of water that had emerged in many – but not all – of the irrigation systems.

The rules have not always been based entirely upon this complex reciprocation. There are those systems that were established in the not very distant days (pre-1960s) when Zamindars (tax farming landowners) dominated the rural areas and had an interest in extending settlement and associated irrigation in their areas of control. System management then tended to take the form of the Zamindar or his agent demanding that a fixed number of hands turned up for maintenance work in each part of the scheme. Landholders or tenants in these areas also had to provide so many days' free labour on the Zamindar's own fields. There must nevertheless have been some sharing arrangements within this general formula for sufficient labour to have been available – particularly in times of crisis when the livelihood of the whole command area would be at risk.

In the Bansbote system there was evidence of a progressive change in the rules of organization, reflecting the more democratic or populist spirit of the post Zamindar era. While the previous Zamindar's agent had, until very recently, been left in charge of day-to-day affairs, the rules of labour contribution had been changed. In the immediate aftermath of Zamindar abolition it had been decided that each landholder, regardless of size of holding, should contribute one labourer for maintenance work. Recent changes had led to large landholders being obliged to provide more than one labourer however, and at the time of the study, there was pressure to further reduce the ratio of acres per labourer.

A current development at the time of the study was the replacement of the ex-Zamindar's agent with a management committee with representatives drawn from different parts of the system. The move had led to the election of a politically ambitious person as chair of the committee and considerable scepticism was expressed as to whether this person's attention would actually be directed towards ensuring timely maintenance work within the system.

There were therefore at least three reasons for seeing ambiguity and paradox in the management environment of this system. The creative and flexible response that was evident in the structures and procedures of these farmers stemmed from the vital role of irrigation in this society and the fact that they were both customers and providers of this service.

A BIAS FOR ACTION

It is with this phrase that Peters and Waterman capture the propensity of modern managers to break formal structures or procedures and, in the face of challenges, to put resources together in new ways. Surely, we may think, this principle will not apply to 'traditional' organizational forms which, almost by definition, are rule-bound. But that is an outsider's definition, a hangover from nineteenth-century sociology which, as a praise song for progress, had to contrast the supposed flexibility of present institutions with the supposed rigidity of the past. In Bansbote it was clear that, should the new 'democratic' committee structure fail to act at the appropriate time, a mass meeting would be called by someone else and the work would proceed regardless.

In looking for the action in farmer managed irrigation systems one encounters two problems. First, there may be a tendency for farmers to legitimize their institutions by describing them as being unchanging 'from time immemorial' (the phrase is not a quote but belongs to the Webbs' study of fenland drainage authorities in England (1922), where origins in time immemorial is equally a myth). Second, outside observers, less familiar with farmer managed systems than are consultants with modern industry, may ask about rules and structure and miss the underlying pragmatic responses. So let us try to see through this tendency.

The whole point about the formal rules of farmer managed irrigation is that they can be seen to be pragmatically derived responses to the action requirements of water distribution. Here we can bring in some of the other Peters and Waterman catch phrases about responsiveness: close to the customer, hands-on management, productivity through people, etc.; each suggests a dynamic relationship between parties to an enterprise and its customers.

Farmer managed systems are not idealized structures and they do not require altruism of their members. Instead they can be seen almost as a result of a discourse between the interested parties, a discourse that might run as follows:

'Over there is a water source, but it is too far for me to dig a canal for myself, will you help?' 'Yes, but how will we share the water?' 'Well, equal shares for equal work would seem to be fair.' 'But that fellow downhill wants to join also.' 'Well, he will have to contribute equally so that the canal can be enlarged and he can look after the last bit for himself since I have no interest in what happens to the water after it reaches my field.'

This dialogue assumes that we are considering an open and participative, if rule-bound, system. Every cultivator contributes labour (either personally or by sending an employee) to the construction or maintenance of the headworks and main canal. They work on the branch canal that leads towards their own fields but not others. They work as far as their own field but not downstream. In return they can draw what water they like when it is plentiful and are entitled to a share when scarcity requires rationing. So there is a perceived proportionality of contribution and benefit as Coward (1979) noted, except that this proportionality is seen from each individual's point of view. Nobody is expected to do work from which he or she does not personally benefit.

In Bansbote and similar systems therefore, people who cultivate fields close to the tail have more work to do than those who cultivate close to the head, because each party has no interest in downstream water. But with this proviso it is important to note that irrigation is perceived as a fair shares business.

So let us return to the question as to why – even in an inegalitarian society like Dang Valley – irrigation systems are open and participative. The answer would seem to be that large-scale labour mobilization is a regular necessity and the only way of securing the necessary commitment to work is to link it to secure benefits. If labour requirements were predictable, some entrepreneur might be prepared to pay the costs and capture the benefits. But mountain environments are hazardous. Rivers are turbulent and landslides common. Irrigation systems are vulnerable not only to silt deposition, leakages and breakdowns but to catastrophic damage. In some valleys there is the provision that if one system among several suffers large-scale damage everybody in the valley must turn out to help with reconstruction. What Coward (1979) refers to as reserve organizational capability can be seen as a loose form of reciprocation – a form of mutual assurance that may even be beyond the capacity of governments to secure (though food aid is increasingly being used to supplement or substitute for local responses to catastrophic damage).

STICK TO THE KNITTING

This discourse leads us increasingly towards a formal analysis of farmer managed irrigation and the second part of the chapter. But first we will examine two points about organizational focus and structure, the first of which, in the language of Peters and Waterman, is the moral injunction to 'Stick to the Knitting'.

Studies of farmer managed irrigation from different parts of the world indicate that, for this vital economic function, farmers stick to single purpose organizations. They do not mix up the distribution of water with marketing of crops, the supply of credit or anything else. The exception is the milling of grain, but only because the miller can be made to pay for some upstream maintenance of the canal that he taps for power. Where this rule does not hold, it is because some outside agency has intervened. I have in mind an aid-assisted project in which small farmers had been mobilized to create a new system through the medium of savings and bank loans, but with vegetable production and marketing added on. Such additions are much favoured by development agencies in spite of ample evidence – for instance, from studies of the cooperative movement – that this creates institutions that will not self-sustain.

SIMPLE FORM, LEAN STAFF

The next imperative is 'Simple Form, Lean Staff'. Irrigation organizations take on an organizational form that reflects the pattern of reticulation of water. This is what Coward (1979) calls a multi-level organizational pattern, but this does not so much imply hierarchy as a structure in which interest/responsibility groups form themselves around the canal branches that are directed to different parts of the terrain. Thus organizational branches with their own leadership and representative structures are there to take charge of canal branches. Some modification of this basic functional organizational pattern can be found where, as in some of the Nepalese cases, representation of different caste groups is deemed necessary.

The only staff employed on Nepalese systems are the messengers who assist the chairman or leader in calling out labour when required and who inspect the system for leakages or water theft. They tend to be paid in kind by all benefiting households.

The organization is also lean in the sense that there are no buildings, no standing administration, in fact nothing to reveal the presence of an organization at times of the year when there is no ongoing activity.

FORMAL ANALYSIS

The gist of a formal analysis has been emerging throughout the text. But it is worth taking it a step further. In this I choose to use some of the organizational insights of the neo-classical tradition rather than the neo-Marxist modes of production theory.

Formal analysis requires some simplification or accentuation in assumptions about human behaviour. In both the above-mentioned traditions, responses to material conditions or maximization of income within a given set of risks are assumed. My source is perhaps an unlikely one: Armen Alchian's analysis of the modern firm and of some 'not for profit' institutions (1977). For me, the value of Alchian's analysis lies in his recognition that team work necessarily involves some elements of common good. There is jointness in the operations or tasks and there are therefore attendant problems:

- the contribution of each individual to the completion of a task is ultimately not calculable;
- shirking (the tendency to 'free ride') will be apparent;
- monitoring of inputs is therefore desirable, but difficult.

All these features are apparent in Dang Valley. In the Bansbote system for instance, when teams turn out to rebuild headworks or clean canals, there is a tendency for some cultivators to under-supply labour. This is recognized, for instance, in the rule that no women are to be sent, the labour of women in this context being considered as less appropriate than that of men (in marked contrast to government employment generation schemes, where women will predominate because neither government nor participants are concerned with the productivity of the labour). Equally, male children are deemed too small if they can pass under a standard measure without touching. Monitoring contributions to canal clearance takes the form of measuring out with a stick the lengths that each individual must clear. Constructing headworks out of stones and leafy branches may require individuals to bring materials in measured quantities (but I am not sure about that). In spite of such devices each party will be aware that contributions are still unequal, both because some tasks will still turn out to be more difficult than others and some people will be more or less able or willing to perform them.

So, how is motivation achieved? In discussing the modern firm, Alchian employs an ingenious interpretation of the right of ownership. My rendering of his argument is as follows:

> Because of the above problems of commonality or jointness each individual in a firm faces the problem that others will be seeking to take advantage of his or her willingness to work, by shirking. This provides an incentive to slow down.
>
> But slowing down is to the disadvantage of all because the productive task is not achieved and the common pool out of which each party is rewarded is reduced.
>
> Therefore it is in the interest of each individual to have a task master who is prepared to monitor inputs, however difficult it is to do that fairly. It may be necessary to accept that monitoring outputs (as in piecework) is necessary instead, but this task is still onerous.
>
> But how is the person who accepts this onerous and socially stigmatized task to be rewarded? The answer is, by granting this person the right to retain what Alchian charmingly calls 'the residuals', in other words the profits.

This does not make profit-taking sound like a very extractive process. It is apparently an interpretation of the firm designed to counterpoise that of Marx. But for me, the slight sleight of hand in this interpretation is the implication that this is the only response to the problems of commonality in team production. The same problems are addressed differently by farmer irrigators, once freed from the proprietary rights of the Zamindars. Yes, they do sometimes find it convenient to hang on to the Zamindar's agent. A problem of leadership does have to be faced. Deviance does have to be negatively sanctioned. So how is it done?

As mentioned above, there was a leadership crisis in the Bansbote system at the time of my visit, an indication that an ideal solution was yet to be found. The immediate explanation was that a politically ambitious person was seeking the status of chairman in order to enhance his political standing in a wider arena. It could be, however, that rewards for leadership under the old regime were insufficient. The only advantage that the leader had over other beneficiaries was the lack of obligation to contribute labour on behalf of his own holdings. This lack of reward contrasts with some schemes such as that in Pul Eliya where the leader is allocated an additional holding of land.

Leadership does entail decisions – about the timing of operations, the extent of repairs and other matters that could be contentious – so there are costs. There is also a role in the settlement of disputes or the enforcement of sanctions, but this is likely to be done as chair of a court of some kind. Sanctions, like other costs, are made acceptable first by being agreed in principle and then by being enforced by the peer group. So there are fines for failure to send labour, and failure to pay the fines leads to the sequestration of property. Both are enforced by the peer group, generally without recourse to the legal authorities of the state.

Self-enforcement – at base an acceptance by members of a work team of chivvying by fellow workers – is made easy by the basic principle in political economy that underlies farmer managed irrigation; that is, proportional rights and responsibilities (though modified by self-interest). This is the *sine qua non* of the massive potential to mobilize labour on a sustained basis. It creates a sense of ownership without owners, because while the land in Nepal is owned individually, the irrigation systems are, in effect, common property. The consequence of the land not being common property is that landlords make their share-cropping extractions as landlords, not as sharers in the irrigation; a nice distinction perhaps, but one that appears to leave the motivation to work hard on the irrigation system intact.

What then is the lesson that these irrigators can pass on? *Co-ownership can work.*

CONCLUSION

The normative dictates of Peters and Waterman have been used to display the management 'excellence' of farmer managed irrigation systems (some of them at least) in spite of the fact that such systems are organizationally very different from 'modern' firms and work in a socio-economic environment that is not that of advanced capitalism. Part of the reason for this fit is that Peters and Waterman's empiricism can in fact be grounded in formal organizational or economic theory and that this theory applies to irrigation systems as much as to modern companies. The other part of the explanation is that farmer managed systems are successful, like modern firms because they are driven by consideration of the needs of the customer – in this case the farmers themselves. In irrigation as in the firm, the complexities of the business will be negotiated by the principal stakeholders to arrive at a workable formula. Negotiation will be an ongoing process as changing factors in the environment influence the system, but everyone recognizes that failure to achieve a successful formula could be catastrophic. Under these circumstances the farmers as owners/labourers/customers have a strong incentive to overcome their differences, find a formula that works, and keep the systems going.

REFERENCES

Alchian, A. A. (1977) *Economic Forces at Work*, Indianapolis: Liberty Press.
Burns, T. and Stalker, G. M. (1961) *The Management of Innovation*, London: Tavistock.
Coward, E. W. (1979) 'Principles of social organisation in an indigenous irrigation system', *Human Organisation* 38 (1): 28–36.
Curtis, D. (1991) *Beyond Government, Organisations for Common Benefit*, London: Macmillan.
Bhadur, T. (1986) *Farmer Managed Irrigation Systems in Nepal, A Case Study*, M.Soc.Sci. dissertation, Development Administration Group, University of Birmingham.
Leach, E. R. (1961) *Pul Eliya: A Village in Ceylon*, Cambridge: Cambridge University Press.
Martin, E. D. and Yoder, R. (1987) *Institutions for Irrigation Management in Farmer Managed Systems*, IIMI Research Paper No. 5, Sri Lanka: International Irrigation Research Institute.
ODI (1984) *Irrigation Management Network*, Network Paper 10c, (three papers: Windanapathirana, A. S., *The Jal Oya Experiment*; Jayewardene, J., *The Mahaweli Programme*; Kathpalia, G. N., *The Nong Wai Irrigation Project, Thailand*), London: Overseas Development Institute.
Ostrom, E. (1992) *Crafting Institutions for Self-governing Irrigation Systems*, California: Institute for Contemporary Studies Press.
Peters, T. J. and Waterman, R. H. (1982) *In Search of Excellence*, New York: Harper & Row.
Webb, S. and Webb, B. (1922) Statutory authorities for special purposes, in B. Keith-Lucas (ed.) (1963), *English Local Government* Vol. 4, London: Frank Cass.

4 Institution building

Examining the fit between bureaucracies and indigenous systems

Trish Nicholson

Reviews and evaluations of development projects have cited institutional and administrative weaknesses within developing countries as a major cause of poor performance. Administrative incapacity affecting both planning and implementation is often described in terms of ineffective management, incompetent or untrained staff, restrictive government regulations, corruption, or simply inefficiency. There has been a tendency on behalf of donors and lenders of development funding to blame the recipients. But other writers, for example Rondinelli (1983) and Korten (1980), have questioned the whole paradigm of development planning and funding. Rondinelli challenges the appropriateness of project 'blueprints' which attempt to predetermine and control development processes that are inherently uncertain and changeable. Korten emphasizes the need for flexibility in achieving a 'fit' between the objectives of a development programme, the needs of the recipients, and the administrative structure and process to articulate the two. Achieving this fit is a process rather than the implementation of predetermined structures.

The establishment of projects as separate administrative units, run largely by overseas 'experts' as enclaves of efficiency, has proved in many cases to be ineffective in the long term. It can create resentment between staff of the host organization and that of the project, particularly where there is a disparity in resource allocation. When project funding ceases, there is little beneficial impact on local management capacities. Such projects can sink without trace soon after completion. An alternative approach, to install new management systems or to reinforce existing bureaucratic systems through staff training, is not always successful either. In many cases, bureaucratic structures in developing countries are a legacy of colonial government, and their ineffectiveness may be in part a symptom of their inappropriateness to indigenous culture. The installation of new management systems is unlikely to be any more effective if they too are designed by 'western' experts who are acting on 'western' values after brief site visits which amount to little more than the type of development tourism described by Chambers (1983).

Insufficient attention is paid by development agencies and planners to a thorough understanding of the cultural base of administration. It is not enough simply to look at the systems and structures and to compare them to some ethnocentrically defined ideal. It is now generally accepted that the availability of an appropriate technology is necessary for successful agricultural development: what is not adopted is by definition inappropriate rather than the result of farmer ignorance or inertia. This has led to the 'farming systems research' methodology which has been a major step towards understanding total farmer circumstances in their cultural context, and identifying appropriate 'recommendation domains'. What is needed in development admininstration is an identification of appropriate management systems, based on the recognition and understanding of the organization's circumstances in its cultural context.

Development targets and time-scales based on optimal turn-around of loans and interest payments are often unrealistic and out of sympathy with social realities. By paying insufficient attention to the cultural context in which institutions operate, the opportunity to be truly innovative has been lost. Instead of assisting developing countries to create structures and systems which are compatible with their changing circumstances, projects mend and make-do with inherited structures, however ill-fitting.

Reinforcement of existing bureaucratic structures inherited from Australian colonial government was the approach used to increase effectiveness of planning and implementation in the institution building component of the West Sepik Provincial Development Project (WSPDP) in the Sandaun Province of Papua New Guinea. (West Sepik Provincial government officially changed its name to Sandaun Province in 1988.) WSPDP was an integrated rural development project funded in part by a World Bank loan. It represented the first phase of a long-term effort to accelerate socio-economic development in the province (World Bank 1984). The five main components were agriculture, education, health, infrastructure and institution building. They became operational in mid-1985. Project status was extended to December 1991 and the completion report was due before the end of 1992.

The aims of the institution building component were to increase the capacity of the province for sustained development by improving standards of planning, management, and service delivery (particularly extension services). To achieve this, sub-components were set up to upgrade the planning and coordination division, to improve financial services, and to create a staff development unit. My role in WSPDP was that of adviser and implementer for the staff development sub-component. The initial remit focused on a training role, but this had to be extended to include input on management, manpower and planning to address entrenched problems in public service structures and systems before training could have any effect.

My status was not that of 'outside consultant'. I was a public servant subject to the same rules and general conditions as my Papua New Guinean colleagues. This chapter is not therefore the result of any attempt at formal research – such would have been inappropriate even had there been time. Rather it is the result of informal discussion and participant observation during the course of my work in Sandaun over a period of five years. My intention is to explore some of the issues involved in strengthening institutions as an aid to self-sustained development, and to identify interrelationships and incompatibilities between indigenous mores and the western model of a public service institution on which the Papua New Guinean public service is based. I shall give some background to the public service structure and the area, and then explore three indigenous systems which have an important impact upon the institutional management process: *wantokism* as a means of resource distribution, compensation as an expression of responsibility, and consensus as a method of decision making.

PUBLIC SERVICE STRUCTURE IN SANDAUN PROVINCE

A major objective of the Papua New Guinea government in setting up integrated rural development projects such as WSPDP has been the creation of conditions for self-reliance in the provinces through the conversion of natural resources and increased participation of its citizens in a cash economy. In this development model, the resources created are believed to achieve equitable socio-economic development through the improvement of health and nutrition, education, infrastructure and other essential services. With few exceptions, provincial governments are dependent financially upon the national government. The mobilization of resources and creation of local revenue to enable provinces to be financially autonomous has been achieved by only a few provinces.

Sandaun was a long way from self-reliance. According to the 1980 socio-economic index of the Papua New Guinea National Planning Office it was the least developed province in terms of land, transport, health status education status, and government staffing. It had the highest malnutrition rate and the lowest per capita income. The latter is notoriously difficult to calculate with any accuracy, but large parts of the province were barely within the cash economy, and hunting and gathering played a significant role in subsistence and semi-subsistence economies. In general terms this description remains true at the present time.

Sandaun is one of the most difficult provinces to administer. Geographically, it ranges from swampy coastal plains, densely forested upland border areas, and rugged mountains with valley settlements. Of its six districts, only two have a road connection between each other, and none has road connections to the provincial capital at Vanimo. There are no overland transport routes to other provinces. Vanimo has limited coastal shipping. The population of 135,000 (1991 census) is widely dispersed in small isolated communities throughout the province, and between them they represent approximately ninety-five separate ethno-linguistic groups. Telephone and radio contacts between the districts and the provincial capital are intermittent and unreliable. Working in these conditions, one hesitates before calling anyone inefficient.

Since the setting up of the nineteen elected provincial governments in 1977, successive central governments have sought to improve the efficiency of provincial administrations. But decentralization has been full of ambivalences and contradictions (Standish 1983). Although new responsibilities and functions were decentralized to provinces, the bulk of the resources and experienced manpower remain in the national capital. At regular intervals the national parliament debates proposals to abolish provincial governments and this remains a major issue. Provincial governments are widely criticized for mismanagement and corruption. Since 1987 at least five provincial governments have been suspended for financial irregularities following reports by the Auditor General. Provincial politicians claim that these problems are on a minor scale compared to corruption in national government which starves provinces of sufficient resources. Similar tensions exist between administrators in national departments and their counterparts in the provinces. Figure 4.1 gives an outline of existing political–administrative structures.

Budgets for both provincial departments and provincial governments are controlled through the National Department of Finance and Planning. For Sandaun it provided approximately 68 per cent of the annual budget. The next largest slice of provincial government income derives from timber revenues (appr⌐ ⌐tely 30 per cent). The general tax base is extremely limited. In some cases the costs of collection exceed the revenue gained.

The National Department of Personnel Management (DPM) controls the employment and conditions of all public servants in Sandaun, to the extent that a DPM representative has to be present at all selection committees, for even the most junior positions. The Department of Sandaun's administrative structure is outlined in Figure 4.2. Like all other provincial departments, the Department of Sandaun is a department of the national public service and is responsible for administration and implementation to both the national and the provincial governments. Functional divisions within the Department of Sandaun reflect those at national level, e.g. education, health, primary industry and provincial affairs, and are influenced to

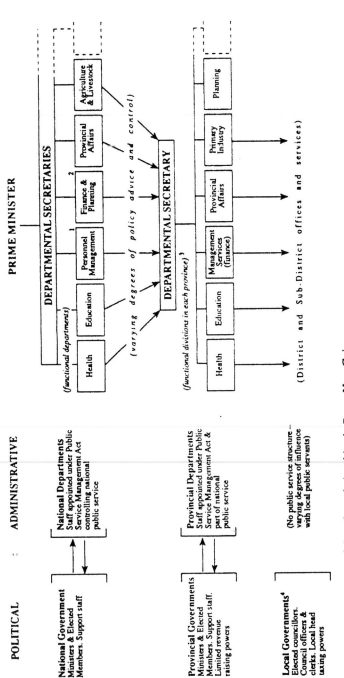

Figure 4.1 Political–administrative relationships in Papua New Guinea

Notes: 1 Department of Personnel Management controls conditions and employment of all public servants and approves all staff appointments up to and including Deputy Departmental Secretaries (Departmental Secretaries are political appointments)
2 Department of Finance and Planning controls budget allocations to all departments and provincial governments
3 There are minor variations in divisional structures between the nineteen provincial departments
4 Not functioning in some areas

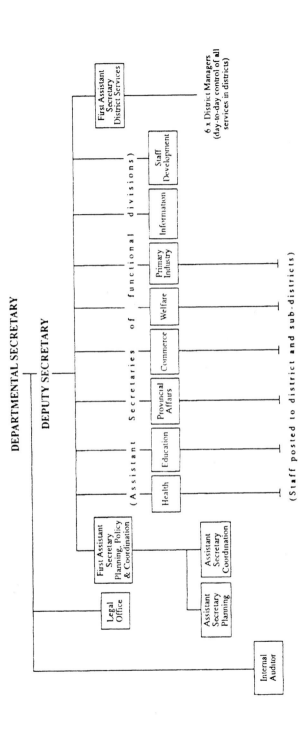

Figure 4.2 Department of Sandaun – administrative structure

varying degrees by their national counterparts. National priorities are sometimes not adhered to due to lack of funds in the province, but during 1991, national government compelled the province to divert its funds to implement certain national health policies within the province. Department functions are carried out by ten divisions representing the different services. Each is headed by an assistant secretary who reports either through a first assistant secretary or the deputy secretary to the Departmental Secretary (more or less equivalent to the chief executive in UK local authorities). Staff from divisions are represented in each district, and since 1991 there have been district general managers reporting to a first assistant secretary. This matrix approach is designed to overcome the lack of management supervision resulting from the isolation of districts. A little under half of the total establishment of 468 public service positions are deployed in districts, sub-districts and base camps throughout the province.

The public service structure in the Department of Sandaun, as in the rest of the Papua New Guinean public service, is a hierarchical bureaucracy based on the Western model which was inherited from the Australian administration. The formal process is similarly inherited. Changes and adaptations developed in the capital, Port Moresby, are heavily influenced by Australian as well as other imported expertise.

MODELS OF PUBLIC ADMINISTRATION

The key functions of public administration in Papua New Guinea are similar to those in western systems. These are the formulation and implementation of government policies, the equitable distribution of provisions contained in these policies, and the public accountability for resources used in the process. The dividing line between the political sphere of determining policy and the administrative sphere of formulating and implementing is similarly a fine one.

As in the western model, the administrative role implies both structure and process which, while differentiated, are closely interrelated. While structure can be viewed as a skeletal framework which describes who has authority over whom and for which functions and groups of activities, process determines the flow of activity through the structure. It includes the methods and systems of communication; where and how power is used (as distinct from authority); and the means by which decisions are made. Also part of process is the interpretation and means of implementing the various statutory instruments to achieve policy objectives. This creates one of the major 'grey areas' in the distinction between politics and administration.

In most organizations both structure and process have an informal as well as formal dimension. While the effectiveness of public management may be gauged to some extent by the congruence between structure and process, and by the reduction of dissonance between the formal and informal dimensions, there are demonstrable benefits in confusion and uncertainty which give managers room to manoeuvre. The dynamics of chaos can be used either to personal or organizational advantage, or both in different situations. Thus attempts at clarity and order and the establishment of clearly drawn boundaries may be covertly resisted from various positions within the structure.

In assessing administrative efficiency Cullen (1992 and Chapter 8, this volume) makes the important point that in most literature, the performance of Third World administrations are compared to the Weberian 'ideal type' of bureaucracy based on legal–rational, formal structures. Her research in the UK demonstrates that this ideal does not exist even in the West, and that various forms of deviance occur, some of which corrupt the values and aims of the organization, but others which enhance policy implementation by reducing inherent inflexibility and inconsistencies in the system. She contends that in the West deviance is not identified in a negative sense as 'corruption'. Rather it is seen as 'initiative' in pursuing the values and policies of the organization, because it is in keeping with indigenous values. In Papua New Guinea various forms of deviance and manipulation are similarly used to overcome inflexibilites and blockages in the formal system to achieve organizational objectives as well as to corrupt its values. The essential difference is that the rational–universal values underpinning the bureaucratic model are part of an ideology imported with the colonial administration and they operate in opposition to indigenous ideologies based on kinship loyalty and obligation. The most widespread forms of deviance are based on this ideology; and they do not necessarily enhance organizational aims and may amount to an alternative system within the structure. Since independence in 1975, successive post-colonial administrations have continued to operate structures and processes of management which originated in Australian and western cultures. This has been reinforced by donors and lending agencies seeking the assurance of familiar models of administration for disbursement of funds and implementation of development objectives before project funding can be negotiated.

Like Cullen, I avoid the term 'corruption' because of its judgemental connotations, and would emphasize that deviance is used here in the sense of acts which deviate from specified bureaucratic rules and their associated ideologies, but which at the same time comply with indigenous cultural norms and expectations. These norms and expectations, while kinship based in a general sense, vary considerably even within districts and sub-districts because of the high degree of ethno-linguistic differentiation within Papua New Guinea and particularly within Sandaun Province. Thus not only are indigenous ideologies at odds with bureaucratic ideologies; indigenous ideologies themselves are complex and varied in the nature and degree of their norms and expectations.

It could be argued that in this situation the rational–universal approach of the western bureaucratic model has an attractive neutrality. In fact there is support from all levels of the public service for this very neutrality, as much from those who practice deviance as from those who do not. This is a reflection of changing values and conflicting interests even within kinship groups, but it is also related to the strength and likelihood of sanctions which may be applied either from within the organization or by kinsmen whose expectations are not met. The relationship between formal and informal systems and their social environments is not static. It is taking place in an arena of social and personal change.

INDIGENOUS MANAGEMENT: 'WANTOKISM'

In Sandaun, indigenous methods for making decisions and distributing resources are based on localized definitions of group membership using concepts of lineage or marriage exchange partnership. Decisions about communal activities and the distribution of shared resources are carried out within the context of clearly defined obligations between specifically identified agnatic or affinal groups. Those of the same 'line' (traditionally a localized residential group) are considered *wantoks*, meaning literally 'one talk', those who share a common language.

This process of resource distribution based on obligation, notably to one's own 'line', has been carried into the public service as an indigenous informal process within an implanted formal structure. *Wantokism* is perhaps the most discussed phenomenon in public service life. Various government acts, and manuals based upon them, prescribe detailed procedures for all public service activities which are designed, among other things, to prevent the influence of *wantokism* in public administration. It is difficult to assess the extent of *wantokism*, or deliberate favouring of relatives in public services, because unavoidably, colleagues are often related to each other or to their clients. This does not necessarily mean that a decision was not made on the basis of criteria justified by rules of equity and accountability. Any unpopular promotion, award of contract or allocation of grant is likely to be described by the unsuccessful applicant as a 'clear case of *wantokism*', when in many instances this is not the case. I participated in the selection procedures for over 400 promotions and appointments in the Department of Sandaun from 1987 to 1991 and in no case did *wantokism* outweigh qualifications and experience as a criterion for appointment.

In some instances it seems that *wantokism* is used as an explanation for any decision the speaker does not like. There is no doubt however that it exists as a major force in public service management, while at the same time it is described openly and frequently by public servants as 'a bad thing', which 'discredits the public service' and 'lowers morale of public servants'. Those who are most vociferous in condemnation are often those most active in practising it in various forms and may genuinely wish to be placed in conditions where they do not have to play the *wantok* system at work.

To one's *wantok* is owed the obligation to share all that one has and indeed all that one has access to, although it may not be one's own, such as government assets, information or employment. The obligation is very strong and is not lessened by urbanization and increasing mobility of employment around the country. As one of my colleagues described it to me, 'The *wantoks* will come to stay in your house for long periods, share your food and pay, probably ask for your watch too, and eventually return home when you have bought them a plane ticket.'

In practice, one government pay-packet will often support several families to varying extents, pay for schooling of brothers, sisters or cousins, and contribute to brideprice and other ritual obligations in the village. It is of course a mutual obligation, but I got the strong impression that those with secure public service positions tended to get locked into the giving mode of an asymmetrical relationship.

As a system of resource distribution, *wantokism* clearly has social value in the economic security of those who are included, both in traditional life, and in the context of development and urbanization where employment and housing are limited. The implication for management process is that the authority vested in the bureaucratic structure, which is intended to enable individual behaviour to be controlled and channelled to the achievement of organizational objectives, can be made ineffective by the power of the informal culturally determined process. When public servants are working in their home districts, it is difficult to withstand the pressure of *wantok* expectations to give priority to their own 'line'. Transfers are often requested out of an officer's home district, and promotions sometimes declined, for the same reason. The informal social process is based on different objectives, which makes it difficult to exercise management control over *wantoks* at work and it is sometimes perceived as dangerous to control the behaviour of non-*wantoks*. On one occasion, a first line supervisor, after successfully completing a supervisory management course, followed the prescribed steps of disciplinary interviews and warnings with one of his labourers whose work performance and attendance were way below the required standards. Getting no improvement, the supervisor eventually sacked him. He subsequently made an urgent request for transfer out of the area as he believed he and his family were being poisoned through sorcery (*sanguma*), exercised by members of the labourer's 'line' as 'payback' for the sacking. At his request he was transferred to the area of his wife's *wantoks*.

The fact that *wantokism* is incompatible with the rules of the public service is generally recognized, but it is not amenable to the popular panacea of management problems – the training course. In many cases it is not that managers and supervisors do not know or cannot carry out what is required; it is simply that the requirements are frequently inappropriate in the social environment of which they are a part.

COMPENSATION AS AN EXPRESSION OF MUTUAL RESPONSIBILITY

The *wantok* system is not only concerned with the distribution of resources. It encompasses an almost limitless complex of mutual obligation; in particular, obligations of allegiance and protection in matters relating to compensation and 'payback', which is an expression of collective responsibility both to defend and avenge. The concept of inclusion and exclusion in defining to whom such obligation is owed is firmly rooted in the village of origin – the *asples*, but it can extend country-wide, however far away one is living from one's own village. There is considerable mobility around the country among public servants. In Sandaun for example, approximately 50 per cent of the department's staff are from other provinces. The definition of *wantok* becomes more inclusive when living outside one's own province. For example, East Sepiks working in Sandaun would consider themselves *wantoks* and have a network for mutual support, even if they are from different villages or districts in East Sepik. But it is likely that this allegiance would be overruled by obligations to support one's own 'line' if a dispute arose between two different East Sepik 'lines'. This may be the case even though the dispute arises back home in their *asples*. If compensation or 'payback' is to be extracted in resolving a dispute, or in pursuit of a clan feud, the network to execute this obligation is equally extensive. In this situation, if a public servant working outside his home province feels vulnerable without the closer support of his own 'line', he is likely to request urgent transfer to his own province.

Not only can this allegiance override that to the institution, but the institution itself can become endowed with the obligation to respond in customary manner as if it were itself a *wantok* group, and in so doing divert resources to which it has access as a public institution to protect its members and avert conflict. This is best exemplified by a brief case study. Public service conditions of employment require that when a serving officer dies, the employing department pays for the repatriation of his body, his immediate family and personal effects to his home province. When a sudden or unexpected death occurs, whatever the overt cause, somebody is to blame. There is usually a great deal of speculation as to who was to blame and from whom compensation should therefore be claimed. The causal links finally identified by the deceased's 'line' often seem extremely tenuous to the outside observer, but they are rooted in the wider social and temporal context of the person and the event, and not just in the death itself.

A public servant who had been working for some years out of his home province was killed while on official duty. His vehicle ran into a fallen tree and he died later that day in hospital from extensive injuries. There was much speculation as to who was to blame for the death, for the tree falling when it did, for him being there at that time and the whole situation which had resulted in the death. As he was on official duty at the time, the role of the employing department also entered into the discussion. Officials of the department were concerned that if people within the province were blamed for the death, a 'payback' killing could be exacted on their own *wantoks* living in the deceased officer's home province. The other concern was that compensation claims might be made against the department or the provincial government. Such claims can be extensive. In either case it was feared that the people of the province where the death occurred, would be perceived by the dead man's *wantoks* to share a collective responsibility for the death, i.e. they would be seen as a *wantok* group in opposition to the deceased's *wantok* group. The burden of responsibility fell heaviest upon the department which represented the province, and was the employer on whose official business the man was engaged when he died. It was important therefore to act in such a way that neither anyone within the province nor the deparment itself could be seen as blameworthy, or display any signs of guilt for the death.

This added to the tension already caused by genuine feelings of loss for a well-respected and liked colleague and friend. A collection was made for his family, and his pay and insurance entitlements were processed with extraordinary speed. It would have been usual to repatriate the body as quickly as possible, but it was decided and agreed with the deceased's relatives that this be delayed until a local funeral service had been held. This demonstrated genuine respect and lack of guilt, and would also allow time for the collection and pay entitlements to accompany the body to his home province.

Just about everyone in the town attended the funeral, which was video-filmed in its entirety to be sent back with the coffin. An unusually large contingent of the officer's colleagues accompanied the coffin to the officer's home province immediately after the service. This required the chartering of two planes, a twin otter and an islander. The party returned later in the day and reported with some relief that his family had accepted the body, the money and the explanation of death. Still the matter remained a preoccupation for some weeks afterwards in case there was a turn-around in events, which might lead to the deceased's *wantoks* claiming compensation or taking retaliation.

There was clearly a genuine expression of grief among those involved, but I can find no other explanation for the timing and manner of repatriation, nor for the additional cost of chartering two planes to accompany the coffin other than the fears about 'payback' and compensation which were expressed at the time. The heads of the department and of the dead man's division (neither of whom were related to him) played a leading role in negotiations with his *wantoks*, and with officials from his home province. These obligations and duties were not carried out on a personal basis, but on behalf of the institution and the people of the province placed in the role of a *wantok* group with potentially collective responsibility for the death. The resources of the institution were therefore used for necessary ritual action to defend it from retaliation or from claims of compensation. In other cases where deaths of public servants from other provinces have occurred, and the employing department has neither been blamed nor feared it might be blamed for the death, the deceased's own local *wantoks* have made all necessary ritual arrangements, and the department has simply paid statutory repatriation costs and entitlements.

DECISION MAKING

A third aspect of indigenous process is that of decision making. As a somewhat task-orientated person, I very quickly learned that the 'Melanesian way' involved a different orientation to time, and a distinctive method of decision making based on consensus, following a democratic process of the full exchange of views. It is possible to short-circuit this process with a more assertive 'boardroom' approach to decision making, but the lack of commitment, which may not be expressed during such a meeting, is likely to result in the decision not being actioned and the whole matter coming up again on a future occasion. This 'timeless' approach to decision making by storying, discussion and oratory is a deeply rooted tradition in Papua New Guinea and an important element of social and political life in the village as in Port Moresby. There is a wealth of literature on the Sepik which describes the significance of debate and oratory, for example in the ritual exchange of knowledge and the articulation of conflict and rivalry.

Speechmaking, and particularly political oratory, is closely associated with the chewing of betel nut, lime and mustard (commonly referred to simply as *buai*). This a symbol not only of friendship and peace between those who share it, but also of personal power, and the power of oratory epitomized in the 'big man'. Despite its importance in the political arena, or perhaps as an attempt to separate more clearly the political from the administrative, *buai* is banned in the public service. A government regulation in 1989 made it a disciplinary offence to chew *buai* within government offices. Persistence in the habit constitutes a serious disciplinary offence for which the ultimate sanction is dismissal. It is, however, widely disregarded.

In other aspects too the characteristics of traditional and political debate are carried through to the process of management decision making. In general, open conflict is avoided and opposing views are aired obliquely. The true meaning may be discerned by the careful listener, and perhaps only in stages through successive discussions. The pidgin term for this form of expression is *tok bokis*, meaning literally 'box talk', to talk with as many angles and hidden meanings as the sides and corners of a box. On one occasion, when an important decision had to be reached and neither the real issues nor a consensus had been openly revealed, despite prolonged discussion, the only way to reach a decision to which the meeting would have commitment, was to reveal the consensus through a secret ballot.

This is a long way from the classic management communications course which seeks to impart the skills of effective two-way communication and the responsibility of the message sender to ensure clear understanding by the receiver. The implications for 'modern' management processes of secrecy, conflict avoidance (rather than resolution) and *tok bokis* are self-evident. Again we see the significance of the informal culturally based process, which in itself carries far less of a distinction between the political and administrative spheres of activity than the formal process and structure prescribe.

THE PROJECT'S APPROACH TO INSTITUTION BUILDING

In spite of the incompatibilities between models of bureaucracy and indigenous systems, and the implications of this which I have indicated, roads and buildings do get completed; babies get immunized; children pass exams and go to high school. Perhaps not as much or as fast as is hoped and planned for, but the fact that so much does get achieved is a great credit to the commitment and skill of public servants in Sandaun.

It is not possible here to give a detailed review of the project's impact on institution development in Sandaun. As stated earlier, WSPDP did not set out to establish alternative structures for service delivery, nor to address specifically the phenomenon of *wantokism* in the public service. It was fairly closely integrated within the existing provincial public service structure, and the overall remit of the institution-building component was to increase the effectiveness of this structure and the processes within it as a means of increasing the province's capacity for self-sustained development.

Through the project, four new public service positions were created: project co-ordinator, project accountant, monitoring and evaluation officer, and staff development officer. All were expatriate positions with counterparts who would take over the principal positions permanently after training (and this was successfully achieved). The original project design envisaged training as a key input to achieve institution building objectives. As the project proceeded it became clear that the chronic structural and operating difficulties within the department could not be cured by training alone, and that the four new positions which would remain for institution strengthening at the end of the project were quite inadequate to maintain these functions and the increased activity generated by the project.

The scope of the institutional development component of the project was radically increased to carry out structural reviews and reorganization (particularly the setting up of district management), and to create positions and install systems which would enable the department more effectively to carry out such basic public service procedures as recruitment, pay administration, accounting and planning (Nicholson 1992). All of these procedures had posed major problems within the department at the time of project start-up, and had contributed to understaffing, confusion over positions and functions, low staff morale and poor performance. These problems were exacerbated by incapacities at national level and the province's isolation from the capital.

To the extent that *wantokism* and other forms of deviation from organizational norms can flourish in a state of chaos and confusion (either because it has become the only way to achieve organizational objectives, or because it provides ample opportunity to pursue one's own objectives), then strengthening systems and skills to operate official processes and structures could enable *wantokism* to be avoided more easily by those who wished to do so. Achievement of results through the formal system can act as a powerful incentive towards its maintenance.

This amounts to providing a workable option, but does not address the core issue of incompatible value systems respresented by the formal and informal dimensions of the public service. Given the external sanctions of international opprobrium (especially where grants and loans are concerned), internal pressures for political legitimization, and the complexity of development administration in multi-cultural environments, it seems inevitable that some form of bureaucratic model needs to be applied. It is equally inevitable that major adjustments and flexibilities will be required to enable the administrative process to engage effectively with different cultures in different localities.

One method of approaching this is by further decentralization of resources and decision making for local services to local communities. There is difficulty here in defining 'community' and identifying local organizations to whom decision making and resource distribution could be devolved. As stated earlier, indigenous decision making groups are based on kinship affiliations which could pose problems for the equitable and accountable implementation of public policies beyond a *wantok* group. Even within a *wantok* group there could be welfare and equity problems, particularly in relation to gender.

The recent setting up of district management allows for the representation of local organizations on the district management teams and, where they exist, local youth groups and women's groups are represented. The extent to which this could provide a mechanism for greater community participation while addressing the problems of equity remains to be seen. Where local organizations do not yet exist, establishing them from outside initiatives can cause difficulties for local legitimization and sustainability. In some cases, local groups have emerged and become moribund because they have neither the power nor the resources to inspire either local participation or official recognition, while power and resources are held, and often perceived to be misused, by both bureaucrats and politicians.

There is no ideal solution waiting to be found and plugged in. Development administration is dynamic not static; in Korten's terms it is 'a learning process', and little learning takes place without experimentation and compromise. Rather than comparing Third World bureaucracies to an ideal model and finding them wanting, it would be more productive to compare them to the cultures in which they are operating and find ways to improve the fit. Whether this results in changes to bureaucratic structures and processes, or involves some degree of devolution to local communities, or both, should depend on the cultures involved and their development objectives. Whether this degree of power sharing will be tolerated is essentially a political issue, but there is a clear role here for anthropologists to apply a holistic approach to understanding organizations and cultures, and the dynamics of negotiation and change between them. In particular, what is needed is a methodology for identifying 'appropriate management systems' at the stage of project identification, and a terminology which would allow effective communication and negotiation of these recommendations at every stage of project planning and appraisal.

REFERENCES

Chambers, R. (1983) *Rural Development. Putting the Last First*, Harlow: Longman.

Cullen, S. (1992) 'Anthropology, state bureaucracy and the community', unpublished PhD thesis, Cambridge University.

Korten, D. (1980) 'Community organisation and rural development: a learning process approach', *Public Administration Review* 5, (40): 480–511.

Nicholson, T. (1992) 'Final report by the provisional staff development officer, Vanimo, Sandaun Province', internal report to the World Bank.

Rondinelli, A. (1983) *Development Projects as Policy Experiments*, London: Routledge & Kegan Paul.

Standish, B. (1983) 'Power to the people? Decentralisation in Papua New Guinea', *Public Administration and Development* 3: 223–38.

World Bank (1984) 'Staff appraisal report No. 5017 – Papua New Guinea', New York.

Part II

Gender and organizational change

Introduction

Michael Roper

In the move to conceptualizing organizations as cultural systems rather than objectively material and technical ones, gender studies have played a large part. Practical rather than theoretical considerations initially led feminist researchers to make this shift, thus challenging the 'positivist faith' in organizational theory. The 1970s in Britain saw the passing of equal opportunities initiatives such as the Equal Pay Act of 1970 and the Sex Discrimination Act of 1975. This legislation and the Equal Opportunities programmes which have followed it focused on removing direct discrimination in pay, recruitment and promotion. They were based on a broadly 'liberal-feminist' perspective, which assumed that women's career advancement would follow once the structure of organizations had been correctly modified. This was coupled with a conception of gender as pertaining to the psychological attributes of individual women and men.

Inequalities in employment have remained in the two decades since the first equality initiatives (Devine 1992: 557; Cockburn 1991: 1). Vertical segregation has persisted, with men occupying three-quarters of all management positions (Hansard Society 1990: 53). The proportion of women managers has increased, but a virtual male monopoly prevails at senior levels (Hansard Society 1990: 60–1). Women and men also continue to be clustered in different kinds of occupations. In the 1980s women's employment grew rapidly in service sector occupations such as finance (Crompton and Sanderson 1990: 89, 127-8). However manual and skilled technical occupations in the manufacturing sector remained largely male preserves (Devine 1992: 559–60; Crompton and Sanderson 1990: 164). The contributions below reflect a sense of disillusionment with the pace of change. The organizations they depict are diverse, spanning the public, private and voluntary sectors. Yet the authors pinpoint similar dilemmas. The question they address is why, after a quarter of a century of reforms, power in organizations continues to be monopolized by men (Bell and Nkomo 1992: 237).

This problem has led to a renewed interest in the role which organizations themselves play in reproducing material inequalities, and to a search for concepts that will reveal fully what is often described as the 'embeddedness' of gender. Organizational logic, it is argued – that is, the design of particular jobs, functions and divisions of labour – is gendered. From an initial concern with material inequalities has emerged an emphasis on the gendered discourses and 'root metaphors' through which organizations are constituted. Gender is viewed as a conceptual category which not only refers to socially produced distinctions between women and men, but, reaching to the very heart of how jobs and hierarchies are imagined, 'infuses organizational structure' (Acker 1992: 253).

The recognition of the embeddedness of gender has resulted in a critique of organizational theory from four linked directions. First, the dominant image of organizations as the principal 'carriers of instrumental rationality' in modern societies (Reed 1991: 128) posed great problems for the first generation of feminist researchers. Following Weber, bureaucratic authority was thought to be based on formally established rules which were exercised in an objective manner, without emotion and 'without regard to persons' (Weber 1948: 215). Whereas (as Pringle notes in Chapter 6 of this volume), bureaucratic rationality presented itself as gender neutral, it actually promoted a particular kind of gender order 'based on the exclusion of the personal, the sexual and the feminine'. The emphasis was on formal rules and technical efficiency. As a consequence, these were the dominant concerns of post-war industrial sociologists. As Burrell and Hearn put it, they were more interested in the 'organization of production' than 'the production of organization' (1989: 10–14). Issues of power; of how organizational structures and processes might have assisted the reproduction of social inequalities, tended to remain marginal (Witz and Savage 1992: 5). Moreover, the assumption that bureaucracies were founded upon abstract principles helped to conceal the fundamentally human and subjective processes facilitating gender segregation.

Not surprisingly, initial attempts to explore the causes of sex-based discrimination during the 1970s were framed in the discourse of fairness and efficiency. Equality initiatives were argued for on the grounds that discrimination was inefficient, as it prevented selection by merit. Strategies for change were seen to depend on the further formalization of procedures, particularly in gate-keeping functions such as recruitment and promotion (Collinson *et al.* 1990: 208; Ramsay and Parker 1992: 262).

Rosabeth Moss Kanter's study of a US insurance firm, *Men and Women of the Corporation* (1977), was one of the very first attempts to study gender segregation 'from within' the field of organizational theory. Still highly influential, it illustrates the limitations of what has become known as the 'liberal feminist' agenda. Kanter identified a number of gendered practices which discouraged women's promotion. A culture of homosociality meant that men tended to choose successors in their own image, and were suspicious of those who were in any way 'different' (Witz and Savage 1992: 15–16). The bureaucratic ethos was also closely bound with generally masculine qualities of calculation and instrumentality, which meant that men saw themselves as particularly suited for organizational success. Despite recognizing the deep-seated nature of male domination however, Kanter emphasized that change could occur through formal mechanisms. Greater use of training, job evaluation schemes, and the introduction of flexible working, she argued, were necessary to achieve equality (1977: 265–87). Whilst showing that the very project of bureaucratization implied a bias towards 'masculine' traits, Kanter nevertheless advocated the further formalization of procedures. Kanter, as Witz and Savage point out, accepted the 'core truths of Weber's account of the rationality and goal directedness of bureaucracies' (1992: 17). She argued that the problem was not gender, but the dominance of men in senior positions. As she put it, 'power wipes out sex' (Kanter 1977: 200).

Kanter's and subsequent studies were presented in the language and concepts of classical organizational theory. They posed the problem as one of 'organizational structure, not gender' (Acker 1990: 143). The emphasis was on removing barriers to talent or labour market distortions (Cockburn 1989: 214; Collinson *et al.* 1990: 208). Liberal-feminist approaches failed to develop the insight that 'organizational rules' were themselves gendered. As a result, many sources of informal exclusion – and indeed the whole question of men's resistance to equality – went unexplored (Cockburn 1991; Pringle 1988: 84; Roper 1994; Sheppard 1989: 141). Such approaches mimicked the technical ethos they were critiquing. Concentrating on the modification of formal rules, they did not explore the gendered symbolism and metaphors which gave shape to these rules. As Cynthia Cockburn has commented, the central concern of liberal equal opportunities policies is 'gaining power, not changing it' (Cockburn 1989: 217).

A second aspect of the embeddedness of gender is that, partly as a consequence of the pervasive myth of bureaucratic rationality, organizational theory has tended to disregard the 'private' sphere of household and family. The liberal-feminist agenda, grounded on this classical theory, concentrated on formal processes internal to organizations. It acknowledged, but did not pursue, the relationship between discriminatory practices within organizations and the 'gender order' of their wider social context. Coming from the opposite direction, radical feminists located women's oppression primarily in the family or state, whilst tending to disregard 'intermediate' institutions such as the workplace (Witz and Savage 1992: 6–7).

In contrast, the interlocking of domestic and workplace gender regimes is central to the chapters in Part II of this volume. They show how it is that a 'job', as Joan Acker remarks, may contain 'the gender-based division of labour and the separation between the public and the private sphere' (1990: 149). Divisions of labour in the workplace and domestic sphere are clearly mutually supporting. Career advancement, in organizational logic, is earned through commitment in time and energy. Yet this level of devotion is often sustained only by a division of labour in which somebody else services the worker's bodily and emotional needs (Finch 1983; Smith 1988). Cynthia Cockburn illustrates this in her study of the union NUPE, which, despite extensive equality policies and a largely female membership, has a male-dominated executive. We need to look across the home/work divide, Cockburn argues, in order to account for this. Men are favoured as organizational workers to the extent that they are able to detach themselves from domestic responsibilities (See also Collinson *et al.* 1990: 88). Cockburn's point is that jobs such as that of union organizer are constructed in a way that facilitates male domination. Habitually unsocial, irregular hours, for example, carry a presumption that the office holder will be a man. Kerfoot and Knights' study of the Pensco Insurance Company (Chapter 7) shows how normative beliefs about who is responsible for domestic tasks help structure the organizational hierarchy. Senior managers allocated certain jobs to women returners in the belief that they would not pursue managerial jobs because of their family responsibilities. The assumption of an inverse relationship between organizational and domestic commitment is fundamental to the gendering of jobs.

Domestic labour thus remains a hidden resource which facilitates the organizational worker. At the same time, however, jobs themselves may be designed around skills which women possess by virtue of their particular life experiences as daughters, mothers or wives. In this way domestic labour divisions may be directly incorporated into the workplace. Kerfoot and Knights provide an interesting example of this. Women insurance workers are often appointed to the job of team leader, a task which involves fostering a 'family feeling' that will enhance organizational loyalties. Emotional work of this kind might be managerial in content but it is seen as intuitive, and is not measured or rewarded. As Hochschild (1983) shows in the case of flight attendants, the product of such emotional labour is not a material good but harmony or 'good feeling', which becomes less visible the more 'efficiently' it is carried out. This is obviously a form of subordination. Yet as Pringle points out in Chapter 6, emotional labour may also engender feelings of pleasure and empowerment. What does the woman secretary gain by bolstering the self-esteem of her boss, the benefits clerk gain by reassuring her client, or the team leader gain through nurturing the careers of younger staff?

Occupations such as this involve a 'public' enactment of supposedly 'private' emotions. This introduces a third way in which gender is embedded in organizations. That is, jobs and hierarchies derive their subjective meanings partly from familial metaphors. Managerial functions may be gendered in a way that mimics the breadwinner/homemaker divide. Line managers in the manufacturing sector, for example, commonly regard themselves as 'organization breadwinners' because their production roles are considered to be associated directly with wealth creation (Collinson *et al.* 1990: 89; Roper 1994). Women, by contrast, tend to be concentrated in what are known as 'support functions', in personnel, finance or sales (Nicholson and West 1988: 190–2). This institutional divide is conveyed and experienced through terms which evoke domestic roles.

Familial imagery is, then, central to the particular type and level of authority which is designated to individual jobs. Metaphoric constructions of gender help to define certain jobs as men's or women's (Acker 1992: 253). Rosemary Pringle establishes a further set of connections between the familial and the organizational in Chapter 6 of this volume. The post-war domestic ideology of complementary roles, she argues, had its counterpart in the discourse of 'office-wife', in which a secretary's job was defined in terms of the carrying out of personal services for a boss. Pringle does not ask what a secretary does, nor where this occupation fits in the labour process. Instead she focuses on what a secretary *is*; on the way the occupation is represented in speech, writing and visual images. This allows her to introduce the sexual and familial themes that structure understandings of this occupation. Pringle collapses the neat distinction between the internal and external environment promoted by organizational theory.

The contributions in Part II also suggest a fourth challenge to the modernist vein in organizational theory, because they depict such radically different gender regimes. The Weberian ideal type was of a one-way transition from patrimony to bureaucracy. Equal-rights feminism argued its case on similar grounds. Professional management practices, it was argued, could help erode subjective – and therefore anachronistic – judgement in matters such as recruitment. The chapters in Part II suggest that there is a complex relationship between patterns of discrimination and particular organizational cultures. The course of historical change is not simply one way from patrimonial authority, conveyed through familial discourses, to the modern bureaucracy characterized by exclusion of the personal, and staffed by rational organization men. Non-bureaucratic modes of authority may persist even in the most professional organization. For example, Pringle shows that although the discourse of 'office-wife' reached its zenith in the 1950s, today, in an efficiency-conscious era where managers are asked to share secretaries, they continue to personalize the relationship by talking of 'my' secretary, and demanding personal services such as the making of tea or coffee.

Industrial restructuring has thrown further doubt on the modernist model of professional versus discriminatory. Trends in human resources policies may well be away from the bureaucratic and formalized procedures favoured by equal opportunities programmes. For example, Peters and Waterman, in their management best-seller of the 1980s, *In Search Of Excellence*, argued that corporate rejuvenation depended on the dismantling of elaborate hierarchies, and the introduction of work teams motivated by 'family feeling'(1982: 8; Kanter 1984: 32). What impact might this celebration of family values have on gender relations? Kerfoot and Knights address this in their study of Pensco. While team working has been introduced with the aim of making the company more 'professional', the effect has been to lock women into familial roles. Described in Weberian terms, Pensco has seen the revival of pre-modern, patrimonial authority in a post-modern context of slim organizational hierarchies and broader job spans. Re-structuring and attempts to professionalize management have gone hand-in-hand with new forms of gender segregation.

The chapters in this book also question the liberal-feminist assumption that a professional organization equals an asexual one. Cullen's study of Job Centre clerks suggests that as this service becomes increasingly geared towards selling itself to employers, dress codes have changed in a way that accentuates traditional femininity. Dresses and skirts have replaced jeans in the management's attempt to 'professionalize' the service. Cullen thus discerns a shift in the Job Centres towards a representation of femininity which is both more professional and more gendered. Dress codes such as this may reinforce gender stereotypes (Sheppard 1989; Ramsay and Parker 1992: 266). However, clothes and appearance can also be sources of personal pleasure. Heightened displays of femininity may even have a disruptive effect, exposing the Weberian myth of the asexual (male) worker (Pringle, Chapter 6, this volume). It is by no means clear that professionalization entails the banishment of sexuality from organizations, nor that an organization in which sexualities are more visible will necessarily be more oppressive (for debates on this see Burrell 1992; Burrell and Hearn 1989; and Witz and Savage 1992: 47–56).

The patterning of gender images varies widely across organizations, from the demure version of femininity presented by the Job Centre clerk to the maternal version valued by employers at Pensco. This variation is perhaps one of the reasons why equal opportunities policies, based on implementing a standardized set of strategies, have met with difficulty. The problem is not only the continued existence of discriminatory practices, but the gendered way in which jobs are envisioned. Furthermore, the skills promoted as necessary for a job derive partly from the experiences of those who fill them. The gender-neutral logic of organizational theory has no way of approaching this fusion of office and person. As Weber commented, the advantage of the bureaucracy was that it could operate 'without regard to persons' (1948: 215).

If gender is as deeply embedded as the contributions in Part II suggest, then one might expect change not just to entail a numerical balance between women and men, but to transform the way that organizations operate. Cockburn's study of NUPE suggests that is the case. In the Northern Ireland office which has simi.ʾr numbers of men and women, negotiations were conducted in a less confrontational way, and power-sharing arrangements had been introduced. Such innovations suggest that equality is not only about the substitution of women for men, a question purely of structure, but that it entails change in 'the nature and functioning of power itself'. Once we accept this then gendered patterns become visible not just in gate-keeping practices, but in the way that hierarchies, functions and individual jobs are formulated. Gender-based inequalities are more deeply embedded than was recognized in the 1970s. At the same time, however, the following chapters show that playing with gender codes – for example, through dress – can be individually empowering. The insight that organizations both produce and appropriate personal pleasures is a politically difficult one. It holds subversive potential, however, for it confounds the 'public' and 'private', 'rational' and 'emotional' dichotomies which have been the bedrock of organizational theory.

REFERENCES

Acker, J. (1990) 'Hierarchies, jobs, bodies: A theory of gendered organizations', *Gender and Society* 4 (2): 139–58.
—— (1992) 'Gendering organizational theory', in A. J. Mills and P. Tancred (eds) *Gendering Organizational Analysis*, Newbury Park, CA: Sage.
Alvesson, M. and Billing, Y. D. (1992) 'Gender and organization: towards a differentiated understanding', *Organization Studies* 13 (2): 73–102.
Bell, E. L. and Nkomo, S. M. (1992) 'Re-visioning women manager's lives', in A.J. Mills and P. Tancred (eds) *Gendering Organizational Analysis*, Newbury Park, CA: Sage.
Burrell, G. (1992) 'The organization of pleasure', in M. Alvesson and H. Willmott (eds) *Critical Management Studies*, London: Sage.
Burrell, G. and Hearn, J. (1989) 'The sexuality of organization', in J. Hearn, D. L. Sheppard, P. Tancred-Sheriff and G. Burrell (eds) *The Sexuality of Organization*, London: Sage.
Cockburn, C. (1989) 'Equal opportunities: the short and long agendas', *Industrial Relations Journal* 20 (3): 213–25.
—— (1991) *In the Way of Women. Men's Resistance to Sex Equality in Organizations*, London: Macmillan.

Collinson, D., Knights, D. and Collinson, M. (1990) *Managing To Discriminate*, London: Routledge.

Crompton, R. and Sanderson, K. (1990) *Gendered Jobs and Social Change*, London: Unwin Hyman.

Czarniawska-Joerges, B. (1992) *Exploring Complex Organizations. A Cultural Perspective*, London: Sage.

Davidson, M.J. and Cooper, C.L. (1992) *Shattering the Glass Ceiling. The Woman Manager*, London: Paul Chapman.

Devine, F. (1992) 'Gender segregation in the engineering and science professions: a case of continuity and change', *Work, Employment and Society* 6 (4). 557–75.

Finch, J. (1983) *Married to the Job: Wives' Incorporation in Men's Work*, London: Routledge & Kegan Paul.

Hansard Society (1990) *Report of The Hansard Society Commission on Women at the Top*, London: Hansard Society.

Hochschild, A. R. (1983) *The Managed Heart. Commercialization of Human Feeling*, Berkeley, CA: University of California Press.

Kanter, R. M. (1977) *Men and Women of the Corporation*, New York: Basic Books.

—— (1984) *The Change Masters*, London: Allen & Unwin.

Mills, A. J. and Murgatroyd, S. J. (1991) *Organizational Rules. A Framework for Understanding Organizational Action*, Milton Keynes: Open University Press.

Nicholson, N. and West, M. (1988) *Managerial Job Change: Men and Women in Transition*, Cambridge: Cambridge University Press.

Peters, T. and Waterman, R. H. (1982) *In Search of Excellence. Lessons from America's Best-Run Companies*, New York: Harper & Row.

Pringle, R. (1988) *Secretaries Talk: Sexuality, Power and Work*, Sydney: Allen & Unwin.

Ramsay, K. and Parker, M. (1992) 'Gender, bureaucracy and organizational culture', in M. Savage and A. Witz (eds) *Gender and Bureaucracy*, Oxford: Polity.

Reed, M. (1991) 'Scripting scenarios for a new organization theory and practice', *Work, Employment and Society* 5 (1): 119–32.

Roper, M. (1994) *Masculinity and the British Organization Man Since 1945*, Oxford: Oxford University Press.

Sheppard, D. L. (1989) 'Organizations, power and sexuality: the image and self-image of women managers', in J. Hearn, D. L. Sheppard, P. Tancred-Sheriff and G. Burrell (eds) *The Sexuality of Organization*, London: Sage.

Smith, D. E. (1988) *The Everyday World as Problematic. A Feminist Sociology*, Milton Keynes: Open University Press.

Weber, M. (1948) 'Bureaucracy', in H. Gerth and C. W. Mills (eds) *From Max Weber: Essays in Sociology*, London: Routledge & Kegan Paul.

Witz, A. and Savage, M. (1992) 'The gender of organizations', in M. Savage and A. Witz (eds) *Gender and Bureaucracy*, Oxford: Polity.

5   Play of power

Women, men and equality initiatives in a trade union

Cynthia Cockburn

The 1980s were characterized by the incursion of the women's movement into major organizations, perceived as sources and sites of male power. The result, for some, was the establishment of policies for equality of opportunity and of positive action measures to achieve equality of outcomes.

The struggle for 'equal opportunities' in organizations followed from the passing of an Equal Pay Act 1970 and the Sex Discrimination Act 1975. More accurately, it sprang from the failure of these laws, unassisted, to produce significant change in women's relative earnings or in occupational sex segregation (Snell *et al.* 1981). Employers were continuing to treat females worse than males. Unions were failing to contest this effectively. Clearly a direct approach was called for in which women could negotiate their needs with those visibly in control. Many organizations therefore introduced 'positive action for sex equality' (Robarts 1981).

The results were still disappointing. By the mid-1980s there was widespread disillusion with the practical achievements of positive action. It was becoming clear that what was involved in sex equality was something less easily achievable than the belated introduction of an unproblematic 'fairness' to working life. Some of the helpful men at the top of the organizations may have seen it as that. However, feminist activists and men down the line saw it, from different points of view, as something more (Cockburn 1989). It was potentially a quite unprecedented, indeed revolutionary, piece of organizational engineering. It is not surprising that there were impediments to change.

This chapter reports one part of a study that examined the positive action processes and male reactions to them in four large organizations, each chosen as an 'equal opportunities' leader in its field (Cockburn 1991). One was a private retail chain, another a large government department, and a third a left Labour local authority. The fourth, described here, was a trade union. The fieldwork on the National Union of Public Employees (NUPE), the trade union in question, was carried out over a three-month period from

June to August 1989.[1] The analysis was completed by the end of 1989. The date is important, because NUPE is changing, and circumstances may well have altered between then and now.

Different types of organization present different problems and possibilities for equality activists. In business companies they are up against the often inflexible aims of profit, productivity, and capital accumulation. In the public sector the balance of service versus cost efficiency can (within governmental constraints) be modified by goals imposed by parties with political control. A trade union is different again. It is a membership organization, usually with a constitution reflecting democratic principles and a perceived obligation to represent its members – in internal transaction of its affairs, in external campaigns and in collective bargaining with the employer. A union is *also* an employer, of paid organizers and administrators, office workers and other employees. When a trade union takes on sex equality it can and must rethink activity in all these spheres.

It may seem at first sight inappropriate, even unfair, to locate a study of power in an organization representative of workers. Is power not something to which the worker is painfully *subject*? There is no intention here to diminish the struggle for survival of a manual workers' union or its members, of either sex, in a hostile political and economic climate. There is, however, one good reason for considering a union, in contrast to state or private employing organizations, from a gender perspective: it simplifies the class context. This is especially the case when the union in question, as is the case with NUPE, represents the lowest of low-paid manual workers. In other organizations it is often difficult to say what effects are class effects and what are gender. In the case of NUPE, a profoundly working-class organization, ruling class pressures (and they were considerable) mostly came from without – employers' practices, adverse changes in the law, political and economic processes. In contrast to, say, a business firm, the membership and the union as an entity could reasonably be read as being of one class and having clear class aims. The dynamics of male power internal to the union are that much clearer.

The relations of gender are, however, intercut with those of ethnicity and racism. Despite operating at the most disadvantaged end of the labour market, NUPE's members, and even more its lay representatives and full-time officers, were disproportionately white. An anti-racist policy had been introduced in NUPE alongside sex equality measures. It is important to remember that in the account that follows, when speaking of low-paid women we are often referring to black women, and when referring to male leaders, usually to white men.

A PREDOMINANTLY FEMALE UNION

NUPE's membership is drawn mainly from the manual workers of the National Health Service. Three-quarters, nearly half a million, of its members are women. They are among the hardest working, most useful and lowest-paid employees of the British economy. They peel vegetables in school kitchens, wash floors in town hall offices, endure the steam of hospital laundries. 'It's built in. Women are in the low grades because that's the natural order of things', said one. Women's position had been further threatened by the recent Tory policy to cut costs and increase productivity in the public sector by selling off the services these women provide to the contractor prepared to cut wages most fiercely.

Women's position at work had not been very substantially altered by the trade unions in recent years. Collective bargaining had gained more for men than for women. Male members were earning on average £3.74 per hour, women £2.96. Inequality in the family had not been challenged by NUPE's reform agenda: it was mainly due to domestic responsibility that 78 per cent of women worked part-time. By contrast, the 11 per cent of men who worked part-time did so in anticipation of retirement.

The disadvantages of women uncovered in the research were not however limited to their position at work. They also suffered markedly unequal status in the union itself. Men, although only 25 per cent of the membership, held three-quarters of the branch secretary positions and 89 per cent of full-time officer posts. The general secretary, deputy general secretary and all national officers were male. Though the union had recently had a woman president and the number of women on the executive council now approached half, women were still only nine out of the sixty-one members on the important negotiating committees.

This unequal status persisted despite more than a decade of campaigning and action by women members. In the mid-1970s, in response to a growing awareness of women's under-representation in the union's power structure, reserved seats had been created on the executive council. In 1983 a women's working party had been set up. Reporting in 1984, it had urged, first, the adoption of many campaigns of importance to women. Second, it had argued for the inclusion in collective bargaining of issues prioritized by women, such as ending low pay, the upgrading of women's jobs, flat-rate rather than percentage pay increases, full-time rights for part-time workers, childcare provision and changes in working hours and holidays (NUPE 1984). On employment, it had pressed for the recruitment of more women to full-time paid officer posts. On representation, it supported adaptation of the representational structure by the setting up of national and regional women's advisory committes and the appointment of a women's officer at head office. If women were to come through in greater numbers to leadership positions, it was clearly vital to get more of them active at grassroots level. The report therefore urged union branches to take many steps to encourage women's participation. Women's liaison officers should be appointed and branch equality committees set up; attempts should be made to negotiate time off with pay, to organize creches or pay for childcare and reconsider meeting venues to enable women to attend. Meetings should become less formal so as not to intimidate inexperienced members.

A curious duality then developed. Formally, most of these recommendations were adopted. Publicly, NUPE's leading men spoke out for women, and the union was well known for a commitment to 'women's issues'. Internally, however, at the time my research began five years later, women activists were bitter that the implementation of positive action was so incomplete. Their unmet demands and hopes make too long a list to detail here. I plan to focus instead on just one issue: *access to and interpretation of certain key offices* in the union. My data gathering focused on two such positions, both highly significant in NUPE: those of branch secretary and full-time paid officer, particularly at area and divisional levels. Women reported difficulty in the related matters of first getting women into these offices and then interpreting the responsibilities involved in a way feasible for women, and appropriate and relevant to them.

WOMEN, ACTIVISM AND THE BRANCH SECRETARY

NUPE women members have little time for union activism because, as noted, 78 per cent of them work part-time. And, as one said, 'they're part-time for a reason. They don't just think, "Oh, I'll be a lady of leisure for half the week." They work part-time because that's all the time they have to give to paid work.' Most go home to a demanding second shift in the household. Indeed many work a third, a 'twilight' shift, for a second employer to make up their earnings to a living wage.

This might in theory be seen as better qualifying women than men for representational and organizational activity in the union. 'Women know more than men' said one woman member, 'because a woman works in the home and has her job as well.' In fact, however, it leads to a situation in which it is almost always men, a minority in the branch, who represent women, the majority. Worse, sometimes the branch secretary is both the women's steward and their 'gaffer', as when a full-time male school caretaker represents part-time female school cleaners. (In principle, he could also be the husband of such a cleaner. We begin to see the multiple, indeed cumulative, nature of the relationships of gender power.) Many women feel a woman lay 'rep' would do more for women. As one said,

I don't want to criticize individual men, but I really don't believe that they can represent the interests of the union because they don't have those interests instinctively at heart, women's interests. And where women come forward and actually put into words the views of their women colleagues at work you get a different slant on issues.

It is not only time that women lack. They also lack confidence and expertise in union matters. It is not surprising if many women vote for an 'experienced' man in preference to an untried woman. How are women to learn? 'Most branch secretaries keep their thumbs on the women,' one woman said. 'Very few men will push a woman on. They don't want them to come on.' It is not difficult for a branch secretary to outflank opposition by ensuring a good turnout of his supporters at the meeting where voting takes place. But often his re-election goes unchallenged. As one admitted, 'So long as no one complains, I'll go on standing.' Another man said,

> I'm part of the geography of NUPE. That's the way NUPE works. It works through me as far as [they] are concerned. . . . People know that I know at lot more than they do. I'm a lot more skilled than them. . . . Those are very big factors that make it very difficult for anyone to run against me.

Not only do men vote for each other, giving each other the 'sponsorship' they withhold from women. When a woman does stand against a man he may fight back, using dirty means – cutting her dead or speaking ill of her behind her back. One woman spoke of the hurtful effects of such aggression on her. 'It's dreadful. It goes very, very deep. You can't believe it's happening to you. When you're only trying to do something well.'

As a result of such practices, as many women told me, too many branch secretaries, characteristically men, stayed in the post for ten or fifteen years, assuming that they had a position for life. Furthermore, the rule book provided for an indirect delegating system. That is to say, the membership voted for the branch secretary, but the branch secretaries voted for representatives at higher levels. Not surprisingly, it was each other they promoted, ever upwards from branch to district, district to division, division to national level. Branch secretaries dominated on all decision-making bodies. They had become a self-perpetuating clique. Consequently, in NUPE, 'getting women represented' was proving easier to effect at the very top (for instance, by reserved seats on the executive council), than towards the bottom: the branch officer stratum. Yet it was here that the great numbers of women existed and where, in many respects, power was generated.

WOMEN AS FULL-TIME PAID OFFICERS

At one time NUPE was acknowledged to be an officer-led trade union. With the growth of the shop stewards' movement of the late 1960s and early 1970s came a democratic awareness that power should shift to the members. External consultants reviewed the union structure and their recommendations were accepted by national conference (Warwick University 1974). A middle-level structure was inserted to effect an administrative and representational link between the workplace and head office. Despite this strengthening of the lay representatives' role, in the 1980s the full-time officer continued to play a very significant part in union activity. The branch secretary and the area officer, working together, were the duo at the heart of the union team.

Of the 180 full-time officers in 1989 only twenty were women.[2] Most had been recruited under the new equality-conscious policy and were still mainly in the lowest grade, that of area officer. This role involves building up organization at the grassroots, aiding recruitment, educating members, motivating activism, and so on. It services branches and committees and develops their work, keeping in touch with lay representatives, responding to their requests for help and intervention, assisting in disputes, appearing at disciplinaries and appeals, backing campaigns and demonstrations, running the office. The work is highly demanding, keeping the officer out two or three nights a week and many weekends a year. It means relentless confrontation and crisis management.

When women overcome their hesitancy to seek the role of officer they face prejudice from other colleagues, employers, lay representatives and members. There is strong, not always muted, opposition to the move to recruit more women in the name of sex equality. There had developed in NUPE a tradition of recruiting officers from a particular culture of socialist working-class men who had characteristically acquired adult education at the labour movement's Ruskin College. Many of the existing male officers thus shared a set of values and a particular relationship to trade unionism. Now the leadership made it clear that the union was looking for a different kind of full-time officer, 'more reflective of the membership'. Internal recruitment was to be favoured, and they would in particular be looking for women to join men on the panels from which officers are selected. Many men suspected that the women coming forward would not be 'really working class', since they were likely to be drawn from the more educated among the female membership, the para-professional social workers and nurses. They felt that by specifically looking for women, the union was 'cutting itself off' from 'the best'. A certain woman officer obtained her officer job in competition with a male branch secretary in her division. This man was (in the words of another male officer) 'very experienced, and the woman was only a shop steward. A lot of people questioned the justice of the decision.' The rejected branch secretary was so resentful that he threatened to leave the union and take his entire branch of 3,000 members with him. The difficulty for the woman in question of building confidence and cooperation in her area can be imagined.

Once in a post, the resistance continues to be felt. One new officer described how her male colleagues were sometimes 'odd' in the way they related to her. 'Extremely polite, deferential even. They treat you like a queen, then undermine you behind your back.' In dealings with employers, also mainly men, she found:

> They play all the tricks that you could get from men in everyday life. I somehow expected it would be different. They'll try and put you down in front of your own members in a way I don't believe they'd ever try to do with a man.

Another woman officer described the difficulty of being in meetings in which you were the only woman present. You got patronizing comments. When you expressed justified anger you were told 'not to get emotional'. Many men were disrespectful, wouldn't hear you out, had to be shouted down. The officer job is thus twice as hard when done by a woman as when done by a man. Many women feel the problem lies in the job and the men, not in the women.

Women themselves play a part in perpetuating these damaging power relations, however. Few women express interest in filling these offices. A minority of women, besides, reject women candidates on principle. 'I won't have her' said one woman branch secretary of a woman candidate for area officer, 'My ladies will never accept a woman'. The reason for women's inactivity or resistance however lies partly in the way men define power and in the hegemonic cultural processes in which they have generated negative meanings for feminism and for strong women. Women, understandably, fail to associate women positively with power. They do not think themselves capable of handling it. And what they want in their full-time officer is a powerful person, not (as one woman said), somebody they see as 'a chit of a girl'. A further manner in which women fail each other is through racism, to which NUPE's white members are not immune.

HOLDING ON TO POWER

Just as it is not all women in NUPE who actively support the equality initiative, so it is not all men who resist it. The male leadership of NUPE pursues national policies that are in many ways favourable to women.

Certainly it has become clear to all trade union leaders that their future depends on courting women, particularly older women and part-timers, the only growth area in membership. The leadership of NUPE at the time of my study purposefully sought a reputation as leading the labour movement on women's issues. They were waging campaigns for a national minimum wage, for childcare and against limitation of women's right to choose abortion. They had been supportive in introducing the women's officer and women's representational structures in the union.

There were contradictions however. First, while the union supported 'quotas' for women in the structures of the Labour Party, the climate of opposition to positive action within the union was such that it seemed impossible even to raise the question of instituting a rule change to create such quotas in NUPE.[3] Second, the union campaigned publicly on 'equal pay for work of equal value', yet the male leadership had been highly resistant to supporting one division's choice to supplement collective bargaining by recourse to the courts in an 'equal value' test case. Besides, the national position on collective bargaining by no means always translated into an equally favourable story for women when interpreted locally. When put to the test even pro-equality leaders felt they must protect the tender feelings of the male activist on whom they saw the effectiveness of the union depending. Some women therefore questioned whether the men at the top meant the same thing by sex equality as they did.

Men in NUPE clearly experienced a conflict between numerical realism (which pointed to a future in which NUPE could truly represent women's interests, be predominantly a women's union, led by women) and their own self-preservation as the powerful sex. Many genuinely respect and like women (in their place). They are proud of 'their' women members and fight fiercely for their rights against the boss. Yet men can say, in moments of honesty, as one branch secretary did: 'I'm very selfish in a way. I want to hang on to the job and I don't want to have to share it with others who may come and compete with me for it. I have to be honest about that.' And of course senior male paid officers, too, loyal as many are to the woman member, still remain firmly in position. As one said, 'as a man you can sometimes feel a bit threatened by it all . . . I'm not sure that I'd happily step aside in my job to allow a woman to come into it.' Clearly 'positive action for sex equality', the women's movement within the labour movement, threatens men, as officers and lay representatives, with loss of position and loss of power.

There are many reasons a man might wish to hold on to office. The advantages of being a representative are numerous. One is simply the authority to decide, to choose the direction taken by an organization. Another is an exciting and interesting life. There is time off with pay from what may be a boring, hard and menial job to do the more attractive work of the union. Representatives get regular trips to attend committees or conferences. Above all, branch secretaries receive a financial commission of 12.5 per cent of the branch subscriptions, which can add several hundred pounds a month to personal income. As for the union officer job, it may not be brilliantly paid, but it is better pay than the member gets in her cleaning job. The roles also enable men to look after men's financial interests in collective bargaining, thereby maintaining the sex differential: '3 per cent on the bonus for the lads'. A fourth advantage is a feeling of personal significance. There is potential in the officer job for some of the self-importance that derives from being someone in the local Labour Party or trades council. They can be a force in the locality:

> There's a lot of ego involved. When you go into a negotiation and the employer has to take you seriously. When your members always listen to what you say. When you have a strike and can bring the whole city to its knees. Yes, it does make you feel powerful.

ACROSS THE WORK/HOME BOUNDARY

One aspect of the power a man exercises in becoming one among a largely male corps of lay representatives and officers is a specifically gendered power: he is a respected member of the dominant sex; those he represents, who look up to him and depend on him, are mainly women.

Relations of sex dominance outside and inside the organization interact and reinforce each other. As we have seen, women in NUPE are mainly part-time workers. Underlying this is the fact that they work many more hours, unpaid, for their partners and families in the home, than do male members. A male activist or officer sees a woman member's domestic life as the source of deficiencies; he sees a man as useful to the union to the extent that he detaches himself from the family. A male officer described the difference.

> A man will be influenced. He'll talk union. He'll go to his pub and talk union. He'll go to a union meeting and talk union. He'll read union stuff at night. He might even do union courses at night. A bloody woman don't. She's got bloody pots, washing, kids, beds, house, mothers. How do you affect that? Women tend to switch off when they leave work. What's in the school cleaner's mind when she leaves work at two? Just got to go to the shops, get home and get the dinner prepared because the kids'll be out at 3.30, the old man's due at 5 o'clock. So she switches off doesn't she.

If a woman sometimes finds herself hindered by a male comrade in the union, she just as frequently stumbles over that other male impediment, 'the old man' back home. A male branch secretary said:

> A lot of women would be put in a very difficult situation with their husbands at home by wanting to take on the sort of responsibility I carry. . . . I've got to be blunt about this. Some of the women shop stewards in our branch are only allowed a certain amount of time to attend meetings, to be active, by their husbands.

Indeed, one husband was reported to me as having said, when his wife thought of standing as steward, 'She'll not start that fucking lark. In and out to the clothes line's enough for her.' A man has to tolerate not only his wife's absence but also the intrusion of union business into the home. The phone rings – and it rings for her. It is not surprising perhaps that, as a woman full-time officer reported, for female lay representatives 'to have support from their partners for what they do is the exception rather than the rule'.

The male interest at home and in the union doubles up. Thus, one male officer felt the union should take care not to step on the toes of husbands.

> If you're going to promote women in the organization and if those women have family commitments, you've got to be very careful to ensure she has the support of her family and partner . . . I've perhaps got a rooted sexism myself. I'd resent my partner – if my partner did my job I couldn't handle that at home.
> [It'd make you feel put down?]
> Absolutely. Absolutely.

Men are right to fear that union engagement may teach 'their' women to refuse subordination: 'My husband doesn't recognize the woman he married.' Getting involved in the union often gives a woman a new confidence. She sees a woman from her branch going to London for a national meeting. She even sees a woman playing the role of president of the union: an ordinary member like herself has become a public figure. She begins to feel, as one woman said, 'I can talk to anyone now. It gives me a wee bit of power.' It can bring a woman a more self-respecting relationship within the family: 'You might interrupt a conversation or say something about a programme on TV in a way you wouldn't have done before.' Another woman lay representative in an interview, looking at her watch, said:

> If I hadn't been in the union now I'd have been thinking I'd better get home to put the dinner in the oven. Now I'll say I've got other things to do. You'll have to wait for your dinner. I think my husband's changed too, because I'm in the union. He can't say things as heavy as he used to. He knows I've a mind of my own.

TRANSFORMING THE USES OF POSITION AND POWER: FEMINIZING THE OFFICER JOB

The NUPE experience shows that loss of office by men and the transfer to women of the power that goes with it is not the only implication, and may not be the biggest challenge, of the equality movement in trade unions. What men quite rightly suspect is that women, in acceding to office, may want to behave differently. They may want to *change the nature of power and the way it is used.* It has been noted elsewhere that an opening to women in the labour movement is often associated with an opening to democracy (Cockburn 1984).

One source of evidence for this change in the nature of power comes from the way women seek to redefine the role of full-time paid officer. Men and women emphasized different things when they specified the qualities called for in an officer. While both sexes described the job as one requiring 'total commitment', 'a twenty-four-hour-day, seven-day-week', technical knowledge and leadership qualities, men more often emphasized toughness and aggressiveness: 'The job's confrontational. It's saying no.' Women by contrast emphasized 'communication', 'relationship', 'devolution and sharing', 'not holding too much information to yourself'. While men rejoiced in the heroic image of the union officer, women problematized it as 'macho'. They deplored this attitude of 'I've worked ninety-nine hours this week and driven 1,000 miles. What have you done?' Women also regretted the competitiveness. One said, 'The ethos is one of individualism. You work alone till you do something wrong, then they come down on you like a ton of bricks.' A curious ethos, she remarked, for a nominally collective movement. The way the paid officer job is designed and carried out makes it a draining job, in two senses. It is a serious health risk for those who hold these posts. It also uses up, unacknowledged and unpaid for, the time and energy of wives and other members of officers' families. One can scarcely do it without support at home. The job is clearly shaped for a male incumbent.

Women of the women's advisory committee of one of NUPE's regions wrote a thoughtful paper on this theme for the consideration of their divisional council. Women were much needed as officers in order to encourage other women. Yet the way the job was done, and its 'male, grey-suited image' excluded women. They argued that a truly equal opportunities policy employer would not permit the lack of respect and support currently encountered by women attempting the job, nor indeed would it create a job that was incompatible with family life. One practical suggestion being canvassed by a number of women was for more cooperation, including job- and 'patch'-sharing, within a divisional team. This initiative, however, received an unsympathetic response from the divisional officer.

He felt the women's comments were inaccurate and unhelpful. He rehearsed arguments I heard from other men:

> Being a full-time officer is a tough job and our members do in fact expect to see full-time officers show some resilience and on some occasions what you call a 'macho' attitude towards management.

He argued that officers needed to be 'firm and decisive characters' because management was increasingly 'extremely macho towards our membership'.

Men in the union widely felt that to do the job differently would be to do it worse. A senior officer felt women must prove themselves to be *like* men:

> Once they've proved themselves, once you've seen them operating in the mire and the dirt where people are kicking each other to death and you've seen they can survive without crumbling – and they can – they'll have respect.

Women on the contrary felt that the pressure on the job came as much from the men as from the employer: 'The way men do it, half the stress is competition.'

RETHINKING THE BRANCH SECRETARY

One division in NUPE, that of Northern Ireland, was unique in having women divisional and assistant divisional officers. Indeed, three out of the team of four full-time paid officers in the division were female. The officer job was interpreted rather differently here from the way it was done elsewhere. Not that the pressure was any less – but the mutual support was greater and there was more openness. The office was run as 'a resource for the ordinary member', indeed for the community. One member said, 'I wouldn't come in if it was men. They think they're the big boss and sit behind their desks.' Equality measures in the union had furnished the division with a women's advisory committee which its members had turned into an effective consciousness-raising group. The equality policy had given formal (if not popular) legitimacy in the division to taking the woman member seriously.

Women of the division had identified the branch secretary role, as traditionally played, as an impediment to the woman member's engagement. As we have seen, some women believe there is a characteristically male way of doing the branch secretary job – hugging the information and the action to yourself, a prescription for early burnout. Women say of such branch secretaries, 'It cripples them, but they won't give it up.' 'It's the great "I am".' Such a representative of course avoids generating any active members who might eventually displace him.

In this division therefore the approach of the officers was to decentralize and devolve, 'to ask new questions, redistribute the roles', and root their policies 'in the reality of our members' lives'. The focus of attention was not the existing 'activist' but 'always the ordinary member'. A smaller proportion of the education budget here was being spent on activities for branch secretaries, more for ordinary members. There were already a number of branch secretaries (mainly women but some men) who shared this aim. As one woman put it, 'every step you take you turn your head and pull someone else along. Not ask them. Pull them.'

There was open criticism here of 'a politics of position', the tendency to see a seat 'not as *a* seat but as *my* seat'. Some shop steward positions had been split into job-shares. The possibility was even mooted of job-sharing the branch secretary role. And could tenure be shortened? After discussion, the women who had been elected to reserved seats for women on the national executive council had voluntarily, as an example, chosen to withdraw their candidacy after the second term of two years 'to make room for others'. In the light of this, a similar reform of the branch secretary role was being discussed among the women. One woman said, 'there'd be huge opposition. That's where the explosion would happen. But if it were accepted, change would flow through the union.' Some worried, would it be a 'waste' of the experience of activism? Others said no, the overall resources of the branch would be increased, provided of course that the displaced branch secretaries were prepared to knuckle down to work without position, to become educators of others.

Even women branch secretaries, however, identified closely with their role. As one woman, who had expressed herself ready and willing to give up various committee seats to make room for others, very honestly admitted, 'my crunch will come when I give up the branch. Because then I'll lose everything. That'll be my moment of truth.' But she affirmed the importance of 'bringing others along' if this local experiment were not to collapse. 'And the union, without that approach, *it*'ll fall flat.'

The results of this policy were already visible. Not a few manual working women here were public figures. Whereas before they had thought of themselves and their colleagues in the way everyone else thought of them, 'it's only the cleaners', 'it's only the home helps', now they began to see their job as useful and themselves as having value. 'I suppose in every woman there's a sense of her own worth. It only takes an issue, or someone else, to bring it out' said one woman domestic.

Some men were changing too. After all, as one woman officer put it, 'enjoying the prestige of being a little higher, having a halfpenny more than someone else . . . it's such a narrow view of being human'. Some of the male branch secretaries had gained a new self-respect, she said, by identifying women as those most in need of the union's efforts. 'Men, who have a little more, thinking first about women who are on the bottom.' Two male manual workers had become willing and supportive comparators in an equal value case. Changes were ensuing in collective bargaining. The priorities had shifted. By a process they called 'participation and democracy' they had uncovered the way previous deals had maintained men's differentials while stitching women into poverty. 'Women had been paying not only for their own rises but for everyone else's.'

The politics of this division were nothing if not strategic and conscious. Both members and officers were rethinking democracy: did it mean everyone should have a vote or that everyone should be enabled to play a part? They were rethinking power. A woman lay representative said,

> Male members have been used to power being taken and used in the one way. The traditional way, the male way. Obviously they must have found it strange when other things started to happen. I mean, we don't so much take power, what we do is start working.

A woman officer admitted, 'to turn the union over to women would be the death-knell of the union-as-it-is'. And despite men's fears, this did not mean less productive trade unionism. This division was widely respected as 'efficient, effective and tough'. What it would mean however, if such an interpretation of power were to spread throughout the union, was changing the union rule book, for 'if you want to hold on to power, the structure offers you the means'. The representational formula would need revision. A limitation of terms in office should be introduced. Rule changes are permitted at biennial national conferences. But the delegates are overwhelmingly male and predominantly branch secretaries. They were unlikely, the women felt, to 'die at their own hand'.

UNDERSTANDINGS OF POWER

How can we understand the power play precipitated by positive action for sex equality in NUPE and other such unions? What concept of power would have resonance for a woman manual worker, a member of NUPE, and which would make sense of all the facets of her experience: at work, at home, in the union? Among the many general theories of power I select for brief mention here two that have been particularly influential and which I believe enable us to debate such issues.

The school of thought that became known as 'critical theory', at its most influential in the period from the 1930s to the 1960s, developed a highly coherent view of the human subject, its domination and potential liberation. The influence of the critical theorists' perception of power was superseded in the 1970s by that of Michel Foucault. Miller (1987) counterposes these two bodies of work. He focuses his attention on what meaning each gives to *subjectivity* and *power*. Both of course are central issues for women, though he does not consider this. Miller characterizes critical theory as proposing that

> For power to operate . . . it must have as its effect the crushing of subjectivity. The subject in such a vision rises up from time to time in a valiant struggle against power, but is constantly turned back.
>
> (1987: 1)

Industrial capitalism is the critical theorists' bogey; the focus of their liberation project is an 'essential subject'. By contrast for Foucault, power 'operates in precisely the other direction, not by repressing subjectivity but by promoting it, cultivating it and nurturing it' (Gordon 1980). If for the critical theorists power smashes (a pre-given) subjectivity, for Foucault it forms, deploys and regulates the subject.

Many cogent feminist criticisms have been made of critical theory's representations of power – indeed, along with Marxism it is the tough material on which new wave feminism cut its teeth. It is a totalizing view that sees but one subject and one kind of power – implicitly a male subject and an ungendered power deriving ultimately from class relations. It discourses unproblematically on justice, truth and freedom – in no doubt as to *whose* justice, whose truth and whose freedom. 'Women' as a sex are not on the agenda, let alone differently situated groups of women – Northern Ireland working-class women, black, colonized, lesbian and other women. These 'others' are invisible, subsumed within 'mankind'. For Max Horkheimer (1974) for instance, the very concept of contemporary 'man' is threatened by the deforming power of industrial capitalism, so heavily does it weigh on him: 'The word man no longer expresses the power of the subject who can resist the status quo' (1974: 4). ('He' however is as yet spared the deconstruction into 'his' gendered parts he will suffer later in feminist critiques.) The family, for Horkheimer, is 'one of the most important formative agencies', but its importance for him lies in its functionality for bourgeois social order, not its part in the reproduction of male power (Horkheimer 1972: 98). For Herbert Marcuse (1968) too, man is an unproblematic category, still the subject of history it seems, and speaking, in self-confident tones, for all of us: 'Concern with man moves to the center of theory; man must be freed from real need and real misery to achieve the liberation of becoming himself' (Marcuse 1968: 72).

In critical theory the Enlightenment project of reason and progress is valid, but it is defeated and mourned. In Foucault's work it is left for dead, the potentially transcendent subject brought down to earth. Power, too, looks different now. Though it still appears to culminate in some shadowy class or state, this power has to be understood, in 'an ascending analysis', starting from its 'infinitesimal mechanisms' in the individual. For Foucault the individual is not the subject of a liberatory project. Rather subjectivity, even the body of the subjugated, is the effect and vehicle of power. In a celebrated lecture he put it as follows:

> [P]ower, if we do not take too distant a view of it, is not that which makes the difference between those who exclusively possess and retain it, and those who do not have it and submit to it. Power must be analysed as something which circulates . . . power is employed and exercised through a net-like organisation. And not only do invididuals circulate between its threads; they are always in the position of simultaneously undergoing and exercising power . . . individuals are the vehicles of power, not its points of application.
>
> (Gordon 1980: 98)

This brings us closer to a woman's reality. Here we can potentially see women being kept down or out, women organizing, but also women as racists, and women denying each other solidarity, of whom there were not a few in NUPE. Foucault supplies us with a meaning for power which is more interesting than brute subjugation.

> What makes power hold good, what makes it accepted, is simply the fact that it doesn't only weigh on us as a force that says no, but that it traverses and produces things. It induces pleasure, forms knowledge, produces discourse.
>
> (Gordon 1980: 119)

We can potentially see a woman's gendered identity here – the attractions of 'being looked after', the pleasures of submission to 'one who knows better'. Foucault acknowledges multiple kinds of power, speaking of 'the manifold forms of domination that can be experienced within society . . . the multiple forms of subjugation that have a place and function within the social organism' (Gordon 1980: 96). There seems to be room here for a specifically gendered power, for male supremacy.

No such specificity emerges, however. Indeed, Foucault is clear that 'in speaking of domination I do not have in mind that solid and global kind of domination that one person exercises over others, or *one group over another*' (Gordon 1980: 96, my italics). In Foucault's work power ultimately becomes simply a pervasive and uniform substance – coterminous with social relations. It is symptomatic that throughout his work Foucault, a man, white, an academic, writes unreflexively, neither recognizing his own sex, ethnicity, or class, nor acknowledging his own embodied part in the *differentiated* processes in the web of power. As Nancy Hartsock says in her essay on Foucault, he leaves women still lacking a stable theory of power. 'Foucault's world' she says, 'is not my world but is instead a world in which I feel profoundly alien' (Hartsock 1990: 166). Oddly, in homing in on the individual experience of power while refusing to identify sex/gender relations Foucault fails to deliver the promise of his approach. The individual remains ungendered. So, as a consequence, does the concept of power.

Not only does this render it inadequate for a feminist understanding of women's gendered relation to power, it allows us no hope of a future beyond that of ever-repeated, doomed resistance. There is no handle on transformation. Ironically, it is the critical theorists, for all their failings, who offer a hope of a different future society, consciously pursued. After all, if liberation is a valid project for 'mankind', the possibility of some future women's liberation movement may just be glimpsed. In Foucault, a feminist future remains unthinkable. Indeed as Hartsock points out, he was of the opinion that 'to even imagine another system is to extend our participation in the present one' (Hartsock 1990: 168).

An understanding of the kind of power play visible in the trade union I have described above, then, may gain from insights from both critical theory and Foucauldian theory. But it means jettisoning many features of both. It requires, I would suggest, at least the following alternative elements.

We need an understanding of power as having more than one identifiable kind of embodiment. Like white power, male power in a trade union or any other organization cannot be reduced to just 'power'. Second, while we cannot *privilege* one kind of oppression over another, nor identify subjects only by their positioning in one set of dominance relations (as was too often done in the case of class), we do need concepts with which to *identify* male power in the lived experience of women; certainly embodied and specified as black or white, of this class or that, but none the less women as a sex. Third, we have seen how the trade union woman moves not only through his or her own life history but across and between several institutions in which everyday life is experienced: family, employment, and union. We need to be able to show patterns of gender power in many institutions and over long historical periods culminating to predispose individual behaviour in the here and now.

This is not to posit unchangeable structures, however. In fact we need to retain an element of intentionality. Foucault admonishes us not to concern ourselves with power at the level of conscious intentions, to 'refrain from posing the labyrinthine and unanswerable question: "Who then has power and what has he in mind? What is the aim of someone who possesses power?"' (Gordon 1980: 97). Hartsock by contrast does not hesitate to begin her article with just such pertinent questions about power. 'Where is it to be found? How is it to be developed? Are relations of power between the sexes comparable to other kinds of power relations?' (Hartsock 1990). Our theory of power has to acknowledge that quite ordinary men (as husbands, bosses, union representatives) in some measure consciously engage in practices that subjugate women and perpetuate male power, that they do indeed (notwithstanding Foucault) 'have something in mind'.

We need to be able to see the part of the dominators in producing people's participation in their own and others' oppression. The acquiescence of women in male power is not 'all our own fault', nor is it universal or inevitable. It is partly the achievement of cultural 'work' by men in identifiable hegemonic processes. An example is their current anathematizing of 'feminism' which is as evident in NUPE as anywhere else (Cockburn 1991).

One reason for retaining a degree of voluntarism in our idea of how power works is that we have seen some men's consciousness transformed. In the Northern Ireland division of NUPE the arguments of women had caused some men to 'change their minds'. You had to 'appeal to a man's best political interests', help him 'reconstruct his identity'. And women had found that men, 'when they think about increasing the value of someone else . . . come to see that it increases the value they have themselves.' A large segment of the women's movement believes that if men are not to continue to be part of the problem, they must be approached as part of the solution.

Most importantly we need a differentiating theory of power that permits scope not only for the sexes to change position in relation to power but for the nature and functioning of power itself to be transformed in that process. Power is not everywhere and always used or experienced in the same way. As Nancy Hartsock has written elsewhere, theories of power are inherently theories of community (Hartsock 1985). Power is commonly domination, but, as some NUPE women show, it can sometimes be reinterpreted as capacity.

Finally, we need concepts of power and subjectivity that do not negate one aspect of many women's everyday experience: the practical viability of a women's movement against male power. The most memorable empirical finding in the NUPE case study was the energy, vision and commitment to change shown by the women's officer, women of the women's committee, 'the ordinary woman member' and their male supporters. There are reasons to believe that women may one day succeed in transforming male-dominated sites of power into organizations with a very different way of going about their business. Trade unions may be more accessible than most organizations to such transformations, since they are membership organizations of a subjugated group: the working class.

Ethical distinctions and liberationary visions did not lose their legitimacy with the critique of the Enlightenment 'man'. In fact there are ever more varied and vocal identities of subordinated women whose claims to parity are calling for a hearing.

NOTES

1 The research was funded by the Economic and Social Research Council and carried out at the Department of Social Sciences, The City University, London. I would like to express my thanks to these organizations, but also most warmly to officers and members of NUPE (as it then was) who so generously contributed information, ideas and encouragement. I wish to emphasize, first, that any errors of fact or judgement in this chapter are my own, not those of my informants; second, that the union has changed in many ways since the time the study was carried out and the date of publication of this account. NUPE is now part of a much larger public sector union, UNISON. The study therefore should be read as a snapshot at a certain point in time of a certain set of tensions and processes.

As is typical of organizational 'case' studies, a range of types of data gathering was involved. Documentation was plentiful. Observation was possible but, as is often the case, lack of time in the end limited the use of this method. The most important source of information was in-depth interviews. Of the total of 200 interviews in the study as a whole, thirty-nine were in NUPE, supplemented by informal conversations with many more people. The findings were later discussed in a seminar with a group of women activists. Of the interviews, twelve were with senior officers, including the General Secretary and Deputy General Secretary. Visits were made to four divisional offices, where a total of twenty-seven interviews were carried out. Of these, twelve were with paid officers and fifteen with lay representatives. In all, fifteen of the interviews were with women, twenty-four with men. Three were with black officers or activists, the remainder with white. The interviews were semi-structured and tape recorded.

2 NUPE asked me to report that by February 1991 the union had appointed two women national officers; women were 28 per cent out of 160 full-time paid officers; and in the most recent six months 50 per cent of newly recruited area officers had been female. They believed this performance would make them the leader in this respect among unions affiliated to the Trades Union Congress.

3 The climate on 'quotas' was however changing by February 1991, when the amalgamation between NUPE and sister unions COHSE and NALGO, that later created UNISON, was in process of negotiation. In planning for the 'new union' the question of proportionality was on the agenda. Women were asking that they be represented on every committee, from branch to national executive, in direct proportion to their numbers in the area or industry with which the committee dealt. And indeed UNISON came into existence in 1993 with a public commitment to sex proportionality throughout the union's decision-making bodies. How exactly it would be achieved was unclear, but women's struggles in preceding years, such as those described here, had clearly begun to reshape power.

REFERENCES

Cockburn, C. (ed.) (1984) 'Trade unions and the radicalizing of socialist feminism', *Feminist Review* 16, April.
—— (1989) 'Equal opportunities: the long and short agenda', *Industrial Relations Journal* 20, 213–25.
—— (1991) *In the Way of Women: Men's Resistance to Sex Equality in Organizations*, London: Macmillan Education.
Gordon, C. (ed.) (1980) *Michel Foucault: Power/Knowledge*, Brighton: Harvester Press.
Hartsock, N. (1985) *Money, Sex and Power: Towards a Feminist Historical Materialism*, Boston: Northeastern University Press.
—— (1990) 'Foucault on power', in L. Nicholson (ed.) *Feminism/Post Modernism*, London: Routledge.
Horkheimer, M. (1972) *Critical Theory*, New York: Seabury Press.
—— (1974) *Critique of Instrumental Reason*, New York: Seabury Press.
Marcuse, H. (1968) *Negations*, Harmondsworth: Penguin.
Miller, P. (1987) *Domination and Power*, London: Routledge & Kegan Paul.
National Union of Public Employees (NUPE) (1984) *Report of the Women's Working Party*, London.
Robarts, S. (1981) *Positive Action for Women: The Next Steps in Education, Training and Employment*, London: National Council for Civil Liberties.
Snell, M., Glucklich, P. and Provall, M. (1981) *Equal Pay and Opportunities: A Study of the Implications of the Equal Pay and Sex Discrimination Acts in 26 Organisations*, Research Paper No. 20, London: Department of Employment.
Warwick University (1974) *Organisation and Change in the National Union of Public Employees*, Coventry.

6 Office affairs

Rosemary Pringle

While I have been doing research on gender and work for some time, my interest in organizations is relatively recent and derives directly from my study of secretaries, on which this chapter is based (Pringle 1989). My earlier work (Game and Pringle 1984) was influenced by Braverman (1974) and concentrated on the labour process and technological change. Somehow secretaries got left out of this study, and it was in the process of reflecting on why this was so that we began to shift away from Marxist labour process theory and towards a greater emphasis on sexuality, culture and discourse. While it is certainly possible to give an analysis of secretaries' work in terms of gender and technology, it makes for a rather limited account. The subject matter actually demanded a change of approach.

Secretaries are extremely vaguely defined: for Australia I was given anything between 25,000 and a quarter of a million, depending on whether I was using census returns or labour force statistics of one kind or another. It seemed impossible to establish a common set of tasks performed; there were no clearcut job descriptions; there were any number of overlaps with other jobs. At first this drove me crazy. But gradually I realized that this vagueness was one of the most interesting aspects, because it said so much about cultural processes. In everyday perceptions secretaries' work is trivialized, treated as not real work. Secretaries are assumed to be on terms of intimacy with the boss, their main function a decorative one. Of course, at another level, no one seriously believes that secretaries spend much time on the boss's knee – and yet the sexual possibilities colour the way the relationship is seen. It is thus difficult to analyse the work that secretaries do in isolation from the heavily sexualized images of what they are. Therefore I could not look at secretarial work as a series of tasks, independently of their social meanings. It became important to look at the construction of the occupation. One of my criticisms of labour process theory is that it misses this level: if it talks about occupations at all it assumes that they just follow naturally from the division of labour, and it pays no attention to their discursive construction. Once we start looking at occupations, the terrain quickly shifts to organizations.

Rather than tracing the history of secretaries in the labour process, I therefore tried to trace the dominant discourses about what secretaries are, noting their important cultural presence. I use 'discourse' rather similarly to Wendy Hollway, whose account of the discourses structuring hetero-sexual relations provided a model. Hollway uses the term to mean a 'system of statements which cohere around common meanings and values . . . a product of social factors, of powers and practices, rather than an individual's set of ideas' (1984: 231). A discourse structures and constrains our constitution of meaning within a delimited field, defines a legitimate perspective for the agent of 'knowledge' and, through its inclusions and exclusions, banishes alternative possibilities as unthinkable. In presenting itself as a direct description of reality, it disguises the fact that it has constituted its own 'reality'.

Secretaries are not sitting at their desks waiting to be counted and it is not self-evident who they are or who should be included. 'Secretary' should be understood rather as a term which has not one fixed meaning but a variety of meanings produced within different discourses. There were three which I took to be predominant:

- The *office-wife* emerged early this century and had its origins in the debate about whether (middle-class) women should work outside the home. It may be found in 'serious' journals, teaching manuals, the practices of a good many secretarial studies teachers as well as the more 'traditional' bosses and secretaries. It was based on the assumption that woman's primary place was in the home, that her other tasks would be redefined in relation to this and restricted to support roles. The office-wife is portrayed as the extension of her boss, loyal, trustworthy and devoted. The discourse has been modernized to shift from the deferential mouse, or the prim, 'spinsterish' figure with the bun, to the more sexy, liberated wife who insists on sharing the housework. But debate about changes in secretarial work is still often cast in terms of how far office marriages are changing. Are they being transformed into more companionate and egalitarian relations where the wife might have other interests or refuse to do certain aspects of the housework?
- The *dolly bird* with long blonde hair, large bust, miniskirts and high heels is an image which appears regularly in the tabloids of the 1950s. Where the office-wife had been a workhorse, putting order into the office, the dolly was presented as a source of chaos and diversion. The office-wife is subservient, passive and reserved, but the dolly is cheeky and loud and is represented as having an active sexuality and a degree

of sexual power over the boss. She appeals particularly to working-class men who may have least contact with office life and who enjoy seeing the boss's authority flouted. What the two constructions had in common was their definition in gendered and familial terms. Secretaries could be wives, mothers, mistresses, dragons or spinster aunts.

* The *career woman*. This third set of meanings struggled to emerge in the 1970s, largely in reaction to the earlier sexualization. It resists the familial and sexual definitions, treats secretaries as having serious careers, emphasizes skill and experience, and plays down the special relationship between boss and secretary in favour of viewing both as part of a management team. However, there was some debate about whether secretarial work itself was to be seen as a career or a stepping stone to one. Was 'femininity' compatible with professionalism?

Most feminist writing has located itself within the third 'equal opportunity' framework: secretaries as career professionals. I have argued that this is not enough. As long as the other representations persist, they have to be addressed and deconstructed. There is no point in just talking about skills and pay and technology while these discourses exert power, and continue to construct secretaries in familial and sexual terms.

If the boss–secretary relation is organized around sexuality and family imagery, this seems to place it outside the modern bureaucratic structures that are a feature of all large organizations. According to Weber's 'ideal type', bureaucracies are based on impersonality, functional specialization, a hierarchy of authority and the impartial application of rules. The boss–secretary relationship contradicts all these criteria. By having direct access to the powerful, secretaries are outside the hierarchy of authority. Far from being specialized, they can be called upon to do just about anything. The relationship is based on personal rapport and involves a degree of intimacy and shared secrets unusual for any but lovers or close friends. It is capable of generating intense feelings of loyalty, dependency and personal commitment. Not surprisingly then, the relationship is often conceptualized either as archaic or as marginal to the workings of bureaucracy 'proper'. I argue that, on the contrary, the boss–secretary relationship is the most visible aspect of a pattern of domination based on desire and sexuality. Far from being an exception, it vividly illustrates the workings of modern bureaucracies. Gender and sexuality are central not only in the boss–secretary relation but in all workplace power relations. Sexuality in the workplace is not simply repressed or sublimated or, as Marcuse (1968) suggested, subjected to controlled expression. It is actively produced in a range of discourses and interactions.

Of course, organization theorists have long been aware of the importance of the personal in the workplace. And yet the discourse of 'bureaucratic rationality' has remained central. I think we can re-read this in order to bring out the underlying assumptions. While the rational–legal or bureaucratic form presents itself as gender-neutral it actually constitutes a particular kind of masculinity based on the exclusion of the personal, the sexual and the feminine. This does not mean that men are in fact 'rational' or that women are 'emotional' but that they come to recognize themselves in these conceptions.

Feminists have talked a lot about sexual harassment. While this has been important I want to situate it as part of a larger pattern. Power is not necessarily organized around coercion – indeed this may be a weak form. Power operates a lot more effectively when it operates around patterns of desire and pleasure, when it is not experienced as power at all, or where its exercise is enjoyed by both parties. As Foucault (1980) has reminded us, power is not exercised simply as a prohibition but as an incitement to act, to take on certain identities and pleasures. Secretaries derive pleasure from their femininity, and far from being directly oppressive they may feel empowered by it. Where coercion itself is defined as pleasurable, and based on consent, can it any longer be regarded as 'coercive'? The debates about sadomasochism, particularly as they have been applied to gay and lesbian relationships and to pornography, can be usefully transposed both to everyday life and to the office. It does not require whips and chains, leather and dungeons to identify the patterning of relations that is being described here. Emotional sadomasochism, if not the 'real' thing, is part of everyday power relations. The twist in the tail is that it is not necessarily the sadist who exercises total power; there is scope here too for reversals of 'normal' gender relations. Sadomasochism therefore provides a conveniently flexible way of understanding the ebbs and flows, the volatility, of power. That is, it captures elements that are obscured by a simple notion of 'power structure'.

METHOD

I have often been asked, how does one go around talking to people about their innermost thoughts and fantasies, about their sexual behaviour and desires? The flippant answer is that, if you say you're researching secretaries, that is what people expect you to do, and you are already the subject of some mirth before you arrive at the organization. In fact I usually found it harder to get people to tell me their salaries than to talk about sex. Needless to say, I showed some discretion in raising the subject directly. It was more a matter of talking around it, and then doing a 'reading' of my transcripts. I taped my interviews, and people rarely objected. This was important for analysing the way people said things, the repetitions and the contradictions. If one takes notes, one not only has difficulty concentrating on what is being said, but one corrects for contradictions. If one is trying to identify discourses of the sexual, one will find them regardless of what is being said – so it is not a matter of asking directly about it. I would usually ask questions about clothes and appearance, about relationships, about gossip and flirtation, about whether the gender of one's boss/secretary mattered, and about what gave them pleasure at work. People would often talk freely about other people's relationships, and about the content of office rumours. Often they spoke in more detail about previous jobs than their present one. Sometimes people did reveal secrets about themselves and the interview became something of a confessional. The tone which they used to talk about other people, and the way they were with me, all provided clues. The interview has, I think, to be seen as something of a microcosm. At the same time, I am aware that the form of the interview affected the results. I mostly chose to interview people separately. Had I interviewed bosses and secretaries together, or spoken with groups, I may have generated a different kind of information.

I and my colleagues interviewed large numbers of people – about 300 secretaries, managers and other office staff. The interviews took between thirty minutes to about two hours and most were carried out at work. In retrospect we did a lot more than we needed for detailed textual analysis of the kind I eventually opted for. At the same time, it enabled me to sample a very wide range of workplaces and thus give my own discourse the authority of empirical detail.

I identified three main discourses which structure the boss–secretary relationship – which does not necessarily exhaust the possibilities. The three may be characterized as master/slave, mother/son and reciprocity or team discourses. The first normatively has the man as subject, the woman as object. The second has the woman as subject, the man as object. But the two do not balance each other. While 'mother' is symbolically the most powerful role for a woman, it is still a subordinate one. In this context it has service functions which might suggest 'nanny' as a more accurate term. She may have to pick up after a 'messy little boy', but the latter does not necessarily feel disempowered by this. That might be exactly what he pays her for! The third, the team discourse, was evoked the most frequently as the appropriately 'modern' form. But as people talked, it was obvious that in most cases the other discourses were operative, even dominant. Where 'team' seemed dominant, it was actually difficult to identify this as a boss–secretary relationship. It seemed more like two or more people who happened to be working together and there may not be any obvious hierarchy. A photograph in *Cosmopolitan* (which I was forbidden to use) illustrated this beautifully: two well-groomed women at a desk, one sitting, the other standing behind her. Which was which? The image of secretary at the keyboard was counterpoised brilliantly with boss at the terminal. But this shared identification is unusual. What is interesting is the way that boss–secretary discourse is maintained. The one-to-one relationship is becoming increasingly rare, and most secretaries now work for more than one person. Nevertheless, managers speak of 'my' secretary while secretaries usually differentiate 'the boss' from others they only 'work for'.

The first two discourses set up normative gender positions for bosses and secretaries: only the team discourse does not. I have been particularly interested in what happens when the boss is a woman and/or the secretary is a man. Sexuality operates between members of the same sex, without necessarily being classified as 'homosexual' in contrast to 'heterosexual'. The least common combination was male boss/male secretary. Many male bosses, when asked, felt discomfort at the idea of a male secretary. Sometimes reference was made to the explicitly homosexual connotations this might have; male secretaries, it would seem, cannot be treated 'as secretaries' and would have to be redefined as assistants or colleagues. (Men who do broadly secretarial work are, in fact, rarely called secretaries.) Female boss/female secretary was the most common, and raises interesting questions about how women assert authority. Women cannot take the subject position of 'master' without being labelled dragon or worse; only rarely (Mrs Thatcher perhaps) can they invest themselves with erotic power in this way. They can of course take up the position of 'mother', and often seemed in competition here with their secretaries. Where a secretary can assert herself by mothering a man, she is ambivalent about doing this for a woman. At the same time, if the boss lays claim to 'mother', the secretary may be relegated to 'daughter' and 'servant girl'. Basically, women bosses cannot use coercion and have it defined in terms of pleasure. They have to rely more on persuasion and reciprocity (as many men do too). Women's power over secretaries is often organized around mother–daughter relations, or is about narcissism – encouraging the secretary to admire her and strive to be like her. In the film *Working Girl* this strategy backfired badly and we saw the secretary take over job, clothes, boyfriend, apartment and future.

We can also see sexuality, power and pleasure as they structure women's relationships at work around what I call 'the bitching discourse'. This can be unravelled in terms of who is said to bitch, who is bitched about, and who, if anybody, really does the bitching. 'Bitching' obviously constitutes a source of pleasure at work, as well as operating to control behaviour. It marks out power and status categories: men put women down for bitching, thus trivializing women while their own behaviour goes unscrutinized. Secretaries are supposed to be 'above' bitching which they seek to relegate to the typing pool or more junior staff. But all women are constructed as 'potential' bitches and neither women bosses nor secretaries are immune. On one occasion ten women – three-quarters of the office – declined to be interviewed, apparently because they did not wish to discuss their attitudes and behaviour towards the woman in charge. They resented her because she went by the book whereas her male deputy was more easygoing. He was rewarded with his favourite chocolate cake for morning tea while she was left out in the cold. This woman was rather brittle and obviously hurt by the level of hostility. Even her secretary kept a discreet distance. Women bosses may be either bitched about, defined as 'bitches', or alternatively go in for bitching themselves. Given the ways in which women's relationships are structured by familial discourse, all of these are possibilities.

Finally, what happens where there is a female boss and male secretary? There were not enough examples to comment with any great authority. But one case which I analyse in detail indicates the extent to which gender may modify the kind of power that a female boss is able to exercise over a male secretary. While the boss denied that gender mattered, her secretary was well aware that it did. He very much resented being called a secretary and had repeatedly tried to get his title changed, to no avail. He talked at length about the way in which she exercised power over him. But as he talked it was clear that the flow of power between them fluctuated very much more than is the case with female secretaries. He talked freely and personally about her, in a way that women rarely did. He claimed the power to read her accurately, literally placing her via a detailed description of her clothes and moods. He even said that there had been a mutual sexual attraction and he had decided not to take advantage of her. The implication was that she depends on his gallantry and cooperation. Given his unease at being called a secretary, he has turned the situation round in fantasy, and to some extent in practice, to make it acceptable to his masculine ego. Her counterstrategy was to deny that his masculinity had any relevance to the situation and to try and ensure that it brought him no extra privileges. The example indicates just how much gender does matter.

POLITICS

Because I have moved away from a labour process approach to the analysis of organizations, I have been criticized for 'abandoning politics', and I should like to conclude with some political observations. I do not deny the existence of structured inequalities at work. But I do not believe that power relations can simply be read off these structures. It is through discourse that strategies of power (and resistance) get worked out. I do not want to see secretaries as victims of structures. Rather I want to explore the strategies that are available to them within discourses and the possibilities of shifting discursive terrains. This means that I take seriously the apparently trivial. The issue of 'who makes the coffee', for example, came up regularly and spontaneously, and was obviously a window on to the dynamic of the relationship. It was here that so much of the discourse of reciprocity, for example, was created and confounded. Secretaries wanted to believe that making coffee was a reciprocal task, and continued to claim this even if the boss had made coffee only once in living memory. They also distinguished between serving the coffee and clearing away – the first could be interpreted as hospitality, while the second amounted to servitude. While bosses usually declined to discuss such 'trivia', it was instructive to learn what detailed orders might be given about what they wanted and where it was to be placed. It is in such details that mastery is often imposed. I also note the pleasure with which stories were shared about how to disrupt such patterns. Rather than simply refusing to comply, they might make it too cold or too sweet, or insert salt or cleaning powder. The demands for coffee usually stopped very quickly. I think a broader point can be drawn from this about pleasure and strategies of resistance.

I do not deny the importance of 'equal opportunity' strategies at work. But the solution to men's sexual domination at work cannot simply be to try and ban sexuality from the workplace, even if this were possible. Given the way in which women are regarded as 'the sex', to ban sexuality from work is analogous to banning women – a move that would undoubtedly be welcomed by sections of the new right. It seems more important to mount struggles in the domain of sexuality itself that would contest men's sexual power and expand the possibilities of pleasure and subjectivity available to women.

The emphasis on sexuality at work thus suggests two important points. The first is the importance of making male sexuality visible and accountable. Currently it is largely invisible, which is ironic given men's role as sexual predator. All those bureaucratic structures that masquerade as gender-neutral need to be exposed. Second is the exploration of female sexuality and power. What might it mean for women to be sexual subjects rather than objects – and to derive both pleasure and empowerment from their sexuality? I hesitate to use Mrs Thatcher as a role model, but I find some of the writing about her at the time of her fall from office to be irresistible:

> She is, and remains in her late sixties, a woman of considerable appeal. In part it derives from the aura of power. François Mitterrand once said: 'She has the eyes of Caligula, and the legs of Marilyn Monroe'. Her manner, when relaxed and contented, is sometimes almost brazenly flirtatious. Without ever compromising her honour, she can so revel in her attraction that few men can help but respond.
>
> (*Independent*, 23 November 1990)

At the peak of her power, Mrs Thatcher was frequently put down by her enemies as an 'honorary man'. In decline, her feminine qualities were praised. It would be easy to read this feminization as part of her loss of power: she was reduced to a mere woman. I prefer to think, however, that if anything positive came out of the Thatcher period it was that it became more possible to acknowledge strong women as women rather than as honorary men. While there is little evidence of this in the House of Commons itself, and certainly Mrs Thatcher made no effort to ensure that there were women following her, it can be argued that changes have taken place in the wider community. Female authority is no longer inevitably regarded as a contradiction in terms; and female sexuality may be assertive rather than passive and reactive. Hopefully women will increasingly have an opportunity to define their own pleasure and not restrict it to pleasing men on terms defined by men. Were these changes to flow through to the workplace, the boss–secretary relation would surely be replaced by the team mode and office affairs would be fundamentally changed.

REFERENCES

Braverman, H. (1974) *Labour and Monopoly Capital*, New York: Monthly Review Press.
Foucault, M. (1980) *The History of Sexuality*, Vol. 1, New York: Vintage.
Game, A. and Pringle, R. (1984) *Gender at Work*, London: Pluto.
Hollway, W. (1984) 'Gender difference and the production of subjectivity', in J. Henriques, W. Hollway, C. Urwin, C. Venn and V. Walkerdine, (eds) *Changing the Subject*, London: Methuen.
Marcuse, H. (1968) *One Dimensional Man*, London: Sphere Books.
Pringle, R. (1989) *Secretaries Talk: Sexuality, Power and Work*, London: Verso.

7 The gendered terrains of paternalism

Deborah Kerfoot and David Knights

This chapter draws on empirical data from an in-depth case study of a UK mutual life insurance company given the pseudonym Pensco.[1] The company was undergoing a period of transformation: in their own terms, they were evolving out of a system of 'paternalistic' managerial control towards a more 'professional' and commercial mode of management. This was happening within the context of a changing environment for personal financial services. We are, however, less concerned with these changes in the industry *per se* than with the employment effects flowing from them and their relevance for an understanding of gender relations at work. Financial services are merely a site for empirical research rather than the intrinsic object of investigation. Through an analysis of some aspects of current employment practice within one organization, our purpose is to demonstrate how a gendered division of labour may come to be reproduced as an accidental outcome of a range of often unrelated processes, both formal and informal.

In the context of our case study company, these processes arose from concerns to satisfy recruitment objectives and strategic customer service goals that, while having little direct relationship to each other, coincided at certain points in their articulation. Yet as was so clearly the effect in Pensco, these practices served to reinforce gender difference at work, and the sexual division of labour. For part of the argument is that, despite having a formal equal opportunity policy designed to prohibit sex discrimination, in seeking to resolve certain recruitment problems in a tight labour market Pensco inadvertently falls upon practices that are discriminatory.

Our focus is upon the employment of what were described in the company as 'mature' women. Initially recruited to fill clerical positions in a scarce labour market, these women's tacit and formally unacknowledged skills were found to be 'valuable' in newly developed working groups. Both their recruitment and the use of their skills was an unintended consequence of localized recruitment difficulties. However, their employment soon began to be recognized, at least by certain personnel managers, as especially compatible with the growing demands for an improved customer service and with the corporate strategy in which those demands were embedded. In practical terms, the translation of these demands was made through 'team working' where, by virtue of their domestic roles, experience, social skills and previous work histories, the women came to assume an informal leadership/disciplinary function.

At first, this recruitment policy appears to be consistent with equal opportunity in providing employment opportunities for women returnees at later points in their life cycle. However, when the informal skills of these older women are consistently exploited, yet unrewarded, to meet the team working demands of the corporate strategy, the company's 'mature entrant scheme' can be seen to follow in the footsteps of the sex discriminatory paternalism to which this management has traditionally subscribed. Personnel managers' belief in the ideal-type team, together with their assumption of the value of what were held to be the social or interpersonal skills of older women, led to their attempts to reconstruct work groups in line with a 'family' metaphor. The point here is not that all older women are the possessors of social skills; indeed some mature entrants were moved elsewhere in the company, or left altogether of their own volition as a result of being dissatisfied with or unsuited to the work. It was personnel managers' belief in social skills as the essential property of the 'mature lady' that led them to their informal strategy of redesigning teams.

Here we find parallels between the employment of 'mature' women as informal leaders in clerical work teams in Pensco, and Davies and Rosser's (1986) analysis of women returnees to the health profession. Drawing on their concept of 'gendered jobs', we thereby illustrate how the mature entrant scheme in the company had the effect of reinforcing and reproducing gendered divisions of labour. Davies and Rosser's term refers to those jobs that function largely by virtue of the extra-curricula gender experience of their incumbents that is not formally acknowledged or rewarded. In our study, they are jobs filled by older women whose experience of domestic labour and/or child rearing is especially useful in relation to certain informal and tacit skills required for team working. Despite attempts to 'modernize' and 'professionalize' management in ways that ought, in a company with a declared equal opportunity policy, to have resulted in an erosion of traditional gender divisions, it transpired that the mature entrant scheme was a major contributor to their maintenance.

The principal objective of this chapter is to analyse this phenomenon by way of what we term the 'gendered terrains of paternalism'. This refers to an analysis of how the paternalistic legacy of the company leaves unresolved the gender divisions historically embedded in this form of management. The phrase 'gendered terrains of paternalism' is used meta-phorically to depict the sense in which paternal, or what might be seen as 'protective' forms of management, occupy a space or territory that takes for granted and thereby reproduces traditional gender categories and distinc-tions. More than this, it maps out a terrain in which women, like the young, are treated as fragile and vulnerable 'creatures' in need of the protective and fatherly care of paternal managers. Here, our argument is that, partly as a consequence of the gendered terrains of paternalism upon which these practices are superimposed, the skills of mature women are brought into the service of management, but remain both unrecognized and unacknowl-edged and thereby unrewarded. For the 'realization' or rather the un-questioned assumption, that older women possess social skills which fit conveniently with the demands of team building in the company, makes their recruitment, but not their career progress, more likely.

Here we note the discontinuity between particular 'modern' managerial ideals such as human resource management[2] and equal opportunity, and those management and work practices that evolve in the day-to-day milieux of everyday workplace relations. This is partly to illustrate a weakness in the managerial literatures which, we would suggest, not only assumes too close a continuity between intention and effect and attributes too much intentionality to practitioners, but also fails to capture the ways in which 'modern' management practices are often a coincidental outcome of solving more immediate problems (e.g. recruitment difficulties). As a result, the practice of management may often be inconsistent with, or in direct contradiction to, some officially designated corporate policy built upon abstract ideals handed down from 'above'.

The chapter is structured as follows. The first section provides a brief report on the contextual and methodological background to the case study. The second section presents the empirical data on one aspect of personnel practice – the conditions and consequences of employing mature entrant women, and its relationship to team working in the company. In the third section we explore how older women came to assume an informal leadership/disciplinary func-tion within newly reorganized family team work groups. In conclusion we summarize our findings on the gender implications of the scheme in relation to paternalistic management. For the moment, some introduction to the case study and a note on our research methods is appropriate.

THE CASE STUDY IN CONTEXT

Pensco is a medium-sized insurance company which has operated very successfully in a niche market within financial services over several decades. At the time of the research, the geographical region in which the company was located enjoyed almost full employment. School leavers drawn from the surrounding area had satisfied much of the company's need for new recruits to the existing clerical workforce of over four thousand people. Yet a variety of factors coincided to disrupt what, for the Personnel Officer, had been a relatively straightforward task of finding an appropriate number of 'bodies' at each intake. These factors included accelerating competition in both product and labour markets; an increased concern for labour productivity and efficiency in the company linked to accelerating salary costs and high staff turnover; recent reorganization and restructuring of the company; and, as alluded to earlier, a concern at the top of the new management structure that the company should be managed more professionally. Moreover, expansion of the clerical function within the company, together with higher salaries in other areas of the region, had combined to produce a situation whereby the company could not fill a substantial proportion of available vacancies from its usual school-leaver sources.

Traditionally the company had been managed in a highly paternalistic fashion[3] without major crises, largely because of an expanding market for its products. The new Chief Executive, however, was determined to modernize the company by promoting a system of what he regarded as 'professional management'. Although this lacked concrete definition, it could be discerned as an ideal which entailed the conduct of management affairs through a systematic recording and quantifying of all objectives and their measurement against specific achievements. Indeed, before this professionalization began, the Chief Executive had implemented a number of replacements in the senior ranks, in line with his desire for the company to pursue a more commercially orientated and dynamic approach to management. His determination was reinforced by the development of an increasingly competitive marketplace that had been stimulated by government deregulation, and new companies entering the product market in which the company specialized.

The rationale behind his decision to create a central strategic role for Personnel was one of ensuring that the organization should develop skills in its staff which would enable them to implement other elements of the corporate plan. Yet the plan to give Personnel a central strategic role failed as a result of disruptions caused by conflicting political objectives. In an attempt to force one of his senior managers to a point of resignation, the Chief Executive moved him to Personnel where he was destined to fail, but also in the process, he undermined the strategic plans of the division (see Kerfoot and Knights 1992a for more detail).

The Chief Executive's notion of professional management included a commitment to strategic personnel planning of the human resource, and a two-year programme on 'team building'. The latter was seen as facilitating greater efficiency of working practices and productivity, and improving customer service quality standards (Kerfoot and Knights 1992b). The team approach was adopted partly because it was seen as a more 'professional' method of organizing routine clerical production but also as a means of both increasing productivity and retaining an increasingly scarce labour force. This was seen as achievable by means of inducing 'ownership' of the product, promoting social ties within teams, and generating camaraderie among members of each team by encouraging competition between teams. Clerical production had been organized in the company around what was colloquially described as work groups, in that people were gathered in one area of an office around a specific type of task or stage in administrative processing. Work groups were composed of small numbers of staff organized hierarchically and by task with each person carrying out one stage in, for example, processing an insurance claim. Work was passed on to other group members in turn until that group's input was complete, including checking for errors. The new team system meant that instead of clerks each having a separate task to perform the end result of which was partially hidden from them, teams of usually six to ten members would work together in processing a particular set of documents (e.g. client proposals or claims relating to life or pensions policies) from start to finish.

Our study adopted a variety of methods of research over a period of three years: semi-structured in-depth interviews with managers and staff, tape-recorded management meetings, documentary investigation of records and participant observation. For the focus on clerical work in the research, seven visits of two to four days' duration over a four-month period were made in which group and individual interviews were conducted and frequent participant observation of team working took place. In addition a small number of staff were interviewed informally outside working hours. A total of 135 Pensco managers and staff took part in the research during this period; twenty-four were older females and sixteen of the total were employed on management grades up to the level of Assistant General Manager. As part of a wider project in the company, all senior management were interviewed, including the Chief Executive, many on several occasions. Access was also given to management meetings, company training exercises and more generally to the office floor.

As indicated earlier, 'team building' and a revision of traditional working programmes in line with this were a component of senior management's strategy of seeking competitive advantage. Yet in terms of any improvement in customer service, this succeeded in part as a result of certain contingent and accidental lower-level decisions taken to resolve particular clerical employment and recruitment difficulties, a product of which was the 'mature entrant scheme'. It is to this that we now turn.

MATURE ENTRANT WOMEN AND TEAM WORKING

In response to the labour shortages described above, middle management in the Personnel Division devised a stopgap scheme to recruit female 'returners' locally. These were older female employees aged from their late 20s up to retirement, although with an average age of approximately 35–45 years. Each had current or past experience of significant domestic and/or childcare responsibilities, together with some history of clerical or office work. Most had been married for several years and were returning to work after a period of child-rearing. Throughout the duration of the research project, no exact figures were available anywhere in the company as to the number of mature entrants, although an estimate within the Personnel Division suggested that a minimum of over seventy people had been recruited onto the scheme. Due to the immediacy of the scheme's implementation, no job description or job specification existed or was to be devised: job content was at the discretion of immediate line management with a minimal degree of intervention by the Personnel Division.

Some mature entrants worked part-time, either permanently or during school term time only, but the majority were full-time, permanent staff. Due to an immensely complex salary system, no two staff members were paid at exactly the same point on the same scale (see also Edwards 1979: 133–4). Pay scales overlapped and annual individual merit payments which were calculated on a percentage basis and added to basic pay, created additional difficulties in determining pay levels, not least in the Personnel Division for those attempting to determine the scheme's cost. The only point of agreement to be found concerning salaries was that recruits drawn in under the mature entrant scheme were on a separate pay banding, with a lower ceiling, distinct from other clerical staffs.

It was not just their comparative 'cheapness' and availability that attracted the company to these staff. Older women were also seen as suitable candidates for team working since, after an initial recruitment exercise, they came to be regarded by personnel management at Pensco as in possession of a variety of 'personality factors' and 'social skills' deemed central to this way of organizing work. Acquired through a period of family and domestic responsibility, 'mature' women were seen as able to employ a range of fully developed behavioural skills which facilitated their acting as informal team leaders, with an informal responsibility for motivating and disciplining younger members and dealing with a diverse range of customers. Defined by the company as self-discipline, stability and co-operativeness, these behavioural skills minimized the need for extensive and costly formal training in what was known as 'training for team work', within an under-resourced training department.

The recruitment drive was thus especially advantageous to the company's interest in improving working practices under the new team structure and quality of service to the customer. It transpired that, with few exceptions, the previous work experience and general organizational and tacit skills of these supply workers 'fitted' them, both for the new team working structure of clerical processing, and for dealing with customers. Indeed, these duties eventually became informal requirements of the post, and what had been a temporary *ad hoc* solution to local employment difficulties was turned into a formal recruitment policy by the Personnel Division. There was some increase in productivity and employment stability: for example, in the company's largest division, turnover rates fell from a high of almost 50 per cent a year to around 13 per cent, while the increase in productivity measured by time targets for processing each document increased from around 70 per cent to a consistent target of 95 per cent. Moreover, the success of this initiative, as measured by performance targets, error rates and processing speeds, was then appropriated by senior management in the company to confirm the 'success' of the overall team building programme, and the efficacy of team working.

Although production had for some time been ordered pragmatically around task type and employees had been grouped accordingly, the traditional team structure took on a new emphasis with the concern to improve customer service as part of the company's pursuit of a strategic competitive advantage. In order to elaborate on the developing role of mature entrants within teams, it is necessary to expand on some of the recent changes in the organization of clerical working practices and to draw attention to the new 'family-like' layout of teams.

Personnel managers in the company described the most efficient or 'ideal type' work group as composed of a mixture of male and female employees of varied ages. In practice, and given the company's reliance on school leavers, this translated to an age range of 16–18 years on average but always with one mature entrant or occasionally two, depending on the size of the team. In comparison with other clerical workers, older women were often deployed in low level clerical work or more usually in a support function such as correspondence clerk or messenger. Few mature entrants were expected to attain promotion or otherwise move up the pay scale, aside from annual pay increases. At the time of the research, two out of approximately seventy mature entrants had been advanced to team leader grade by means of removing them from the scheme altogether, and re-employing them on the main clerical pay grades. These individuals were seen by management as exceptional cases, whose circumstances related to their having held previous positions of some seniority in the company's clerical hierarchy, prior to maternity leave.

Work groups were referred to as 'family-like' in the sense that they had small numbers of young people and one or two older adults. Mature entrants were viewed as acting out the 'maternal role' and of nurturing, counselling and facilitating their work group. For example, before appointment they found themselves 'interviewed by someone who says to them "I really like having mature entrants, you can look after all these youngsters I recruit in the summer"' (Cindy: Personnel Assistant).

For management, the team building programme and team working practices that flowed from it involved discipline and morale. Older women were regarded as able both to spread the corporate message of loyalty and commitment and to bind the localized work group in a dual integration function: 'their attitude is so positive . . . they are fantastic motivators, natural leaders' (Peggy: Personnel Manager).

Older females were identified as already fully conversant with social or interpersonal skills required for team working in that they were seen to draw on resources of social capital gained outside the workplace in the family. This obviated the need for expensive and time consuming 'training for team work'. This was especially valuable given the discontinuity between management's intention to introduce social skills training as part of a human resource management programme, and the reality of events within the 'crisis-mode' operation of an overstretched training section as indicated earlier. Further, 'mature ladies' were noted to be 'a tremendously stabilizing influence' on the rest of the workforce in that they had significantly lower turnover rates, higher productivity with fewer errors, and were 'so committed . . . [since they were] so grateful to be given a job'. Management regarded this configuration of factors as increasing the productive efficiency, discipline and motivation of team organized employees, typically expressed by one manager in the following way: 'They've got this tremendous burden of responsibility that they've had with children, and it just comes into their working life – it's brilliant!' (Cindy: Personnel Assistant).

By restructuring teams and the combinations of people within teams, management in the Personnel Division believed it possible to mimic authority and trust-based social links as in the non-work domestic setting. Given that clerical work in the company was organized around groups of people working together, efforts to construct the 'family team' could be seen as an attempt to manipulate the social relations of clerical production, where older women were key figures. The desired result was a shift from teams as merely many pairs of hands to teams as collections of personalities mutually functional to production. Reordering work groups around the family team model was crucially dependent on the development of social ties between types of employees selected and deployed in deliberate combinations: 'We've got to get the mix right, get the balance right . . . groups have to "gel"' (Peggy: Personnel Manager).

In short, by reconstructing teams to resemble idealized family-like relations, the employment of older women was seen by management to be conducive to improving efficiency and service standards. The concept of the family is used in its metaphorical sense rather than in any literal one. Tasks are accomplished through a set of informal practices in which are embedded the tacit skills of the older women. In this sense the women exercise power from the 'base' of the hierarchy, reproducing a 'maternal role' without necessarily understanding themselves to be so doing, or it being obvious to others.

Moreover, such 'improved' working arrangements were an important part of the development of a 'corporate identity' which was being promoted by senior management. Coincidentally and by default, the practice of locating mature entrants in teams came to support and reinforce the notion of human resources as 'strategically manageable'. Drawing on an image of matriarchal leadership, 'mothering' and nurturing drawn from domestic life, or, as Cindy put it, utilizing what she saw to be their 'mother-henning' characteristics, these 'mature' women were useful in a productive sense to the organization. In this instance, the unintended consequences of recruiting older women produced effects which were coterminous with the desired aims of the 'total corporate identity' philosophy and with team working practices. The 'social skills' and 'personalities' of mature entrant women both regulated and lubricated team-centred production.

Yet as we have stated, there were certain conditions which, although not in themselves sufficient to bring about the mature entrant scheme as an employment practice, were necessary for it to be realized initially. We have directly discussed some of these conditions above, including the new management regime, local labour scarcity, and intensified competition in the financial services market. The coincidence of these conditions, combined with the growing discourse on human resource management as the strategic management of employees, provided an impetus for the development of team building and team working. Applying the concept of a 'gendered job' (Davies and Rosser 1986), the following section begins to explore 'the gendered terrains of paternalism' through which the practice of team working was acted out and took form in Pensco.

THE GENDERED TERRAINS OF PATERNALISM: TEAM WORKING AND GENDERED JOBS

A fundamental requirement and common denominator of team working and the mature entrant scheme is a range of tacit social skills. In the case study company, these were seen as 'logically' best found in 'mature ladies'. Given that mature entrants are older as opposed to younger women, what becomes necessary is a consideration of why the labour of females at particular life cycle points is of special value. This entails breaking down that which is encapsulated by the word 'mature' and directly linking this to tasks performed. Davies and Rosser's concept of a gendered job illuminates this, and the underlying dynamism of gender differentiation in how 'women's jobs' come to be created. This emerges from the notion that gender is implicitly 'written in' to the design of a job before that job is filled. If the gendered job theory is applied to Pensco, then only older women can fill mature entrant clerical posts, since job design and content predetermine who will occupy that post. But centrally, Davies and Rosser's argument is that job design and content *per se* are dependent on the informal, unacknowledged qualities of women at a particular life cycle stage. Pensco has capitalized on the social skills of older female staff and 'developed' this to become concretized in the mature entrant scheme, aided and accelerated by the emphasis on interpersonal skills generated by team building and team working within the discourse of strategic human resource management.

At the core of a gendered job lies the necessary possession of a range of skills essential to the performance of the task. The jobs of older women in Pensco are so constructed as to capitalize on the assumed qualities and abilities of the job holder, merely by dint of her description as mature female. The euphemism 'mature' thus describes a range of formal and informal skills as prerequisites for mature entrant work. These skills go largely unrecognized and unspoken but are at the same time essential to the work group and team structure, and to the general smooth running of clerical production in 'the social office' (Braverman 1974; Downing 1980).

The concept of 'gendered jobs' is useful in indicating how certain skills, while of importance, remain tacit and unrewarded when practised by, for example, older women. It contributes to an understanding of skill as gendered (Sturdy *et al.* 1992). Mature entrant jobs come to prescribe a range of skills found only in the labour of mature women: a fusion occurs that at once predetermines who will fill the post, and simultaneously confirms and recreates the specific 'abilities' of the holder. In so doing, this acts to deny the social worth and thereby lower the financial reward of mature entrants themselves:

> It is not that women do the job and that it gets done in 'a woman's way', it is not even simply that the qualities of the job and the capabilities of the job holder have become fused. It is rather that the fusion has occurred and that the fusion itself denigrates and dismisses women's skills.
>
> (Davies and Rosser, 1986: 110)

Mature entrant women's skills are twofold. First, those technical skills either taught on the job through (albeit limited) training, or acquired in previous clerical or office environments. These skills may be highly task-specific relating to the operation of a piece of equipment, for example, a visual display unit, or to the ability to repeat information over the telephone in answering customer enquiries. Second, mature entrants are expected to possess a range of non-technical (Manwaring and Wood 1985) or supplementary skills (Kusterer 1978) seen as fundamentally dependent on the woman's later life cycle stage, and acquired by virtue of the roles she has played in her life as a woman (Davies and Rosser 1986: 103). Older women are selected who can draw on a variety of abilities and dexterities roughly lumped under the term 'mature'. These are capitalized on by Pensco, yet described by management in the company under the loosely generalized, informal and ambiguous heading of 'getting on with people'. Moreover, the tacit skills of mature entrants are not in practice distinctly separable from technical skills, since the performance of the latter hinges to a greater or lesser extent on the possession of the former. Thus, for example, answering telephone queries draws on both technical and tacit social skills simultaneously.

Within the paternalistic management culture which has traditionally characterized Pensco, women – as predominantly clerical staff – have been 'protected' from responsibility for managing work as opposed to merely executing tasks. Regardless of attempts to introduce professionalism through human resource management and the extent to which older women assume informal leadership responsibilities, this 'gendered terrain of paternalism' impedes the formal acknowledgement of these women's contribution to the management of human resources. At the point when the unspecified skills of older women become a requirement for clerical posts and their recruitment under the scheme accelerates, the association between those skills, the job, and the women themselves becomes further reinforced in self-generating momentum. Moreover, this process sustains a definition of those skills as the generalized all-round attributes of all older women as a category of labour. The following paragraphs explore further our concept of the gendered terrains of paternalism through which the mature entrant scheme is articulated in ways that reproduce gendered social divisions and jobs.

In our view, paternalistic management represents a way of controlling employees through the use of family imagery, thus providing space for the manager to act as 'caring and protective' head of the industrial or commercial 'household'. While having a long history in industrial philanthropism, paternalism remains a legacy of management in a great many organizations and especially those mutual institutions (e.g. savings banks, friendly societies, insurance companies) which grew out of an ideology of prudence, thrift and self-help designed to avoid the stigma of falling on 'hard times' or becoming dependent on public welfare in the nineteenth century. Since such organizations were unconstrained by the voting rights of shareholders, this elite group felt the need to develop some system of internal self-regulation and control. Consequently, membership of this elite tended to be based upon certain 'gentlemanly characteristics' (sic) derived from notions of social class acceptability supposedly indicative of high standards of personal conduct. The impact of this 'ethic of guardianship' with respect to the financial well-being of customers was one of projecting highly specific and narrowly defined duties upon employees, on the grounds that staff of a lower status and 'respectability' could not be treated with the levels of social responsibility presumed to reside in high office.

As a mutual life company, Pensco has its history in, and represents a modern counterpart of, these institutions of financial self-discipline. Despite every effort of the new Chief Executive to 'rid' the company of the 'old ways', the paternalistic legacy remains and, although without intention, is given a new lease of life in the form of the mature entrant scheme. Typically, paternalism facilitates a reduction of the tension surrounding the management of subordinates by simulating patriarchal, family-like relations where power is exercised for the 'good' of the recipient. Far from being dispelled by management, the view of mature entrants as lacking occupational skills and therefore 'lucky' to have a job, a view the women themselves largely shared, was fodder for the company's paternalistic belief in doing the women a 'good turn' by employing them.

But the pretence of exercising power only for the benefit of the employee, in the guise of helping and protecting those who are ostensibly less fortunate, means that paternalistic forms of management also have the effect of relieving tension in management–subordinate relations. We believe this tension derives from the conflict or incompatibility in contemporary employment relations between the discourse of 'rights' of individual autonomy and 'choice', and the 'reality' of hierarchical control in organizations where employees are expected to subordinate their individuality to the authoritative demands of their managers. There is the obvious fact that the reduction of tension renders employees more compliant and predictable and therefore makes the lives of those exercising the power more comfortable. However, equally important is the sense in which adopting a paternal role helps to legitimize managerial prerogative both in the eyes of those who are 'protected' from the harsh reality of decision making, and the decision makers themselves.

Paternalism is a mode of management that is to a degree 'comfortable' for both sides and this may account for its longevity and resilience to erosion from the more commercially aggressive systems that our case study company, amongst many, was seeking to instigate. For management, it provides an illusion that their practices are an act of enlightened self-interest which eradicates the need to feel guilty about denying or curtailing employees' 'rights' to independence and self-autonomy. For subordinates, the illusion is that compliance to managerial command is no more than an act of self-interested realism. The company's paternalistic management culture is of course a contradiction, not only in relation to the ideals of human resource management, but also with respect to the long-term concerns to resolve labour market difficulties by recruiting and retaining women 'returners'. This legacy of paternalism in Pensco left management oblivious to the sense in which they colluded in a denial of the need to recognize formally, rather than merely acknowledge and exploit informally, the skills that these women were thought to possess.

The collusion was not difficult, given that many of these women had a lifetime experience of perceiving domestic labour as subordinate and inferior in status to paid work outside the home, and of accepting a definition of 'pin-money jobs'. In these circumstances, it is not surprising that many felt themselves 'privileged to be in work', and self-deprecating about, or more usually unaware of, their own socially acquired abilities to manage activities and people: 'They come to me with all the little squabbles in our group, about targets – oh, and boys, and things – you know ... Jenny's a nice girl [Team Leader] but, well, they come to me' (Shirley: mature entrant).

Paternalism in Pensco simply reinforced the authoritative undermining of their own self-worth and status partly because, not unlike the father in the family, management is seen as the fount of all wisdom. Since it is believed to exercise managerial power always within the constraint of protecting and improving the lives of its employees, the majority of mature entrants did not suspect any sense of being 'used' or denied the full rewards for their work.

SUMMARY AND CONCLUSION

This chapter has given an account of one company's attempts to create a team identity over the whole organization and at the level of individual work groups. A number of conditions coincided around which the discourse of strategic human resource management began to take hold. Simultaneously, a new and viable category of clerical workers (i.e. mature entrant women) emerged which in effect acted to reinforce the 'success' of the Chief Executive's strategy, evidenced in the minds of senior management by higher productivity and lower turnover. Although not directly planned with such purposes in mind, this mode of recruitment had the effect of assisting and elaborating team working, and ultimately the 'success' of managerial initiatives surrounding 'team building' throughout the company.

We have argued that both the emphasis on social skills, and the new family-like structure of teams, had implications for the recruitment and deployment of older females, viewed as conversant in social or behavioural skills. Applying the stereotypical image of older women as essentially nurturing and motherly, these workers came to be seen by personnel management in the company as suitable candidates for team working, and as performing informal yet unpaid leadership roles within teams in what was constructed by management as a 'parental' function. We have argued that this in turn sustained what we have described as the 'gendered terrains of paternalism' on which the relations between employer and employee are acted out in the company. The consequence of what was an *ad hoc* and unplanned low-level human resource strategy was therefore to reinforce and reproduce gender inequality at work.

It has been argued that both the emphasis on social skills, and the new family-like structure of teams, have implications for the recruitment and deployment of older females viewed as 'experienced' in the use of such skills. In effect, their skills are exploited in such a way as to sustain the gendered terrains of paternalism upon which the relations between management and staff have traditionally been conducted, and through which gender divisions in work are continually created and recreated. For as we have suggested, a central feature of a paternalistic management culture is the self-fulfilling assumption that women are less than 'rational'. Accordingly, they must be 'protected' from the realities of managerial decision making in a 'harsh' commercial world. Although their ability to sustain a team-like solidarity within the work group is recognized informally, this is not a 'rational' skill which the formal hierarchy acknowledges in terms of career progression. In short, the patriarchal household where men provide financial 'protection' and women emotional 'stability' for the family spills over into the work situation wherever a paternalistic culture prevails.

We have observed how groups of workers organized into teams and informally supervised by older women gave the appearance of becoming more self-regulating in terms of discipline and motivation. But since the older women were not formally recognized in the hierarchy, this 'matriarchal power' operated as a less visible, and both socially and financially as a more economical form of supervision within the work group. This coincided with the company's team building programme of creating an organizational identity for the workforce; without a formal and explicit attempt to do so, the effect was to integrate business strategy not as a corporate policy but at the level of everyday workplace practices. In the eyes of senior management, work teams became self-disciplined, flexible and committed to the productive goals of increased output, quality and customer service – all important features of Pensco's corporate strategy. Thus the mature entrant scheme in Pensco was found to have unintended consequences whose effects were consistent with, and facilitative of, team working and team building. Yet only an in-depth analysis would be able to reveal the gendered terrains of paternalism in which gender inequality is its condition and consequence.

We have argued that women in the organization were drawn into the scheme not on the basis of a gender-neutral disembodied service capacity such as the ability to process paperwork or maintain mathematical accuracy, but on the basis of their identity as women at a particular life cycle stage. In Pensco, the hiring of older women as clerical workers takes a gendered character such that what are in effect 'new jobs' become defined around the women concerned, linked to the specific effects of changes in the industry, the way in which those changes take hold in the organization, and the continual redefinition of the task content of clerical work. This is not to suggest that these are 'new jobs' in the sense of more or 'better' jobs, but rather that existing jobs are defined and redefined in new ways contingent upon a fluid and amorphous concept of what clerical work is at any one time and who does it. What determines the form and content of posts under the mature entrant scheme is not a pre-existing or emerging requirement for a specific technical function or component of clerical operations, but a stereotypical and common-sense notion of who 'is good at' different types of work and why. What is illustrated by the case study here is the process by which the content of a job comes to define the type of person doing it and, simultaneously, how the type of person doing it becomes confirmation of that job, the post itself, and the rationale for sex segregation. In short, the mature entrant scheme is articulated and finds concrete expression through a highly gendered framework which acts to reinforce and reproduce gender differentiation in the workplace and to sustain clerical work as 'women's work'.

NOTES

1 We would like to thank our sponsors the TSB-funded FSRC at UMIST and the ESRC as well as the anonymous company and staff which allowed us access into their lives to conduct this research. Thanks also to Mike Roper and Sue Wright for helpful editorial comments, and to Hugh Willmott at UMIST who was involved in the ESRC part of this research that provides some of the background material. An earlier draft of this chapter was presented at the GAPP Conference, Swansea University, 4–6 January 1991; participants' comments are gratefully acknowledged.

2   Human resource management (HRM) is designed to transform personnel management into a more 'professional' and strategic set of practices, attempting to restructure the personnel function so as to give it a central role. In doing so, HRM seeks to ensure that staff/employees discharge their responsibilities in such a way as to integrate with the overall strategic objectives of the company.

3   Paternalistic management is a legacy from nineteenth century Quaker and religious movements having a tradition of moral responsibility for what are seen as the weaker members of society. In industry, it has involved managers feeling a moral responsibility to 'look after' their workforces much like a father may care for his children. In this sense, it protects them from having to make decisions, thereby reinforcing precisely the weakness and vulnerability that it assumes workers to exhibit.

REFERENCES

Braverman, H. (1974) *Labor and Monopoly Capital: The Degradation of Work in the Twentieth Century*, New York: Monthly Review Press.

Davies, C. and Rosser, J. (1986) 'Gendered jobs in the health service: a problem for labour process analysis', in D. Knights and H. Willmott (eds) *Gender and The Labour Process*, Hampshire: Gower.

Downing, H. (1980) 'Word processing and the oppression of women', in T. Forester (ed.) *The Microelectronics Revolution*, Oxford: Blackwell.

Edwards, R. (1979) *Contested Terrain: The Transformation of the Workplace in the Twentieth Century*, New York: Basic Books.

Kerfoot, D. and Knights, D. (1992a) 'Planning for personnel?: Human Resource Management reconsidered', *Journal of Management Studies* 29 (4): 629–43.

—— (1992b) '"Managerial evangelism": quality management in financial services', paper given at the European Institute for Advanced Studies in Management (EIASM) Conference, Workshop on Quality Management in Services, Maastricht, The Netherlands, 21–22 May.

Kusterer, K. (1978) *Know-how on the Job*, Boulder, California: West View Press.

Manwaring, A. and Wood, S. (1985) 'The ghost in the labour process', in D. Knights, H. Willmott and D. Collinson (eds) *Job Redesign: Critical Perspectives on the Labour Process*, Aldershot: Gower.

Sturdy, A., Knights, D. and Willmott, H. (eds) (1992) *Skill and Consent: Contemporary Studies in the Labour Process*, London: Routledge.

8 Culture, gender and organizational change in British welfare benefits services

Sandra Cullen

This chapter is about cultural variation not between societies, but between office workers in three different aspects of the welfare benefits system in the UK. It also examines how these variations influence the construction of gender relations within the workplace. These cultural differences may not be immediately obvious to the casual observer who passes between the different offices, but the staff involved were acutely aware of them and actively engaged with the public in such a way as to demonstrate these differences, both to themselves and to their colleagues. The processes which created this variation also produced different gender relations, but although these gender relations were constructed in very different ways in different contexts with very different types of femininity appearing, the net effect was always to subordinate the women's position within the workplace.

I should add that the organizations discussed here had comprehensive Equal Opportunities programmes, which included flexible working hours, adequate maternity leave provisions, opportunities for part-time working and job-sharing, as well as a policy of actively encouraging managerial staff to sustain a heightened awareness of the indirect discriminatory effects of assuming male or female work patterns such as timing office meetings when part-time workers could attend. This heightened awareness was reinforced in the Employment Service by the task of monitoring local employers for unlawful discrimination.

There is no doubt that women were making progress within the organization. Staffing figures for the Employment Service as a whole show that in the year up to April 1992 the number of women in most junior and middle management grades either grew faster than that for men or fell more slowly. But despite this gradual trend the overall pattern remained one of women being over-represented in the lower grades and under-represented in the higher grades. Women were entirely absent from the most senior grades, comprised approximately 25 per cent of the middle ranking grades, and approximately 75 per cent of the most junior grades.[1]

My intention here is not to belittle the substantial advances women have made in the recent past, but to look more deeply at the cultural underpinnings which produce such strong resistance to change. Given the high priority that Equal Opportunities policy has had in these organizations the fact that women are making some progress is not surprising; it is the slowness of this progress that requires explanation. In this chapter I examine the cultural underpinnings found within the organizations and their wider environment which cause women to be disadvantaged at work. It is only by bringing culturally embedded issues to light that Equal Opportunities policies can be developed further.

Changes in structure and policy are likely to have cultural consequences, especially when they involve the amalgamation of offices which have developed separate workplace cultures. These in turn have repercussions on the way the public is perceived and dealt with, and ultimately on the way the public reacts to staff. In short, organizational change may affect the way policy is implemented in unanticipated ways unless the culture of the services in local offices is considered.

THE ORGANIZATIONAL SETTING

The following ethnographic account is based upon observations in 1989–1990 within offices which had responsibility for local implementation of financial welfare policy in Britain.[2] Two central government departments were primarily involved in the administration of the welfare benefits system, the Department of Social Security and the Employment Service.[3] The latter was a component of the Department of Employment Group, which included both Unemployment Benefit Offices and Job Centres.

The Department of Social Security was responsible for payment of two main types of benefit, one contributory and the other means-tested. Contributory National Insurance benefits were paid to clients on the basis of the number of payments made into the National Insurance fund during a specified qualifying period. However, National Insurance benefit rates had been declining in value and the qualifying conditions had become increasingly difficult to meet. As a result most clients relied on means-tested benefits which had become a major means of alleviating poverty in Britain. This shift has been heavily criticized because means-tested benefits are expensive to administer, they are daunting in their complexity for claimants, and they are socially divisive and stigmatizing so that take-up is low (Townsend 1976; Deacon and Bradshaw 1983).

The Department of Social Security had ultimate responsibility for payment of benefits, but the Unemployment Benefit Offices acted as agents for the payment of both contributory and means tested benefits to unemployed people. Their main task was to identify clients who were 'genuinely' unemployed; that is, those who met the legal criteria for qualification to benefit entitlement as unemployed people. Unemployed people were treated with more circumspection within the benefits system than other categories of clients such as sick people, retired people and lone parents. This was because unemployed people could more easily have made bogus claims. It was more difficult for them to provide objective evidence of involuntary unemployment, and opportunities for working within the 'black economy' were not necessarily diminished by economic recession, although there was some dispute over the extent to which unemployed people were able to participate in the informal economy (Pahl and Wallace 1985).

Both the Unemployment Benefit Offices and the Department of Social Security offices required their staff to be vigilant in detecting potential offenders. Thus the work of both involved a substantial element of policing. Unlike other clients, unemployed people were required to visit the Unemployment Benefit Office regularly to 'sign on', usually every two weeks, at a prescribed time which was during normal working hours. This procedure was in part a check on clients who would have found it difficult to attend if they were employed. Staff were expected to look for evidence of work such as clients with grease-covered hands, paint-splattered overalls, etc. In addition to this welfare role the Employment Service was also concerned with labour market issues. They also provided advice on employment legislation and local job opportunities, advertised vacancies for employers free of charge and actively 'sold' government training schemes, such as employment training.[4] Many of these functions were usually performed within Job Centres.

THE AREA

The study took place in two cities and one town in one county of England. One city was characterized by a buoyant 'high-tech' and service sector and a low-paid sector with few middle-range jobs. The other city, thirty-five miles away, had a manufacturing engineering base which was in decline but had successfully attracted many new employers from the service sector, off-setting the worst effects of the decline. The town was a small market town in the centre of an agricultural area. One of the cities had several ethnic minority groups including Italians, Gujuratis and Ugandan Asians, mostly Muslims. Neither city had a serious unemployment problem, but the offices of both served a larger rural population, where employment opportunities beyond agriculture were more limited.

Agricultural work was largely casual and seasonal and typically organized by gangmasters. Farmers sub-contracted work to gangmasters who formed gangs of casual workers through personal contacts, transported them to the farm and paid them for piece-work, often cash in hand. The system was becoming increasingly common, extending beyond land work to pre-packing and some seasonal factory work, such as food processing. Many seasonal workers also came into the area during the summer in search of land work. The gangmaster system was notorious for encouraging benefit, National Insurance and tax fraud, because of its casual mode of operation. Accurate records were not always kept and all parties stood to gain by keeping the officials of the state at bay. For example, wages could be kept low if workers' pay was being subsidized by state benefits.

The Department of Social Security and the Employment Service responded with mobile fraud teams who were very active in checking on the activities of the seasonal workers and the gangmasters. The extent to which they were successful in detecting and deterring fraud was difficult to assess given the potential scale of the problem.

This mixed urban and rural area was clearly very different from the majority of areas which have been studied under the general heading of 'unemployment'. Jobs were available but they often required specific high-level skills or were low-paid and of low status. In the rural areas the 'black economy' was well established although under periodic surveillance. Many of 'the long-term unemployed' (over six months) remained unemployed, not through a simple lack of jobs, but through factors which made them unattractive to local employers. Many had prison records, or a history of alcoholism or drug addiction, or suffered from psychological problems or illiteracy. Rather than having a regular paid job some clients expressed a preference for the relative autonomy of occasional, seasonal, casual work, with state benefits to fill in the gaps between jobs. Certainly within the rural area it was possible to live very cheaply with neither food nor housing being particularly expensive.

COMMON FACTORS

Before examining the differences between the various types of workplace it is necessary to consider what they had in common. All three were dealing directly with the public and were responsible for the delivery of government policy. All of these workers were 'street-level bureaucrats' (Lipsky 1981).

One unremarkable feature, unless considered within a global context, was the lack of any obvious corruption by staff. In comparison with the Weberian legal–rational ideal type, these offices deviated from the formal rules and regulations in similar ways to non-western bureaucracies (Blau 1963). Numerous informal short cuts and rules of thumb were considered necessary for the effective delivery of policy. Informal staff practice rendered the necessary degree of flexibility that could not be built into a system of rules. This also added a moral component to the policy delivery, in that staff made greater efforts to be flexible with clients that they believed to be 'deserving' of benefits whereas they applied the rules more rigidly with those judged to be 'undeserving' (Handelman 1980). Arguably the value to administrative systems of the myth of Weberian bureaucratic orthodoxy of impartial, rule-following bureaucrats is to legitimize the administrative system by demonstrating the impartiality of its policy delivery apparatus. However, when legality and rationality could not deliver policy with the necessary level of responsiveness and flexibility, the informal system was essential but had to remain unacknowledged.

Thus the role of the informal system both enhanced government legitimacy by delivering policy, and simultaneously undermined it by being partial, value-laden and difficult to control. While these local officials were not 'corrupt' in the conventional sense, they did deviate from the Weberian model in similar ways to those in which the 'corruption' of most non-western bureaucracies has been measured. The main difference seemed to be that the deviation tended to reinforce policy objectives rather than undermine them in that they prevented many 'rational' yet illogical outcomes from occurring. In this sense the deviation was described as 'initiative' rather than corruption, and the crucial difference seemed to be that staff believed the system to be just in its aims.

Most staff shared a belief in the need for a welfare benefits system, but thought that system to be 'under attack' by unworthy clients who were trying to 'milk the system'. Defects in the benefits system in which innocent clients were subjected to intrusive questioning and placed under suspicion were blamed upon these potential 'freeloaders'. It was thought that if everyone behaved in a socially responsible manner 'the system' would meet all 'genuine' clients' needs.

'Corruption' in the sense in which it is found in other parts of the world was largely absent because the organization had legitimacy. Staff also had a personal interest in protecting the welfare system within which they worked. Local office staff were drawn from the community they served. They did not represent an elite within the community by virtue of their work: rather the work was considered to be relatively low-grade and stigmatized by its association with unemployment and poverty. A majority of staff had personal experience of unemployment, at least for a short time, and were aware that ultimately they may have had need of welfare benefits themselves. Thus personal and professional interests coincided. Staff protected 'the system' for the 'deserving' clients, which potentially included themselves and their families, and sought to save 'the system' from the 'undeserving' clients who were believed to be undermining it (Howe 1985; 1990).

Most local officials were to some extent alienated from the larger bureaucracy hierarchically arranged above them. They saw themselves as being ultimately responsible for the delivery of policy to their clients and often felt hampered by the layers of bureaucracy which impeded their freedom of action. They voiced suspicions that the higher levels were inadvertently sabotaging 'the system' for personal ends, or were simply out of touch with the reality of clients' problems, tactics and local office pragmatics. Front-line staff felt themselves to be undervalued within the bureaucracy and unpopular with their political masters. As one said, 'You try to do the job properly but they keep chipping the ground away from under you.' For local staff the essential failing of the higher levels was that they did not regularly meet the public and so had an artificial, simplified and naive picture of what the work entailed. Furthermore, they complained that higher level staff did not often seek their advice. The articulation of this complaint may have been in part a response to my presence as observer.

Politicians were regarded with considerable suspicion and particularly criticized for initiating organizational and policy changes which appeared to be circular and therefore pointless. In response to news of changes being introduced during my fieldwork, one supervisor voiced the mood of the moment: 'They [the government] really hate us'. Such comments were consistent within local offices whether staff worked in the Department of Social Security, the Unemployment Benefit Office or the Job Centre.

INFORMAL RANKING OF THE THREE TYPES OF WORKPLACE

Staff in these three types of office operated a simple, informal ranking system between them which placed the Job Centre at the top, Unemployment Benefit offices next, and the Department of Social Security local offices last. This went beyond the obvious conditions of the work, but also provided a means of evaluating the people who worked there. It was in effect a set of symbolic boundaries, as described by Cohen (1986), who argues that complex, mass societies have erected symbolic boundaries to preserve their sense of distinctiveness. Cohen's argues that

> The search for boundaries of identity goes deeper than between ethnic groups, localities, class, gender and generation. It extends even more insistently into smaller entities; within small local communities; between and within households. The compelling need to declare identity is social as well as psychological.
>
> (Cohen 1986: ix)

This ranking of offices can be analysed as the creation of symbolic boundaries within the workplace. The ranking system was openly acknowledged and challenged. The lower-ranked workers wished both to change the ranking order and to move to a higher ranked workplace; that is, despite complaining about the ranking they 'voted with their feet' if an opportunity arose to move into a higher group. The contradiction was not difficult to explain. It was accepted that certain 'plumb jobs' existed; that is, jobs which commanded more organizational resources, better working conditions, demanded less effort and paid the same as other more difficult jobs. While denying the legitimacy of the evaluation which determined this difference, it made perfect sense to try to avail oneself of the advantages. However, once established in the higher group the privileges were justified and so perceptions changed and divisions remained.

This workplace culture was constructed out of different ideas of professionalism and different ways of relating to clients. In each office, gender relations were constructed differently. I will set out the culture of the Job Centre, the Unemployment Benefit Office and the Department of Social Security in turn, before considering the way these cultures and their gender relations were reworked in the face of organizational change.

JOB CENTRES

The Job Centres were a creation of the early 1970s when the then Labour government policy was to remove the stigma of unemployment from the task of job broking. Labour Exchanges had previously been responsible for both the payment of unemployment benefit and the servicing of job vacancies. The intention had been to match unemployed people with suitable vacancies. But unemployed job seekers had suffered discrimination from employers who preferred to take candidates who were already employed. By separating job broking from the payment of unemployment benefits, Job Centres were able to provide a service which incorporated both employed and unemployed job seekers as clients. They also provided various services for employers such as sifting potential applicants for suitability, matching job seekers with appropriate skills to notified vacancies, and provision of premises for interviews. Registration at the Job Centre became voluntary to ensure that only seriously interested clients would be sent to employers. There was to be no question of 'testing' a client's intention to find work by sending him or her to a vacancy and risking wasting an employer's time. Thus Job Centre culture developed out of a conscious attempt to raise the status of their work by removing it from any association with the payment of benefits to unemployed people, and by identifying more closely with the private service sector.

Although Job Centres were not profit-making enterprises their continued existence depended on their ability to attract both job seekers and notifications of job vacancies. This ultimately depended upon attracting sufficient numbers of high calibre job seekers to register, i.e. those who were those most valued by employers. Thus 'customer care' and 'public relations' were of paramount importance, as in any other business dependent upon attracting 'customers' in the competitive market.[5] Presentation and 'professionalism' became key ingredients. When one Job Centre was burgled and the police asked that nothing be tidied away until their investigators had visited, the overriding concern of the manager was how this would look to the public. Offices were located in town centres and were furnished to a relatively high standard with an open-plan, welcoming and accessible office layout. Staff and clients shared the same physical space. Staff were encouraged to wear smart, formal, gender-specific clothes.

Job Centre staff were also encouraged to develop what was called a 'professional' mode of behaviour towards clients, which could be summarized as detached politeness. Interactions were friendly but reserved. During one training session staff complained that such behaviour was 'dishonest and unnatural'. They were told that 'professionalism' was 'a cloak within which to hide true feelings'. This provided a good metaphor for Job Centre culture, which was centred on presentation and service provision. The paramount criterion of success was to communicate with clients without any suggestion of conflict and to 'sell' the service.

This had an important influence on the way in which gender difference was constructed. Although both men and women were engaged in similar work, the majority dealing directly with the public were women (about three-quarters of the clerical staff). They looked and behaved like saleswomen (Benson 1986), secretaries (Pringle 1989) and air stewardesses (Hochschild 1983); that is, they dressed and behaved in ways which enhanced a restrained, non-assertive style of femininity which they described as 'civilized' and which extended beyond their surface appearance. They moved relatively elegantly, spoke softly using moderate language, and shared 'respectable' gossip about families, holidays and domestic issues, even during breaks when they were out of sight of the public. The minority who did not conform to this standard were quietly marginalized and isolated. Staff frequently contrasted this 'civilized' behaviour with that thought to be prevalent at the Unemployment Benefit Offices. It had become a 'symbolic boundary' to protect their higher status, but it was also instrumental in creating a particular form of femininity which went beyond the 'cloak of professionalism' advocated by the trainers, to be incorporated into the office culture.

It is relevant here to consider the work of Peta Tancred-Sheriff and Arlie Hochschild. Tancred-Sheriff (1989) identified a concept of 'adjunct control' which described a series of occupations providing the bulk of women's employment, in which staff mediated between management and workers (e.g. secretaries and clerks) and producers and consumers (e.g. saleswomen). These women participated in the authority of management but had little personal authority. Their sexuality was utilized by management to facilitate control of clients, customers or workers. Job Centre staff seemed to fit this pattern and thus the construction of femininity here may be construed as enhancing a conventional, passive, supporting type of female sexuality which was used to attract and control mainly male clients.

Hochschild (1983) explored the idea of 'emotional work' whereby staff feelings were artificially manipulated through control of bodily expression and manufactured warmth. She argued that 'emotional work' alienated workers from their own emotions and reduced the capacity for spontaneous warmth. There were obvious links here with staff unease expressed during training about the 'cloak of professionalism'.

It can be argued therefore that Job Centre culture, by constructing clients within a 'service' metaphor, generated a type of passive, compliant femininity in which both sexuality and emotionality were utilized by management. The Employment Service wished to extend this interpretation of 'professionalism' to the Unemployment Benefit Offices. The overt aim of this policy was to improve customer relations, but a consequence of it was to reinforce women's subordination within the workplace.

UNEMPLOYMENT BENEFIT OFFICES

After job broking was removed to Job Centres, the residual part of the work of the old Labour Exchanges was to assess, calculate and pay benefits to unemployed people. Clients were required to call into the renamed Unemployment Benefit Office regularly to sign on. The staff had a dual role: to deliver accurate and prompt payment to those with entitlement, and to detect and deter false and cynical claims. But this was not an easy balance to achieve.

To qualify for payment unemployed people had to be fit, available and actively seeking work; they should not have made themselves intentionally unemployed by either leaving an employer voluntarily or securing dismissal by misconduct. Evidence of a client's state of health and the reason for his or her leaving previous employment was relatively easy to obtain from independent sources such as the client's doctor or the previous employer. But evidence of availability (having no other commitments which preclude employment) and of actively seeking work were more difficult to prove, because it depended to a large extent on the client's own testimony. This placed the benefit staff in an investigative and judgemental position in relation to their clients' behaviour, and thus structural conflict was built into the relationship regardless of personal prejudices. This latent conflict had to be managed by staff and was reflected in the way benefit culture constructed clients and gender relations within the office.

Clients were involuntary; they needed financial support throughout the period of unemployment and the Unemployment Benefit Office was the only source to which they could turn for access to state resources earmarked for this purpose. Without the need to attract clients there was no necessity for expenditure on a pleasant environment. Offices were often located in less central locatiﾭas than Job Centres, and until recently little effort was made to furnis'ﾐ the public areas, which were large, virtually empty signing halls originally designed to accommodate long dole queues. The boundary between staff and public was a large, high counter often completely sealed with protective glass screens. Out of sight of the public the staff working environment was frequently shabby yet functional. Staff tended to dress informally, and the younger ones often wore unisex jeans, sweatshirts and trainers. Hair and make-up showed greater variation than at the Job Centre; some women paid little attention to their grooming, others exhibited extreme styles. This was in marked contrast to the conservative consensus of style at the Job Centre. This unisex style extended to their behaviour and gossip. Women again formed the majority of the clerical staff, but here talk was often sexually explicit and language unrestrained. Staff acknowledged the existence of a 'benefits humour' which they described as 'crude and vulgar'. Gossip was often about the sexual orientation of senior staff and interactions between staff were peppered with jokes. These ribald women were in marked contrast to the 'civilized' women of the Job Centre and were very conscious of the difference, which they did nothing to diminish.

Benefit staff often expressed the opinion that despite their pivotal role in welfare policy they were not valued. Within the Employment Department group as a whole, 'welfare' work, the province of the Department of Social Security, was less central than work which involved employment issues. Thus the removal of job broking served to diminish the status of Unemployment Benefit Offices within the organization. One means that staff used to distance themselves from their welfare function was to emphasize the legal side of their work; to ensure that the complex rules and procedures determining payments were strictly observed. As one manager explained, 'All that was left to do was to make benefit payment an art form'. Benefit offices developed a culture in which accuracy of payment and procedure took precedence over 'customer care'. Work interest centred on the application of the letter of the law by which staff efficacy and professionalism was judged, at least amongst colleagues. When case papers were transferred from another office, staff gleefully searched for errors in the paperwork. Less than perfect examples were deemed to be 'a mess' and much debate between staff about how cases should be conducted were common. Staff spoke of 'the system': an overarching set of laws and procedures which had a logic beyond human understanding and should not be tampered with.

This tendency towards legalism was moderated by the 'moral component' present in welfare-related work in which the 'justice' of the outcome was important (Handleman 1980). It led to a creative manipulation of the rules where skilled operators worked within the system to produce the desired outcome. This contrasted with the Social Security offices where staff were more willing to relax rules and procedures relating to payments. Thus Unemployment Benefit Office culture had two distinctive features; it was highly legalistic and clients were slightly peripheral and under suspicion. Knowledge of the rules and procedures conferred both power over clients and informal status with colleagues. Knowledge was power and power over clients was 'professionalism'.

This cultural milieu had important implications for gender construction. Many of the women working in the Unemployment Benefit Office were mothers of young children who had 'chosen' to limit their career aspirations to accommodate the double-bind of domestic responsibility and paid work. As a result women were the most experienced, most knowledgeable and therefore most powerful within the Unemployment Benefit Offices. However, this merely served to confirm the stereotype that women were most suited for clerical work which entailed a bureaucratic, unimaginative concern with trivia, an image which did nothing to enhance their prospects of promotion. Less experienced men who were prepared to bend the rules were seen to have greater initiative. Furthermore, men with family commitments saw their responsibility to seek promotion actively rather than limit their workload, as the women did, since for the men family responsibilities required them to earn a higher wage and did not involve increased domestic labour.

When dealing with clients women were valued as being better at containing conflict, but this was attributed to the reluctance of male clients to engage in verbal or physical abuse with women. However, my observations suggest that these women contained conflict and controlled clients through use of the strong gender role of 'mother'. In this role they were able to control clients through a less provocative 'caring' stance, which reduced the potential for conflict. Vulnerable clients confronted with a knowledgeable, strong woman who represented an intrusive state demanding to know personal details were likely to find this threatening. But if the encounter was mediated through the familiar, or more accurately familial, metaphor of mother and child, the threat was reduced. This in turn enhanced the officials' power because as mother she could admonish, instruct and socialize client behaviour and represent the action as being 'for his own good'. As mother she also had the back-up of 'father' in the more coercive power of the state: police, courts, etc. Not surprisingly, clients preferred to deal with the woman on the counter and to place themselves in her capable hands.

Thus the construction of gender within benefit culture was very different from that of the Job Centre. Here women were active, capable and powerful and were not required to be sexually attractive to their clients. Indeed, attraction would have served to undermine the women's authority since it would have shifted the power balance in favour of the male client. This was clearly reflected in the way benefit women dressed, their unisex style and their ribald sense of humour. These women actively used their sexuality to embarrass male colleagues and undermine the authority of management with their gossip, highlighting their inadequacies as 'real men'. By undermining the position of men who did not match an aggressive, dominant form of masculinity they were affirming its efficacy and, by implication, their own subordination. Neither their power as women over clients nor their active use of sexuality within the office could prevent the reinforcement of their subordination as women at work.

Thus there were two very different workplace cultural milieux in which gender difference was constructed, yet in both women were subordinated. Both involved women engaged in 'adjunct control' tasks but only in the Job Centre was sexuality used by management to attract and control clients. Benefit culture constructed women who denied any sexual attraction between themselves and clients in favour of the stronger gender role of 'mother'. Here sexuality seemed to be more under the control of the women themselves and yet it still reinforced their disadvantage in that it defined them as domestic and passive. 'Emotional labour' was more evident in the Job Centre than in the benefit culture where control of clients depended upon knowledge of law and procedure rather than on 'manufactured warmth'. These cultural differences which emerged with the separation of job broking from payment of benefit were being challenged by further organizational change as the two were to be reintegrated.

THE DEPARTMENT OF SOCIAL SECURITY

Department of Social Security offices had a similar relationship with clients to that in Unemployment Benefit Offices. They had the additional problem of administering a means-test, which created a far greater potential for staff–client conflict. Department of Social Security policy has been to minimize face-to-face contact between staff and client, and as a result Department of Social Security benefit culture arose within a workplace where clients were seldom visible. They were contacted in writing and would occasionally telephone or call into the office, but most staff had minimal contact with their clients. The offices were larger than Un-employment Benefit Offices and proportionately more men worked there. The style adopted by staff was similar with varied, casual and unisex clothes. Informal conversation was jokey and sexually explicit, although it was more often the clients who were the subject of the jokes. (See Cullen and Howe 1991 for a discussion on the use of jokes to create client stereotypes.) Women often actively used their sexuality to undermine men with jokes impugning their masculinity, although being a larger office with more senior grades present, the men were more likely to respond in kind.

All three types of workplace were being changed, the Department of Social Security was being computerized, and both benefit paying organ-izations were being given agency status.[6] I did not study this in great detail but concentrated on the move towards the reintegration of the Job Centres and Unemployment Benefit offices. I will look at the ways their ideas of professionalism, construction of clients and gender relations were begin-ning to be re-worked. The process of re-integration was at an early stage, but there was one newly created work role which cut across the symbolic boundary between the two: the role of counsellor.

COUNSELLING

During the 1980s the role of the Job Centre was substantially reduced in line with the Thatcher government policy to 'roll back the frontiers of the state'. Job Centres were to provide only a minimal service. Their other functions were left to private employment agencies. Thus while Job Centre staff retained their veneer of 'professionalism' their work had become largely routine. Their employment-advising role was transferred to coun-sellors who provided the service exclusively for unemployed people, and which incorporated a substantial element of policing of the continued entitlement to benefit payments. The 'professionalism' of the Job Centre staff in part had been based upon their knowledge of the local labour market acquired through continued contact with local employers advising vacancies. This pool of knowledge had been seriously diminished as employers had forsaken Job Centres for the more comprehensive services available from private employment agencies. Counsellors continued to use the Job Centre definition of 'professionalism' based upon an emphasis on 'customer care', but unlike those of the Job Centre their clients were not voluntary, nor did they have a fund of employment advice to offer. Counsellors used Job Centre style and Job Centre language, but they were engaged in policing the benefits system which created a relationship between staff and client more akin to that of the benefit office.

Counsellors retained the style and presentation of Job Centre culture, but were engaged in the task of controlling (called 'influencing' within the department) and re-socializing clients. The task of counsellors was not to identify clients whose benefit was to be stopped, but to use the ultimate threat of benefit suspension to effect certain changes in behaviour; changes which it was believed would enhance the clients' prospects of finding work. In effect, counselling staff were presented with a contradiction. They were to exercise control over clients to a greater degree than that exercised by benefit staff, but without a fund of specialized knowledge which was the immediate source of the benefit staff's power. It is true that counsellors, like benefit staff, could call upon the indirect power of the state, but that was most effective as an ultimate deterrent. Counsellors were required to persuade and convince their clients, not blatantly to coerce them.

How did counsellors achieve this compromise, and what effect did it have on the construction of gender relations within the workplace and with clients? Counselling, being a higher grade job than those already discussed, was not wholly 'women's work'. Men and women were represented in approximately equal proportions which gave an opportunity to compare how men and women resolved the problem. There was also the question of how staff practice was evaluated. In training, counsellors were told that their primary task was to help unemployed people get back to work with the implicit suggestion that quality of service was paramount. In practice, strong emphasis was placed on reducing the numbers on the politically sensitive Unemployment Register by whatever means were legally available. This had a strong quantitative evaluative element with demanding targets being set for counsellors to achieve in terms of the number of interviews they completed and the number of 'sign offs'.[7] In the trade-off between quality and quantity the former, having a higher political profile, was given greater emphasis by management.

Counsellors retained the style and behaviour of Job Centre 'professionalism', but used it to facilitate client control rather than 'customer care' *per se*. To do so, counsellors could not remain wholly detached as Job Centre staff did within the 'cloak of professionalism', but needed genuinely to empathize with clients without relinquishing control. This was a difficult balance to achieve. Some counsellors succeeded in building a relationship with their clients to such an extent that they became advocates for them, negotiating with other government agencies, landlords and employers long after the client had left the Unemployment Register and was technically no longer the counsellor's responsibility. Others failed to empathize and found themselves in unproductive disputes with clients. Some clients were intimidated into agreeing to co-operate but failed to act on the agreements. Counsellors were particularly frustrated by this latter category of clients because they represented a considerable investment in time to little effect. Counsellors were obliged to interview these unfortunate people again and again.

The retention of Job Centre 'professionalism', although officially encouraged, also served the counsellors well because it gave them the veneer of higher status occupations such as solicitors or doctors. Their formal, gender-specific style of dress and middle-class mannerisms enhanced this image. The office layout provided many counsellors with private interview rooms which were relatively well-furnished. This image of 'professionalism' suggested a semi-independence from the bureaucracy which in practice did not exist. Training encouraged counsellors to enhance this impression by teaching social skills not usually employed by bureaucratic administrators such as greeting clients with a handshake and a personal introduction, and various interviewing techniques designed to put the client at ease within a controlled environment. Counsellors often expressed surprise that clients would reveal so much of themselves during interviews and assumed that counsellors would not inform the benefit and fraud sections. Counsellors dealt with this conflict of loyalties in different ways. Some who preferred to retain the trust of the clients said nothing, but others saw it as a valuable source of information for the department as a whole, and passed the information on to their colleagues. This image of semi-independence had very little basis in fact; counsellors received only minimal training and had little specialized knowledge, but it was important in enabling counsellors to retain control.[8]

This Job Centre style, as adopted by counsellors, lacked the use of sexuality to attract clients. Counsellors' clients were not voluntary; they were compelled to attend the interviews and failure to do so would result in suspension of payment of benefit. Despite their appearance, women counsellors adopted the gendered role of 'mother' in a similar manner to that of their benefit colleagues. Counselling, which sought to incorporate empathy with and re-socialization of clients, was an environment in which control through care was a very effective strategy. Men could and did use a similar strategy but often voiced a discomfort about 'getting too involved'. They were more likely to avoid emotional displays by clients, often making friendly jokes to 'lighten the atmosphere'. The emotion most commonly expressed by male counsellors was that of anger in response to lack of cooperation – 'You have to sit on your fists sometimes' – but this was relatively rare.

Once again the women's strategy was valued less than the men's. Association with motherhood and emotionality stigmatized women's attempts to provide a high-quality service for clients. It often meant that women counsellors spent a disproportionate amount of their time with clients who had serious problems, unemployment probably being the least. By contrast the more emotionally detached approach favoured by more of the men enabled them to complete more interviews and gain more positive outcomes which looked better on the office statistics. We have here again the simultaneous exploitation of women's mothering skills, which provided a higher-quality service to unemployed people, and the devaluation of those skills in favour of alternative methods which delivered a higher quantity of interviews.

CONCLUSION

I have described the recent history of part of the Employment Service in which the dual areas of employment and unemployment policy implementation had been split and were being reunited. The initial split generated two very different workplace environments in which client and gender relations were constructed in very different ways and for different purposes.

Women working at the Job Centre developed a style which provided them with a higher status. However, this style also served the needs of management in that women's sexuality was part of the package designed to make the Job Centre attractive to potential clients. Within the Unemployment Benefit Office, clients were involuntary and placed under suspicion. It was more important for staff to be able to control clients. Women here did not use their sexuality with clients since it would have undermined their authority. They did however use their sexuality within the workplace as a means of undermining individual men, although this reinforced male authority in general. With clients they adopted the non-sexual gendered role of 'mother' which enabled them to control clients through 'care' and thus defused possible conflict.

As the two policy areas (employment and unemployment) were brought back together there was a need for adjustment, particularly in view of the fact that official departmental policy was to impose Job Centre 'professionalism' on Unemployment Benefit Offices. But the structural underpinnings of that approach, the need to attract clients, was no longer paramount. Counselling gave an indication of how this adjustment might occur. Counsellors used Job Centre style to enhance their prestige, but Unemployment Benefit Office metaphors to effect control through care.

However, the one single issue which has remained consistent throughout these organizational changes has been the subordination of women. Whether as sexualized objects to help attract clients, or as sexualized subjects teasing male colleagues, they reinforced conventional forms of sexual stereotypes in which men were dominant and active while women were submissive and passive. When they utilized their skills as 'mothers' in order to enhance authority over clients without exacerbating conflict, although they were serving organizational ends, these skills were undervalued as belonging to the domestic sphere and not entirely appropriate within the workplace.

Women's subordination persisted relatively unchanged despite gender relations taking different forms throughout this period of organizational change. Furthermore, the Employment Service is part of the government department responsible for the implementation of Equal Opportunities policy and has a heightened awareness of these issues. What this demonstrates is the extent to which culturally embedded gendered power relations have resisted both structural and cultural organizational change and an active Equal Opportunities policy programme. Awareness of cultural underpinnings to unequal gender relations within the organizations is an essential next step in the development of policy. Existing policy has aimed to create an environment in which individual women could compete with individual men on equal terms. What is needed is a greater recognition of the social and cultural processes which produce the gendered categories that constrain and limit the choices of individual men and women.

NOTES

1 These figures were obtained from *Tempo* (December 1992: 4). *Tempo* is the Employment Department Group staff newspaper.
2 This ethnography is based on a period of twelve months' continuous fieldwork in four Unemployment Benefit offices, three Job Centres and one local office of the Department of Social Security between 1989 and 1990. I attended two staff training courses, during which time I met staff from similar offices over a much wider area. I also spent three weeks at this same Social Security office in 1987.
3 In 1988 the Department of Health and Social Security (DHSS) was divided. The change made no noticeable difference at local level, so for the sake of simplicity I have used the term Department of Social Security throughout.
4 There were a number of government-funded schemes available to people who had been unemployed for more than six months. The most extensive of these was employment training which offered in-house training and placements with local employers for a period of up to one year. In practice, good employer placements were difficult to find.
5 Competition was with private employment agencies. Furthermore, local employers could simply advertize in the local newspapers and not inform the Job Centre that a vacancy existed.
6 Agency status is part of a general government attempt to make the Civil Service more flexible and responsive to local conditions. Its main effect on local offices is a possible change in management structure and the introduction of different types of statistics for local staff to collect.

7 People left the Unemployment Register for many reasons other than finding a job. They transferred to alternative benefits such as those for sick people, or they joined a government training scheme. Such people would still be paid state benefits but they were no longer counted as 'unemployed and claiming benefit' on the government statistics.

8 Training consisted of two weeks and three days training at Regional Office in interviewing techniques and sales skills to influence client choice and behaviour.

REFERENCES

Benson, S. P. (1986) *Counter Cultures: Saleswomen, Managers, and Customers in American Department Stores 1890–1940*, Urbana and Chicago: University of Illinois Press.

Blau, P. (1963) *The Dynamics of Bureaucracy*, Chicago: University of Chicago Press.

Cohen, A. P. (ed.) (1986) *Symbolising Boundaries: Identity and Diversity in British Cultures*, Manchester: Manchester University Press.

Cullen, S. and Howe, L. (1991) 'People, cases and stereotypes: a study of staff practice in a DSS office', *Cambridge Anthropology*, 15 (1): 1–26.

Deacon, A. and Bradshaw, J. (1983) *Reserved for the Poor: The Means-test in British Social Policy*, Oxford: Basil Blackwell.

Handelman, D. (1980) 'Bureaucratic affiliation: the moral component in welfare cases', in E. Marx (ed.) *A Composite Portrait of Israel*, London: Academic Press.

Hochschild, A. R. (1983) *The Managed Heart. Commercialization of Human Feeling*, London: University of California Press.

Howe, L. (1985) 'The "deserving" and "undeserving": practice in an urban, local social security office', *Journal of Social Policy* 14: 49–72.

—— (1990) *Being Unemployed in Northern Ireland: An Ethnographic Study*, Cambridge: Cambridge University Press.

Lipsky, M. (1981) *Street-level Bureaucracy*, New York: Russel Sage Foundation.

Pahl, R. E. and Wallace, C. (1985) 'Household work strategies in economic recession', in N. Redclift and E. Mingione (eds) *Beyond Employment: Household, Gender and Subsistence*, Oxford: Basil Blackwell.

Pringle, R. (1989) 'Bureaucracy, rationality and sexuality: the case of secretaries', in J. Hearn, D. L. Sheppard, P. Tancred-Sheriff and G. Burrell (eds) *The Sexuality of Organisation*, London: Sage Publications.

Tancred-Sheriff, P. (1989) 'Gender, sexuality and the labour process', in J. Hearn, D. L. Sheppard, P. Tancred-Sheriff and G. Burrell (eds) *The Sexuality of Organisation*, London: Sage Publications.

Townsend, P. (1976) 'The scope and limitations of means-tested social services in Britain', in P. Townsend (ed.) *Sociology and Social Policy*, Harmondsworth: Penguin Books.

Part III

Clients and empowerment

Introduction

Susan Wright

From the 1950s to the 1970s, modernization in the West involved a rapid growth in the number and size of service industries and bureaucracies (both regulative and redistributive). Danet (1981: 303) shows that by 1970 in the United States, service workers were 62 per cent of the labour force, with the greatest growth in government. In other western countries over 50 per cent of the labour force was in the service sector, with a similar trend in some parts of the Third World (ibid.). In interacting with these organizations, people were constructed as 'clients'. As Collmann puts it '"clients" are bureaucratic creations' (1981: 105).

In becoming clients, people are classified according to only that narrow segment of their lives which is relevant to the organization's policies and activities; people's own construction of themselves and their problems is subordinated to this classifactory framework. As people's welfare problems rarely fall entirely within the remit of any one organization, this can produce a situation where different 'bits' of a person are relevant in different ways to different organizations, thus fragmenting the person (Wright 1982). Sociologists and anthropologists have tried to conceptualize the contradictions in relations between clients and bureaucracies. Tapp and Levine (1977) suggested that it was characterized by a combination of competence and compliance. Competence refers to the ability of clients to understand the bureaucratic system and activate it in an appropriate way in pursuit of their rights and interests. Compliance refers to passive acceptance of the behaviour required by the organization. Handelman approached this contradiction by suggesting that clients are always constructed as both individuals and as objects. As individuals, it is their 'personal failings' which cause them to come into contact with bureaucracy; and they are considered to be objects in that they are to be acted on and bureaucratically moulded (Collmann 1981: 110). He argued that bureaucratic work can only proceed unproblematically if clients accept this falsification of themselves. They are to accept passive objectification for ease of administration and yet to be active agents, correcting their 'personal failings' as this is the purpose of bureaucratic intervention. The two constructions play off against each other: 'A client is supposed to become rehabilitated; but self-motivated, rehabilitative actions produce sanctions which enforce clientship' (ibid.).

McCourt Perring's chapter in Part III (Chapter 9) exemplifies this contradiction. In this case it is between care and control. The move of patients out of large mental hospitals to community-based group homes was intended to enable patients to live more independently and engage in more active self-definition. Yet, when this involved activities which were difficult to control, the institution defined these individuals as 'problems'. With reference to Collmann (above), it seems that clients' 'competence' may include knowing that they have to appear 'compliant' with these contradictory definitions of themselves.

This complexity in client–organization relationships raises many questions about power. The earliest studies concentrated on face-to-face interactions and attempted to classify these into different types. Blau and Scott (1962) distinguished four types of organization according to their primary beneficiaries, and posited that clients would have different relationships with each. In 'commonweal organizations', such as tax collection or the police, the beneficiaries were the public at large, in whose interest the individual client's behaviour was regulated. Service organizations, such as health clinics or social welfare agencies, were established to benefit individual clients. In mutual benefit organizations, for example, trade unions or cooperative societies, members were the primary beneficiaries, whereas in service sector businesses (hairdressers, shops, banks, airlines) the primary beneficiaries were the owners or shareholders. Katz and Danet (1973) hypothesized that clients would feel they had different kinds of power in relation to each of these four types of organization. They expected that people would use different kinds of appeals (ranging from altruistic to normative) in trying to obtain service from them.

Ethnographically, the situation is much more complicated. For example, the social services department of a local council is both a commonweal organization, responsible to the public at large through their elected councillors, and a service organization, benefiting individual clients. The growth of such organizations has also been accompanied by the institutionalization of professions. That is, people who have specialized knowledge of how to handle clients' problems and with sanctions or resources to apply accordingly. However, a considerable distance can be established between a profession's knowledge, culture and language and that of the lay people for whom they are working. This is exemplified by Collins' account of lawyers and divorce proceedings (Chapter 10, this volume). To overcome the gap in communication and power between clients and professional bureaucracies, there has been a growth of voluntary pressure groups which further complicates the institutional picture. Edwards' account of Housing Aid (Chapter 11, this volume) is an example of such an intermediary voluntary organization.

Not only is the institutional picture more complicated than the early attempts at classification allow; the analysis of power in client–bureaucracy relations can no longer rely solely on characteristics of face-to-face interactions. One of the main contributions of anthropology has been in showing how these are informed by an interaction between the conceptual systems of bureaucracies and clients. Cullen (Chapter 8, this volume) has already introduced the idea that people working in organizations have patterned ideas about their clients into which individuals are fitted. Howe (1989) studied employment offices in Northern Ireland and showed that desk officers had a classificatory system of 'deserving' and 'undeserving' poor. Certain indicators were taken from the dress, mien and speech of clients to fit them into these categories. This had material outcomes, as it affected the information that clients received and their access to benefits. From a socio-linguistic approach, in a variety of bureaucratic settings it has been shown in detail how the discursive styles of clients from ethnic minorities were misunderstood by white officials and how they were disadvantaged in these interactions (Gumperz 1982). Such studies show that underneath the surface of objective processes for determining access to resources, concepts and linguistic symbols are operating to the disadvantage of particular sets of people. As Gumperz argues (1982: 14), although clients are adept at monitoring and negotiating meaning in interactions, they are disempowered when the conceptual and symbolic grounds for negotiation are obscured by an appearance of bureaucratic neutrality.

From the late 1970s in Britain, people of all political shades were discussing the ways clients were made powerless in the face of large state bureaucracies which had been established for their welfare. The word 'empowerment' was central to all sides of the political argument. It was a strange word to use, as it suggested that power was in the gift of those who had hitherto been disempowering. It already had currency in the Third World, where its meaning was informed by a much clearer analysis of the differential distribution of benefits and non-benefits from capitalism, and of connections between economic change and the role of the state. Hence 'empowerment' referred to the development of economic activities under the control of the weakest (for example, homeless or landless people), or women so that they had their own resources for development. It also meant the growth of their organizational capacity and confidence to demand treatment by the state as equal partners with professionals and officers in a process of development (Marsden and Oakley 1990).

These emphases on process and on linkage between economic and bureau-cratic systems did not accompany the word 'empowerment' when it was used in a British context. The new right borrowed from a model of private sector service industries where people were 'empowered' by their ability to choose between competing organizations in a market. The word 'client' was replaced by 'consumer' and legislation was used to remodel public sector organizations and construct an appearance of market choice, for example, in state schools and the National Health Service, and to set up direct competition between public and private sector provision of other services through compulsory competitive tendering. However, these changes to institutional structures were not accompanied by economic measures to ensure that the most disadvantaged people had the resources to participate in this 'market' or engage in develop-ment under their own control.

The left tried to hold on to the redistributive aims of the welfare state whilst recognizing that so far large state organizations had rarely had that effect. *In and Against the State* (London to Edinburgh Weekend Return Group 1979) was an account by welfare state professionals of the ways in which their interactions with clients were disempowering, even though they were committed to achieving the opposite. This set up a search in Labour local authorities for strategies to 'empower' the public and clients. For example, Islington decentralized service departments to neighbour-hoods; Sheffield engaged in locally-based economic development; Cleve-land emphasized community development. Hoggett and Hambleton (1987: 1) reported that forty local authorities had decentralization strategies.

Both left and right concentrated on organizational structures rather than practices. There was a transfer to the public sector of some ideas from 'empowering' new management systems which were being introduced in industry at the same time (Whyte 1991). This broke down the old Taylorist vertical separation whereby planning and decision making was done at the top of the management hierarchy, controlling and coordinating workers at the bottom. In the new system horizontal links were stressed. Middle managers were 'thinned out', and the remaining ones were placed close to workers in a supportive role. It was workers who took responsibility for ensuring that operations were continually improved and linked in an un-interrupted flow to the processes before and after them. Workers were 'empowered' to take initiatives to improve work processes and organ-ization. Such 'empowerment' also meant that workers took on the stress of this tightly strung system (Whyte 1991: 139). In service industry it meant that the system should, in theory, be driven by front-line workers' experi-ence of client (dis)satisfaction.

Ideas from this new management system were introduced, often piece-meal, into the public sector. It was piecemeal because some authorities, while introducing the language of 'empowerment' and various forms of 'horizontal' and 'total quality' management, still clung to an idea of 'efficiency' associated with strongly centralized, top-down decision making. Hoggett argued that 'each layer in an organization tends to reproduce, in its dealings with the layer below, the way in which it is addressed by the layer above' (1987: 164). If chief officers felt they were rendered powerless by the councillors, they did still have the ability to silence the layer below. This pattern of each layer feeling powerless and unsupported by the layer above and suppressing the layer below would continue down to the front-line workers. To empower clients they required the opposite management characteristics: the ability to respond to initiatives from below and to feel empowered themselves by a supportive line management. It was contradictory to maintain centralized decision making at the same time as expecting front-line workers to empower clients. Hoggett therefore argued for empowerment not by localizing a bit of service delivery but by changes to the whole structure and practice of the organization (1987: 159).

So far there are few ethnographic analyses connecting the structure and practices of an organization's management to the ways front-line workers relate to clients (Wright 1992). Stanton (1989) made a participatory study of the introduction of self-management into Newcastle Family Service Unit, a semi-independent unit within a conventionally hierarchical bureaucracy. Within this impressive study, there was insufficient space to investigate whether the staff's more participatory management system enabled them to be more empowering of clients. Lipsky (1980) concentrated on 'street-level bureaucrats" relations with clients. He argued that this street-level interaction created an organization's policy, to some extent regardless of the echelons above them, with whom relations were 'intrinsically conflictual'. But he did not explore in ethnographic detail whether the different management systems of welfare, school and police departments affected street-level bureaucrats' interactions with clients.

The three chapters in Part III combine the different dimensions of anthropological work outlined in this introduction. They bring together fine-grained ethnography of organizational arrangements with a study of the symbols and concepts through which officials negotiate their interactions with clients. Collins (Chapter 10) studies changes to surface features of judicial rituals, notably the removal of wigs, to try and make people feel more in control of their divorce cases. This was coincident with legislation to equalize women's rights in the division of marital property. She shows that the layout of the room, the use of space in the court and, more importantly, the linguistic and other practices which sustained an inaccessible boundary around the legal profession, continued to make people feel disempowered and to maintain gender inequalities in the material outcomes of divorce.

McCourt Perring (Chapter 9) studies the impact of care in the community legislation. She shows that although the closure of large mental hospitals and the transfer of people to group homes did result in improvements in their lives, these were limited by the metaphors for social relations in the new organization. By contrasting the old 'patriarchal' system with new 'family' homes, an image of caring and sharing equality was evoked. But 'family' also implied hierarchy, by gender and age. It was through the use of this metaphor that the disempowerment and infantalization of clients were maintained.

Edwards (Chapter 11) draws on another British cultural concept, that of 'class'. She shows how it was used in managing relations between clients, the Housing Aid organization and housing bureaucracies. The Housing Aid workers transformed the binary oppositions of working class/middle class and us/them into 'ordinary people' (which aligned them with clients) as against 'bureaucracy'. She shows how, whilst maintaining this binary classification, individuals could be placed in different ways. Thus a 'bureaucrat' who was immediately helpful and who appeared to share the long-term aim of changing unequal social systems (a different definition of empowerment) became an 'ordinary person'. Edwards argues that the establishment of fixed categories, like classes, and the flexible allocation of individuals between them, is the operation in one organizational context of a widespread cultural process in Britain.

As exemplified by these three studies of British organizations in the 1980s, an anthropological approach can combine a grasp of the structure and operations of large-scale bureaucratic systems with not only the fine-grained ethnography of interactions between officials and clients, but also the analysis of the symbols, concepts and cultural processes that is needed for a critical evaluation of who is empowered by 'empowerment'.

REFERENCES

Blau, P. M. and Scott, W. R. (1962) *Formal Organizations*, San Francisco: Chandler.
Collmann, J. (1981) 'Postscript: the significance of clients', *Social Analysis* 9: 103–12.
Collmann, J. and Handelman, D. (eds) (1981) *Social Analysis. Special Issue: Administrative Frameworks and Clients* 9.
Danet, B. (1981) 'Client–organization relationships', in P. C. Nystrom and W. H. Starbuck (eds) *Handbook of Organizational Design* Vol 2, pp. 382–428, Oxford: Oxford University Press.
Gumperz, J. (ed.) (1982) *Language and Social Identity*, Cambridge: Cambridge University Press.
Hoggett, P. (1987) 'Going beyond a rearrangement of the deckchairs: some practical hints for councillors and managers', in P. Hoggett and R. Hambleton (eds) *De-*

centralization and Democracy: Localizing Public Services, pp. 157–67, School of Advanced Urban Studies Occasional Paper No. 28, Bristol: University of Bristol.

Hoggett, P. and Hambleton, R. (eds) (1987) *Decentralization and Democracy: Localizing Public Services*, School of Advanced Urban Studies Occasional Paper No. 28, Bristol: University of Bristol.

Howe, L. (1989) 'Social anthropology and public policy: aspects of unemployment and social security in Northern Ireland', in H. Donnan and G. McFarlane (eds) *Social Anthropology and Public Policy in Northern Ireland*, pp. 26–46, Aldershot: Avebury.

Katz, E. and Danet, B. (1973) 'Petitions and persuasive appeals: a study of official-client relations', in E. Katz and B. Danet (eds) *Bureaucracy and the Public*, pp. 174–90, New York: Basic Books.

Lipsky, M. (1980) *Street-Level Bureaucracy: Dilemmas of the Individual in the Public Services*, New York: Russell Sage.

London to Edinburgh Weekend Return Group (1979) *In and Against the State*, London: Pluto.

Marsden, D. and Oakley, P. (eds) (1990) *Evaluating Social Development Projects*, Oxford: OXFAM.

Stanton, A. (1989) *Invitation to Self Management*, London: Dab Hand Press.

Tapp, J. L. and Levine, F. J. (1977) *Law, Justice, and the Individual in Society*, New York: Holt, Rinehart & Winston.

Whyte, W. F. (1991) *Social Theory for Action. How Individuals and Organizations Learn to Change*, London: Sage.

Wright, S. (1982) *Parish to Whitehall: Administrative Structure and Perceptions of Community in Rural Areas*, Gloucestershire Papers in Local and Rural Planning No. 16, Gloucester: Gloucester College of Art and Technology.

—— (1992) *Evaluation of the Unemployment Strategy*, Sussex University and Cleveland County Council's Research and Intelligence Unit, series of seven papers, Middlesbrough: Cleveland County Council.

9 Community care as de-institutionalization?

Continuity and change in the transition from hospital to community-based care

Christine McCourt Perring

UK social policy has pursued radical organizational changes since the 1980s; amongst these is a planned shift from institutional to community-based care for people who are categorized as dependent and/or deviant.[1] This shift stretches across different sectors of public services from acute medicine to social care and the criminal justice system. In all cases it is assumed that by releasing individuals from large institutions and by placing them in settings constructed as 'the community' or 'family-like' they will be both more independent and more integrated socially. My analysis focuses on mental health services but invites comparison across a wider range of institutions. My central argument is about the concern of such institutions with the related but conflicting functions of care and control. I suggest that, although individuals have been empowered to some extent, the planned changes have encouraged reproduction of the structures which were the object of reform.

These planned changes provoke questions about the meaning of the word institution. In psychiatry, *institution* has come to be symbolized by *hospital* (as a built environment), rather than, as in Douglas' (1987) wider use of the term, the models of thought and action which sustain it. Thus one can plan to close an institution and imagine it is being replaced by something other than an institution, by evoking the notion of community. My aim in this chapter is first, to explore how social institutions are developed and maintained and how this relates to the experience of individual members; and second, to show how resistance to change operates in social institutions beyond the hospital.

THE CASE OF PSYCHIATRIC HOSPITAL CLOSURE AND RESETTLEMENT

The idea of community care in psychiatry has been debated over a long period, but it is only recently that a large-scale run-down of hospitals has taken place. The policy is generally traced to the Royal Commission of 1930, which introduced the principles of voluntary treatment and of after-care in the community. Gradual changes in hospital regimes and in social thinking reduced the number of long-term inpatients from a peak in the 1940s (Scull 1977), but it was only in the 1970s that an alternative structure was envisaged. The White Paper *Better Services for the Mentally Ill* (DHSS 1975) set out a broad framework for community mental health services, which still relied strongly on a medical model but which gave increasing responsibility to local authority social services and voluntary agencies for planning and providing care. It expressed great caution, however, about the prospects of closing hospitals in a period of increasing financial stringency. In the 1980s, pressure to close the larger hospitals was stepped up. It was assumed that the treatment functions of psychiatry would be transferred to local health services, while care functions would be managed in a community setting making increasing use of voluntary and private care (Ramon 1992). The consultative document *Care in the Community* (DHSS 1981) advocated closure of one-third of the Victorian asylums.

In 1983 the regional health authority which is featured in my study announced its decision to close two of its six large psychiatric hospitals. The motivation for the decision included financial, value-for-money considerations as well as the mounting criticisms of long-term hospital care. However, clear aims and philosophy have never been agreed between the different interest groups involved. Broadly speaking, there are three strands to the motivations for change which remain quite different in their implications for the nature of mental health services. First, sociological critiques of 'total institutions' in the UK and the US had led to a rethink of the supposed therapeutic value of the asylum. Institutionalism (Barton 1957) and labelling of patients (Scheff 1966) were recognized as major problems. Second, medical professionals saw the shift as a means towards greater integration with biomedicine through the location of psychiatry in district general hospitals and local clinics. Third, planners saw the policy as a solution both to criticisms of psychiatry and to the increasing economic burden of maintaining or improving the asylums.

Strategic plans were gradually drawn up by each district health authority involved to provide alternative places for each hospital's patients. The broad aim was to create a community mental health service. Short-term patients would go to a general hospital unit and longer-term patients to community-based homes, with a smaller number of more 'difficult' patients remaining on the site in a new unit, euphemistically named 'The Haven'.[2]

Through an anthropological study, I explored what these policies meant for the people they were supposed to benefit. Few people had asked the patients themselves what their needs or wishes were and there was much concern and debate about how the moves would affect the long-stay patients in particular, many of whom were elderly. Consequently, I planned a small scale but in-depth study, over eighteen months, of the experience of leaving hospital. The main method used, participant observation, drew on anthropological theory and allowed communication to be established with a group of people who had, in many ways, been isolated and forgotten. The study followed the transition from hospital to community-based care in three group home projects, comparing patterns over time and across the different groups of people or institutions involved. The study took account, therefore, of different perspectives on reality using multiple sources of information about this major development.

My expectation of the research was that change would be considerable and in some ways this proved to be true. Life outside hospital was preferred by the overwhelming majority of former patients, who pointed to the positive changes in their environment, the pleasures of living in a house with their own rooms and more ordinary facilities, and some new freedoms in their lifestyle and activities. However, their accounts and my own observations made clear that this change had to be understood in a very limited and relative sense. Residents felt that important aspects of their experience and identity were still framed in the way they had been as hospital patients.

The psychiatric hospitals had functioned as a living environment for long-stay patients, often over many years, the average stay at these hospitals being twenty-one years. The first hospital to close had been opened in 1851 as a model institution for 1,250 inmates but within ten years had doubled its 'population'. In 1985, when the closure plans commenced, this had declined to about 900 patients. Many of the traditional, self sufficient features of the hospitals, such as market gardens, had long gone and both hospitals had been absorbed gradually into the boundaries of the metropolis from which its patients had once been removed. Everyday life was on a ward scale and shared many features of the system described by Goffman in 1960. Numbers living on a ward had declined from about sixty to thirty but this still allowed little room for the conduct of private or autonomous lives. The main features of the psychiatric ward, from the patients' perspective, were:

- a rigid and childlike routine, ordered by staff roles;
- depersonalization and conduct of life on a large group scale;
- lack of privacy;
- lack of choices;
- barriers to ordinary activity leading to loss of living skills;

- ordinary activity categorized as therapy and rehabilitation;
- distant staff/patient relations;
- objectification of patients by staff;
- a structurally defined inability to 'do the right thing'.

The structure of the hospitals was hierarchical, with levels of authority ranging from the general managers and the consultants at the top, to the patient body at the bottom. It was also pyramidal, in that the higher the status of staff, the smaller the numbers, and the lower the status of staff, the more time they spent in direct patient care. There was also a division between the different professional disciplines, primarily that between medical and other staff. If one of the markers of status within hospitals is the degree of distance from patients, then it is perhaps not surprising that relationships on the ward were rather distant. There is also an issue of what constitutes professionalism in an institution which is defined as a hospital, but where staff are not normally involved in acute medical care.

The decision to close the hospitals had taken place at a high level, with little consultation or involvement by hospital workers, thus adding to rather than resolving the many conflicts of interests, ideas or meanings in the planning of alternative services. The hostile attitudes of many nurses towards the hospital closure was perceived as a major problem by community-based workers in the reprovision programme. This was to some extent a stereotype. Nurses' views were inevitably more individual and I would describe them as primarily ambivalent and defensive. The concerns of hospital staff focused partly on their jobs and position in the closure plans and also on patient care and professional values. The nurses whom I met in the course of the study expressed frustration to me over the way the hospital was run and the way they had to work within it, as well as over the issue of closure. Community-based workers viewed nurses as over-protective and therefore as failing to allow patients to maintain the levels of self-direction of which they were capable. Nurses reflected this in their concerns about the welfare of patients, repeatedly stressing how much had been done for them in hospital, emphasizing their disabilities and expressing doubts about whether they would manage outside.

The structure and routine of the ward system reinforced a dependent status which may be carried over into patients' lifestyles after leaving hospital, even if living conditions are very different. The distant staff/patient relationship was also one of interdependence, with staff having responsibility for and some measure of control over their patients' lives. In community-based homes this relationship persists, but in an altered and in some senses closer form.

GROUP HOMES IN THE COMMUNITY

Patients leaving the hospitals in the first three years were mostly housed by voluntary organizations in staffed group homes and small hostels. These homes provided accommodation, board and care with varying numbers of residents and levels of staff support, depending on assessment of 'dependency' in the hospital. Mostly they were designed to be small – from around four to twelve residents – to facilitate a more ordinary and domestic image and scale of living. The three projects studied involved four houses (with two neighbouring houses run as a single project) for between four and seven residents. They were managed by a voluntary organization with care provided by a small number of workers providing all day (or in one house twenty-four-hour) cover. These workers generally had little experience and no formal qualifications in psychiatry and were generally strongly committed to a principle of community-based care.

The group homes in particular aimed to create a different structure and ethos from a hospital, to provide rehabilitation and to break down institutionalism. There were two somewhat different views of group homes: the formal, policy view of group home living, as presented in policy statements and agreements or in staff reports; and the less formal, everyday view, centred on the experience of the residents. The attitudes of care workers generally reflected the formal view, but the closeness of sharing in the home led to some ambiguity for them between this and their closer proximity to the residents' daily lives.

Domestic activity formed a basis of group home life, through a routine which structured time and activity. It was less rigid than that of the hospital and allowed more opportunity for activity within and outside the home. However, like the hospital routine, time was structured by the staff for the residents, and there was considerable unspoken resistance to allowing residents to adopt more personal and loosely structured activities. The contradictions of a routine which appeared very different, yet shared a basic hierarchical pattern with that of the hospital, were brought out particularly clearly in two areas of group home policy: those around managing medication and the use of psychiatric day centres.

All the residents were expected to attend psychiatric day centres, the majority of which, like the hospital's industrial therapy units, concentrated on packaging and assembly work. They were considered an important aspect of rehabilitation, to prevent boredom and possible recurrence of symptoms and to simulate an ordinary working life. However, these centres remained segregated and provided routine work which was poorly paid and could be described as alienating. Problems arose around the issue when several residents in the homes studied, all of whom were over retirement age, attempted to resist the policy. They felt that the work was unrewarding and boring and argued that in ordinary life they would be retired and not expected to work. Although the policy was described by managers as flexible and not compulsory, workers found themselves having to 'persuade' unwilling residents to attend, against their own judgement. In effect, those residents who continued to argue logically against attendance were categorized as 'difficult', through the use of illness labels.

Medication was regarded as the treatment which enabled patients to live outside hospital. Among care workers, this view was not derived from experience of medication effects, but was learned via public knowledge and via other staff in their on-the-job training. It was felt that these views were based on experience that medication makes community care more workable by controlling pathological symptoms, even though the way in which medication was administered made it very difficult for them to judge its effects. Consequently, the medication routines which were so important to hospital life were reproduced in the group homes. Policies of self-administration of medication and reduced dosage, sanctioned by community psychiatrists and pharmacists, were resisted. Residents remained ignorant of the purposes and effects of their medication, except in the vague sense that it was to 'make you better'.

Just as the homes were modelled in opposition to the hospital regime, so the care task was conceptualized in opposition to that of hospital staff. The ideal qualities of a residential care worker – 'caring, practical common sense, stability, patience, flexibility' – tell us something about the ideals of what group home care should be like. They were not classed as *professionals* and were not generally drawn from highly trained or experienced groups. Qualified nurses were occasionally employed, but not generally regarded as appropriate. Managers saw the workers' skills as a matter of personal character – naturalness and an *intuitive approach*. Although staff were given basic induction and training, the main emphasis was on learning from the managers and from other residential group workers during the course of work. There was also a class-based view that professional workers were too socially distant from their clients. The care workers had varied backgrounds but the majority were female and younger than their clients.

The care staff were, on the whole, highly committed and motivated, but during the course of the study frustrations increased which were reflected in an increased staff turnover. They felt that their capabilities were being underestimated in the style and level of training and management adopted. They were aware of a lack of professional identity and status. Some care workers also felt their work was directed in ways they did not value, such as having to spend long hours chasing up DHSS problems,[3] or in having to supervise residents in ways which they felt were unnecessarily controlling.

'Common sense' and the experience of visiting prospective residents in hospital did enable workers to understand some of the main problems facing people who have lived for long periods in institutions. However, they did not have sufficient knowledge or experience to consider how far de-hospitalization in itself would imply de-institutionalization. Changes in environment were expected, in a rather instrumental way, to achieve a great deal. Staff wanted chances to analyse their roles more, perhaps to discuss some of the ambiguities they felt as individuals in their work. It seemed that this was regarded as unimportant, or even as not being a suitable activity for ordinary workers.[4]

In the group home setting, the smaller scale and the valued staff roles ensured that relations between and among staff and residents were closer and less 'depersonalized' than those found in hospitals. This was not simply a matter of being in greater proximity. The main contrast was in the nature of the interaction, with an emphasis on shared activity. Care workers aimed to work with their clients and talk to them in the course of this everyday activity. However, as in the hospital, those who worked most closely with the 'patients' also had the least influence in planning and decision making.

A great deal of progress was made in rehabilitation – residents in all the group homes were able to do more for themselves and for each other, and to make small but important choices in everyday life which they could not manage in hospital. However, the attempts by some residents to become independent in more important aspects of their lives were regarded as problematical, and their activities remained largely segregated rather than integrated in any wider community. Jane, for example, had developed an interest in painting while in hospital and for years had been viewed as difficult because she would not work in the workshops. Now she hoped, with staff support, to join an art class and perhaps put on an exhibition in the local library. Managers simply saw her hopes as unrealistic – symptoms of mania – and encouraged staff to persuade her to attend a psychiatric day centre. Thus the apparent limits of rehabilitation were marked out by carers. Rehabilitation was inward-looking and focused on the group home, or other psychiatric facilities, as a sort of alternative community.

PATIENTS AS PROBLEMS. OR AMBIGUITIES OF CARE AND CONTROL

Why was rehabilitation into 'ordinary' life only partly achieved and why were the group homes an alternative community rather than being part of the surrounding community? How were the changes limited in such a way that the residents, despite the changed forms of address, continued to be viewed in a sick role, in a permanently liminal state? I became interested in the processes by which carers interpreted their responses to 'problems' (anxiety-provoking situations) through projection of problems on to residents.

In staff meetings discussion focused particularly on certain individuals who were thought to be problems. For those residents who tended to question things more, rather than putting up with things that bothered them, their illness was emphasized and their abilities and contributions to the home played down. Their problems in getting on with the group home routines were seen as pathological and as deriving from assumed general characteristics of psychiatric patients. In contrast, for residents who were the most dependent and compliant, staff emphasized their progress and well-being. This view of problems is very significant for philosophies of care, because the idea that mental illness is internal to the sufferer encourages suppression rather than exploration of problems and leads to assumptions that rehabilitation is not going to lead to definitive change. It also runs contrary to the idea that community-based, rather than institutional, care would foster independence.

It could even be argued that certain people or events were problems because that is how they had been defined by those with greater power in the system. Preferring personal interests to packaging work, or preferring retirement to an unrewarding job can be seen as a good thing or as a problem, depending on the viewpoint of the person who is defining the situation. Thus, the ability of care workers to redefine the behaviour of residents may become a way of regulating their behaviour, but also confuses their sense of identity. The residents on moving into the group home were encouraged to make choices, to pay attention to their personal and social identity, to develop their interests. However, when they exercised these choices in a way which was not sanctioned by the carers, they were given the message that they are incapable of making such decisions and have to be told what is good for them, regardless of their intuitions and opinions.

I have argued that problem definition and problem solving by staff focused general and quite understandable anxieties about the running of group homes on certain individuals. In some cases, attempts were made to place sanctions on 'difficult' behaviour by threats of removal from the home.[5] If we think of the range of views as a continuum between the residential and managerial poles, care workers fluctuated between the two. This reflected their working base and roles as both close to the residents' everyday lives and as distanced through their supervisory responsibilities. Over time however, they tended to shift towards a managerial position. Conflict between management and workers' views was rarely directly expressed and tended to be deflected through negotiation or through withdrawal – with some workers leaving rather than shifting and others projecting the source of conflicts on to residents. Parallels can therefore be drawn between the negotiation of experience between managers and workers and that between workers and service users, in which conflicting interests or views are individualized and the overall ethos remains relatively stable.

Care workers were encouraged to feel a sense of responsibility for the general welfare of the residents – with the effect that staff might fret if a resident came in much later than usual, or went out without saying where. The tensions between staff and individuals who were seen as problems brought out the issue of dependency as one which underlies the running of such institutions. Group homes were designed to enable rehabilitation and to develop a new lifestyle, yet they were taking over a regime of care which was established in the history of the psychiatric institution. The uncertainty of staff responses, for example, moving between a view of depression as a normal response to major change or to difficult past experiences, and a use of pathological labels to characterize a problem, points to the ambiguities of caring work in this context. In the group home, the ideology was about caring which promoted rehabilitation rather than control, yet workers' custodianship over the residents and their anxiety to see the home work smoothly contradicted it.

The following diary extract brings out the residents' perspective on such contradictions:

> Jane told me about what the staff had said – that she was the only one to question things. She said she'd met one man in another group home who seemed frightened to do so. She explained that once you've been in an institution you carry it with you, and there is always *fear*, especially fear that you can be sent back in. She is aware that the staff may try to use this fear.

Comparison with Menzies' (1970) analysis of general hospital nursing suggests that community-based care workers experienced similar sets of anxieties and conflicts to those of hospital workers. The anxieties can be linked to a number of contradictions in the role of the care workers. One is the widely held belief that mental illness is permanent, so that only a limited view of rehabilitation or therapy can be formed. Another is the low value placed in British culture on providing and receiving care. A third is the differential status and power in the relations between carer and dependant. One attempt to resolve this was to model the group home as a family and the relationship between staff and residents as that between parents and children.

The group homes were modelled on various ideas of care, but they used notions of kinship for a guiding philosophy. Despite the emphasis in policy on the notion of 'community care', these 'family homes' were inward-looking and little attention was given to social reintegration or to changing attitudes within the family, the neighbourhood, or the wider society. Despite the conscious opposition of the alternative services to the image of the hospital – as caring rather than controlling and as nurturing independence rather than institutionalism – the ideal model of these homes as family-like was notably like that described above for the hospital. In both there was a hierarchical pattern of paternal, maternal and childlike roles. The family model of group home living was a more conscious and positive one, since the gender typing of the hospital was implicit in its hierarchy. The care workers were seen as mothers, charged with resocializing or retraining these metaphorical, special sorts of children. Similarly, managers could be understood as paternal, with a more distant and overarching authority. However the idea of motherhood, like that of all family relationships, was one in which the contradictions of care and control were contained and masked by a model of benign authority.

CONCLUSION

This discussion suggests that attitudes and structures interact dialectically to reproduce or change institutional practices. Consequently we can hypothesize that interventions must address both structural and more personal, role-specific levels of an organization. The viewpoints of service providers attribute a great deal to the perceived characteristics of groups of people who need care – who are categorized alike as dependent or deviant. Professional explanation of the nature of the institution is via the nature of the inmates, using 'natural' principles such as disease and kinship, to articulate the social process. The continuity of practices across a range of settings and throughout a period of planned change confirms the view that it has much to do with workers' role conflicts and ambiguities. It confirms that perception and interpretation of patients' behaviour tends to be guided by the institutional forms. The patient role is moulded to fit with the organizational culture, just as staff roles are through training and cultural learning. We can draw a comparison here with Mary Douglas' discussion of the concept of a 'thought world' and the importance of legitimation. She argues that 'to acquire legitimacy, every kind of institution needs a formula that founds its rightness in reason and in nature', and goes on to say,

> past experience is encapsulated in an institution's rules so that it acts as a guide to what to expect from the future. The more fully the institutions encode expectations, the more they put uncertainty under control, with the further effect that behaviour tends to conform to the institutional matrix.

(1987: 48)

Although, in this analysis, psychological factors cannot account for institutional forms in a satisfactory way, we can see that individual participants use their defensive responses to anxiety in a way that tends to reproduce the institutional system. Thus, while workers may feel trapped by its hierarchical structure they resist changes over which they feel they have no control. Menzies (1970) argues that the social system of a hospital functions as a defence against anxieties experienced in the nursing role, but as she relates, it can be seen as a sort of dysfunction, which inhibits changes sought to resolve such anxieties. In cases of transition from a psychiatric hospital to group home care, we are looking at the formation of new social institutions derived from but modelled in opposition to, the dominant and traditional form. In this context, the pattern of institutional reproduction and change becomes clearer.

The irony is that the community-based workers do not see themselves as passively bound by the organizational culture, but attribute such characteristics to hospital-based workers. The context of ongoing change, calling previous practices into question, suggests that institutional learning occurs in a more active way – a dialectical process – so that the culture is continually reproduced in a form which coheres with its history. As Bourdieu argues in his explication of the concept of 'habitus',

> the unconscious is never anything other than the forgetting of history, which history itself produces by incorporating the objective structures it produces in the second nature of habitus . . . it is yesterday's man who inevitably predominates in us, since the present amounts to little compared with the long past in the course of which we were formed and from which we result.
>
> (1972: 78–9)

Approaches to caring work and responses to its anxiety-provoking situations are culturally acquired. Similarly the worker's concepts of the nature of the mentally ill or dependant person and of appropriate responses are culturally learned and are reinforced through induction into the caring work. These responses are not only recreated out of the nature of the interaction between individual carer and her 'dependent' in the new 'community' context, but from their history. They draw on the life experience of the individuals involved, both residents and staff, and on the previous social structures which set the parameters of their thought and action.

The transition to community care prompted a reconstruction of patients' histories, through the processes of assessment and preparation, of leaving hospital and making a new life outside. However, the assumed history has often been that of a sick role and identity (Parsons 1951; Freidson 1980). Research centred on the patients' experience has shown that people who have lived in institutions for long periods may want and be able to leave them behind, but the structures of the past which order the connections and contradictions of care and control, may continue to frame their identity and so the possibilities for their future lives.

NOTES

1 Other important shifts, not discussed here, include new managerial structures in public services and the introduction of a market model for caring services with internal markets, mixed economies of care and a concept of the service user as consumer (DHSS 1989a; 1989b; DOH 1990).
2 Detailed accounts of the process are given in Tomlinson's account of the administrative process and my account of the process of closure for three groups of patients in Ramon (1992).
3 A substantial proportion of fees for residents of residential homes was funded by the Department of Health and Social Security through a board and lodging allowance. This has changed, from April 1993, through implementation of the 1990 Community Care Act (DOH 1990).
4 During the course of the research I wrote regular reports which I made available to the workers. Although they expressed strong interest in using them for group discussions, managers felt this was inappropriate.
5 In the hospital, which was a place of last resort, other sanctions would have been applied. Among them were the practices of keeping patients in nightclothes or replacing their 'pocket-money' allowance with parcels to restrict their actions. Most important to the patients was the possibility of compulsory medication.

REFERENCES

Barton, R. (1957) *Institutional Neurosis*, Bristol: John Wright.
Bourdieu, P. (1972) *Outline of a Theory of Practice*, Cambridge: Cambridge University Press.
Department of Health and Social Security (DHSS) (1975) *Better Services for the Mentally Ill*, London: HMSO.
—— (1981) *Care in the Community. A Consultative Document*, London: HMSO.
—— (1989a) *Caring for People. Community Care in the Next Decade and Beyond*, London: HMSO.
—— (1989b) *Working For Patients*, London: HMSO.
Department of Health (DoH) (1990) *The National Health Service and Community Care Act*, London: HMSO.
Douglas, M. (1987) *How Institutions Think*, London: Routledge & Kegan Paul.
Freidson, E. (1980) *Profession of Medicine: A Study of the Sociology of Applied Knowledge*, New York: Harper & Row.
Goffman, E. (1968) *Asylums. Essays On The Social Situation Of Mental Patients And Other Inmates*, second edn, Harmondsworth, Penguin.
McCourt Perring, C. (1993) *The Experience of Psychiatric Hospital Closure. An Anthropological Study*, Aldershot: Avebury Press.
Menzies, I. (1970) *The Functioning of Social Systems as a Defence Against Anxiety*, London: Tavistock.

180 *Clients and empowerment*

Parsons, T. (1951) *The Social System*, New York: Free Press.
Ramon, S. (ed.) (1992) *Psychiatric Hospital Closures. Exploring Myths and Realities*, London: Chapman & Hall.
Scheff, T. (ed.) (1966) *Being Mentally Ill: A Sociological Theory*, London: Weidenfeld & Nicolson.
Scull, A. (1977) *Decarceration: Community Treatment and the Deviant: A Radical View*, Englewood Cliffs, NJ: Prentice-Hall.

10 Disempowerment and marginalization of clients in divorce court cases

Jean Collins

INTRODUCTION

The Divorce Reform Act 1969 abolished matrimonial offence as the legal basis for divorce and substituted the principle of irretrievable breakdown. At the same time the Matrimonial Proceedings and Property Act 1970[1] empowered the courts to redistribute between the spouses all the assets owned by them, thus enabling women's contribution to the marriage to be reflected in the financial settlement. These, and subsequent associated reforms,[2] revolutionized both the process of divorce and its financial consequences, especially for women. Nevertheless, the modern emphasis on negotiation and settlement in divorce still does not prevent hostile litigation dominated by lawyers, and does not necessarily lead to an equitable distribution of the marital assets.

This chapter is concerned with the process of disempowerment and marginalization which continues to occur when divorced people attend court to achieve a final settlement of their marital finances and property. The clients' lack of familiarity with legal norms and niceties enables legal professionals to dominate and overpower them, placing them on the very margins of the legal process despite their inherent position, as clients, at the centre of the legal proceedings. A legal culture has developed around the specialist knowledge and experience of legal professionals, providing an environment in which the particular understandings and perceptions of legal experts are held to be superior to those of the lay person.

Drawing on the research ethnography[3] I first briefly describe the circumstances in which people come to court, and indicate the kind of relationship they are likely to have at that stage with both their solicitor and their barrister. I then describe the various discussions and negotiations which take place before the commencement of the hearing, and the way in which the professional role-play of the lawyers excludes the parties from participation in their own affairs. I go on to describe how the continuing role-play of the professionals in the registrar's chambers, combined with their adherence to strict norms of behaviour and use of esoteric language, reduces the parties to the role of non-comprehending and non-participating observers. Although the professionals' intention may well be to defend and further the interests of their clients, in so doing they also extend and reconstruct the power of the legal profession in general.

LAWYERS, COURTS AND ANCILLARY RELIEF

It is not always necessary for the parties to a divorce to attend court in order to achieve a final order on their financial matters, known as ancillary relief. They may reach financial agreement either between themselves directly or through their solicitors, in which case they can apply to the court for a consent order. This does not require the attendance at court of either of the parties or their legal representatives. If they cannot reach agreement, one of them applies for a hearing to achieve a final order through adjudication. In this case both parties must either attend court or send a representative.

Although solicitors are qualified to represent their clients in ancillary relief hearings they often prefer to leave this side of the proceedings to those whom they regard as the professional advocates: the barristers. Many solicitors argue that barristers have far more experience of the court-room than they do, are more thoroughly versed in divorce litigation, and are therefore more adept in the role of court advocate.

From the client's point of view there are two obvious drawbacks to this arrangement. The first is that the barrister is more expensive than the solicitor and has to be paid for in addition to either the solicitor or the solicitor's clerk, who may be sent to court with the barrister in the solicitor's stead. Even where Legal Aid has been granted the fees will in due course be recovered from the client by the Legal Aid Fund under its claw-back procedure, unless the sum recovered or preserved by the court action is very small indeed.

The second drawback is that the barrister will be virtually a stranger to the client, who often feels abandoned at the crucial moment by the solicitor who is known and trusted. Clients feel more involved in their case when in contact with their solicitor, who has probably been advising them for many months and even years. Although the solicitor's specialist knowledge and skills ensure that solicitors and clients do not regard themselves as being on equal terms, a relationship is usually created enabling clients to express their views, even if these are later set aside by the solicitor's advice. As a consequence of engaging a barrister clients are one further step removed from involvement in the conduct of their case. To help overcome this a conference with the barrister is usually arranged prior to the court hearing, so that the barrister is able to clarify the case particulars and has at least met the client. This is by no means always achieved, and barrister and client may well meet for the first time on the morning of the hearing.

The relationship between the client and a barrister is of a qualitively different nature to that with the solicitor. It is highly significant that the barrister is engaged not by the client, but by the latter's solicitor, who is referred to by the barrister as 'my instructing solicitor'. The working relationship is that between the barrister and the solicitor, not between the barrister and the client. The barrister will of course refer directly to the client in order to establish details of the case, will note the client's preferences as to outcome, and will provide guidance as to choices. A client who is resistant to advice, however, will whenever possible be left for the solicitor to deal with. The client is very much the solicitor's problem.

I am not trying to suggest here that barristers work in an underhand way. On the contrary, their role as professional court advocates is clearly defined, and they relate in a specific manner to other members of the legal profession. Their skills are employed in the service of legal-outsiders, but only through the mediation of other legal professionals. In this respect solicitors are legal brokers with a foot in both camps, mediating between clients in need of astute legal expertise and professionals regarded as being able to fulfil that need. Nevertheless, solicitors as lawyers are more closely associated with the legal world than with that of the non-legal. This is a point I shall come back to later in the chapter.

With the solicitor acting as 'buffer' between barrister and client the lawyers perceive no need for the rarified legal atmosphere of barristers' deliberations to be modified in favour of admitting clients to their understanding. Whether in the negotiations between the barristers prior to the hearing, or in the registrar's chambers, clients are excluded from full participation. They are excluded physically from the barrister-only negotiations which precede the court hearing; they are excluded symbolically from the action in the registrar's chambers by their physical separation from the main actors; and they are excluded from an understanding of the proceedings by their unfamiliarity with the procedure and the language.

The position of solicitor as buffer between barrister and client is accentuated by the formal court etiquette which requires that, when before the registrar but not actually in formal examination, barristers ask questions of their client only through the instructing solicitor. The barrister does not address the client directly. The full hierarchy is demonstrated by the common practice of registrars, when they want to clarify a point from the client, asking their question of the barrister, who relays it to the solicitor, who puts it to the client, who gives the answer to the solicitor, who relays it to the barrister, who answers the registrar. Only in formal, open examination does the barrister or registrar normally address the client directly.

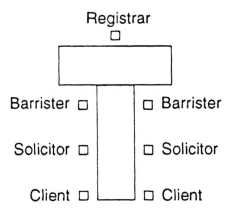

Figure 10.1 Seating arrangements in registrar's chambers

This hierarchy is graphically demonstrated in the seating arrangements in registrars' chambers. In one court studied in the research, for example, there are two tables arranged in a 'T' shape. The registrar sits in the middle of the horizontal part of the T, looking down the vertical part. Everyone else sits along the vertical part: the barristers sit opposite one another nearest to the registrar; the solicitors sit next to them; and the clients sit beside them, furthest from the registrar (see Figure 10.1).

In another court studied in the research the clients are even further removed from the registrar, sitting right at the back of the room. In one case we witnessed the husband had no legal representation in court, whereas his ex-wife was accompanied by both her barrister and her solicitor. To help balance matters the registrar called the husband from the back of the room to sit with the lawyers immediately in front of him, and of necessity addressed him directly throughout the proceedings. This left the wife isolated and alone at the back of the room, ignored and unspoken to. She had the benefit of legal representation, but she suffered much personal humiliation and frustration at what seemed to her the special treatment given to her ex-husband.

In the pre-hearing negotiations clients are similarly marginalized by their confinement, with their solicitor's clerk, to a waiting room. The clients are ushered into separate waiting rooms on their arrival at court, and remain there until ushered into the registrar's chambers. They have no contact with their ex-spouse. All the activity during the pre-hearing negotiations is centred on the barristers. They huddle together in some corner of the corridor or landing and attempt to thrash out a negotiated settlement. From time to time they return to consult with their clients. Such consultation is usually concerned either with checking a piece of information provided by the other side, or whether the client is prepared to accept some compromise deemed appropriate by the barrister. The thrust of this negotiating process is to achieve a settlement and thus make a trial unnecessary.

THE CASE OF MR AND MRS JOHNSON[4]

All these factors are demonstrated in the case of the Johnsons, who were unable to reach agreement on a settlement prior to their court hearing. They had been married in 1973 and had three children. They had both worked throughout the marriage, although Mr Johnson earned the larger salary and Mrs Johnson worked only part-time while the children were small. In 1975 they bought a house in the husband's sole name. Mrs Johnson was given to understand that the house belonged to her husband in its entirety, and that if he were to die it would go, not to her, but to their children. She accepted this because it was her husband who paid the mortgage out of his salary. The fact that she did not contribute directly to the mortgage repayments led her to regard the house as not being joint matrimonial property, despite her own contribution to the marriage in terms of both earned income and unpaid labour in the home. She told me: 'I didn't even think about querying it.'

When Mr Johnson left her by mutual agreement in 1983 it was on the understanding that she and the children would continue to live, for the time being, in his house with his permission. Mrs Johnson described his attitude as follows:

> Well, right at the very beginning he didn't want me to have anything from the house at all. I mean, this was his house, he had worked for it, I didn't contribute anything, this was his idea. I just was bringing up the children!

Neither spouse immediately took divorce action, although Mrs Johnson did seek the advice of a solicitor. However, in the face of her own and her husband's conviction that the house was totally his, she doubted the solicitor's advice that she could successfully claim a significant, and possibly major, share of it. Consequently she felt extremely insecure, and never knew when her right to remain in her home might be terminated.

In 1986 Mr Johnson decided to buy another house for his own use. He agreed with his wife to remortgage the matrimonial home for the sum of £25,000, the original mortgage having already been fully repaid. Mrs Johnson undertook to make the mortgage repayments and gave her husband the £25,000 to use as a deposit on another house. She was happy with this arrangement because she felt that it established, beyond all possible doubt, that she did now have a legitimate claim on the matrimonial home. She felt more secure having visibly purchased a share in the house.

Early in 1987 their three children, then aged twelve and ten, went to live with their father, and in the summer Mrs Johnson initiated divorce proceedings. She was advised by her solicitor that, after payment of the outstanding mortgage, she was entitled to at least three-quarters of the value of the matrimonial home. This took into account the fact that she needed to rehouse herself, whereas her husband did not. Mr Johnson, however, maintained that his entitlement was 60 per cent of the sale price of the house, and that his wife should repay the mortgage out of her 40 per cent. Later he modified his claim to 50 per cent, and later still to 40 per cent, but he persisted in his demand that she pay back the mortgage out of her share. Eventually he accepted that the mortgage should be paid before the proceeds were split, and he then offered Mrs Johnson £45,000 on a putative net equity of £85,000. This was his most generous offer and was still extant when the case came to court in February 1989.

By this time, however, Mrs Johnson had decided that she no longer wanted to sell the matrimonial home. A week before the court hearing her solicitor arranged a conference with a barrister. His advice was that, taking into account the market value of the house at the time it was remortgaged, and bearing in mind the fact that Mrs Johnson had taken full responsibility for that mortgage, then Mr Johnson had already received his full entitlement from the matrimonial home. Indeed, the barrister argued, he had received approximately 60 per cent when his proper entitlement should only have been 50 per cent: it could be claimed that he should repay Mrs Johnson that 10 per cent. The barrister therefore advised her not to offer a further lump sum at all, but instead to offer maintenance for the children.

Mrs Johnson believed that not to offer her husband any further money from the house would jeopardize his willingness to cooperate over access to the children. She therefore decided to compromise, and instructed her solicitor to send her husband a letter offering £8,000 plus maintenance of £10 per week for each of the children. Mr Johnson responded by calling the offer 'a pittance', and by cancelling a meeting they had arranged to discuss the children.

By the time the case came to court both sides were deeply entrenched and the conflict had become highly charged and acrimonious. Undoubtedly, in the negotiations to date, Mr Johnson had made the greater concessions. However, his starting point had been very far from the modern legal concern to give equal weight to the contributions of both spouses. The apparent success of the wife in this case, of wringing from her husband an offer far in excess of either her or his original expectations, still did not represent a settlement likely to be considered as just by the court.

The pre-hearing negotiations hinged, not on whether Mrs Johnson should pay an additional sum, but on whether she could afford to do so.

Mr Johnson's barrister argued that she should sell the matrimonial home in order to release a reasonable sum for him. Her barrister argued that there were no grounds for forcing Mrs Johnson to sell the house, and that no registrar would order her to do so. If she was not to move, had she the financial capacity to increase her mortgage? The barristers went through the figures that Mrs Johnson had provided in relation to income and outgoings. Using a calculator, her barrister initially concluded that she had no capacity for an additional loan, not even the £8,000 already offered.

All these negotiations, including the discussion of Mrs Johnson's personal income, expenditure and life style, took place in the busy thoroughfares of the court's public corridors and stairways. There is minimal space provided at the court for private meetings, and these detailed exposés of intensely personal data are commonly conducted within the hearing of passers-by. Totally excluded, however, were the parties themselves, as they sat in separate waiting rooms with their respective solicitors' clerks. The barristers returned to them from time to time for consultations, but the parties were in no way involved in the discussions.

Mrs Johnson afterwards admitted that she was overwhelmed by what was going on and did not fully comprehend the implications. The calculations of her income and outgoings were so tight that there was no room for error, and yet error there was because she had failed to list all her expenses. She later told me:

> At that time, when he was working out the figures, if I was to give £10,000, he worked out on a monthly basis how much I'd have left. And he was working out I'd have about £30 left every month. I mean, £30! He said 'You could have a holiday with that!'. I can't even . . . it's a struggle. There's not £30 left any month.

In representing their clients during these negotiations the barristers habitually don the mantle or persona of the client. In respect of their own client they talk about 'our income', 'our mother', 'our holiday', and so on, whilst in respect of the other party they say 'your bills', 'your boy-friend', 'your new house', and so on. Although this usage sounds very strange to the lay person's ear, for the barrister it is part and parcel of the job. The use of 'our', 'we', 'you' and so on accentuates the identification of barrister with client. The barrister is not only acting for the client but as the client, underlining still further the responsibility of the client for the negotiating strategy pursued by the barrister.

Mr Johnson's barrister eventually proposed that Mrs Johnson pay a lump sum of £10,000 plus £10 per week per child. Her barrister tentatively agreed but stipulated that only half should be paid now, and the remaining half in a year's time provided that her salary had increased sufficiently. He also demanded that Mr Johnson pay all the costs of the hearing, since it was his fault that agreement had not been reached beforehand. We need to remind ourselves at this point that it was her barrister's original contention that Mrs Johnson need pay nothing further at all to her husband, and that indeed he owed her a small lump sum. Although it was at Mrs Johnson's insistence that a further offer was made to her husband, that offer was then increased by her own barrister.

Throughout the negotiations it was clear that Mrs Johnson's barrister was in the strongest position. Whenever the other side repeated an untenable offer he threatened to take the case straight into the registrar who was, after all, waiting for them. Mr Johnson's barrister progressively modified her demands in the hope of avoiding the trial threatened by her opponent. So desperate did she become that at one point she physically barred his exit from the discussions by standing in the doorway.

After nearly two hours of this the barristers had agreed that Mrs Johnson would pay £8,000 immediately and £2,000 in a year's time, provided that her salary had increased sufficiently. The registrar had now summoned the case and, as they proceeded down the corridor, Mr Johnson's barrister continued to badger her opponent for more child maintenance. She only desisted as they literally crossed the threshold into the registrar's chambers. Maintenance was 'agreed' at £10 per week per child.

In the registrar's chambers the parties played no larger part than previously. The common courtesies of introductions and greetings are not part of the court procedure, and were totally dispensed with. Mrs Johnson later commented: 'We don't know who they are anyway, judge or registrar or whatever.' The parties were given no opportunity to acknowledge, or be acknowledged by, the principal power figure in the room. He did not address them directly, and throughout the encounter they said not one word except in one or two whispered exchanges with their respective barristers. Mrs Johnson afterwards told me: 'I may as well not have been there, really. I found that very frustrating.' In accordance with the usual seating arrangements at this court they were placed opposite each other across a table. They contrived to totally ignore one another, sitting sideways on to the table and looking steadfastly at the registrar. I never saw either of them so much as steal a glance at the other.

Mrs Johnson's barrister briefly summarized the circumstances of the case for the registrar's benefit and then explained the terms of the settlement just reached. The registrar responded that he would not interfere nor withhold his benediction from what had been agreed, but added: 'what an awful pity that this couldn't have been agreed last week'. There was some further discussion about the detailed wording of the order, and the need for some administrative tying up. Mrs Johnson said about this part of the proceedings:

I don't like all this jargon. I mean, when the barristers got together and started talking without involving you, it sort of made you feel inferior, really. And they're talking about you. I know we do it in our profession [medical], but not like that, we do involve the patient, it's their body you're talking about.

Without any explanation the case was pronounced finished and the parties were dismissed. Mrs Johnson had some further discussion with her barrister outside in the waiting room, during which he attempted rather unsuccessfully to explain the full implications of what had been ordered. They then departed.

Despite his protestations during the actual negotiating, Mrs Johnson's barrister did not mention in court the proviso, agreed informally outside, that the additional £2,000 only be paid if she had received an adequate pay increase. Nor did he ask for costs. Mrs Johnson told me that her barrister 'did say to me in court "I don't really now like asking them for costs". So I had no say in it, really. I think I said "That's alright". I don't know what I was saying!' The final agreement therefore, after two hours of bargaining, left Mrs Johnson in a worse position than her offer of the previous week would have done, which her barrister had already described as over-generous. Moreover her costs had been increased by this additional appearance at court.

Mrs Johnson afterwards felt very unhappy about the settlement. She told me:

I'm very angry now, very angry. At the time I was a bit relieved I suppose, because it was over, and that's what concerned me. But after a couple of weeks you start thinking . . . he [husband]'s done really very well and I shouldn't have had to offer that £8,000 or £10,000 really. I tried to get out of it, but now it's too late. . . . I did write to my solicitor, saying – well, how badly I felt, really. And all she said was 'What about reducing the maintenance payments?' You see, I don't really want to do that, because that's affecting the children. What I wanted to do is get out of this paying the £10,000.

On reflection she wished that the case had actually gone to trial, as she had expected it to. She believed that, judging from the advice given her by her solicitor and barrister before the hearing day, she would probably have achieved a more beneficial order had the registrar been called upon to adjudicate. Although on the day she had felt pleased that it was over, she afterwards felt cheated and aggrieved. Could she have done any worse by having had the case tried?

THE PRESSURE TO SETTLE

It may seem strange that the lawyers, having prepared the case for trial and being ready to conduct their clients' case, should on the very morning of the hearing be keen to negotiate a settlement. The example provided by the Johnsons is by no means an exception to the rule. On the contrary, there is almost always a last-ditch attempt to achieve settlement on the morning of the trial, and registrars customarily wait patiently while this is attempted. If registrars feel that insufficient effort has been made by the lawyers to achieve settlement, it is not uncommon for them to exhort the lawyers to even greater effort before finally accepting their defeat and agreeing to try the case.

This is because there is a strong preference within legal culture for settlement in divorce. This preference is not enshrined in legal statute, but it has become established as a principle in the legal conduct of divorce cases. Broadly speaking, settlement, where it is achieved before application for trial, saves time: solicitors do not have to prepare cases in the extensive detail necessary for trial, and courts do not have to set aside time for a hearing. Even when the case is ready for trial and the registrar is waiting to begin, settlement is still seen as preferable for the clients because it avoids the open expression of grievances and anger in the court-room. Settlement at the door of the court might mean that a lot of time has been wasted on the preparation for trial, and the registrar's time might have been wasted, but it also means that the various lawyers can return to their offices sooner than expected and work on other cases.

Many lawyers hold the view that clients often tend to want 'their day in court', but they believe that the experience will not in fact benefit clients. Settlement, they argue, is better for the clients because they agree to the final outcome rather than having it imposed on them by an outsider. The thesis is that, since an agreed settlement must by definition mean that the clients are mutually satisfied, it will be more beneficial to them than an order made following hostile cross-examination in court, which will not have the implicit acceptance of both parties. Mrs Johnson's solicitor summed up a very common belief when she said, 'I like the idea of calculation in negotiation, because obviously if you settle, I think you've won. If you have to go to court and have a stranger decide what each should get, I think you've lost.' Of equal importance, in lawyers' opinions, is the advisability of avoiding the exposure and aggravation of deep hurts and resentments which is almost inevitable in the trial process.

The adversarial principle which characterizes full hearings on financial matters in divorce is typical both of the British legal system in general, and of the system's approach to all aspects of divorce prior to the Divorce

Reform Act of 1969. Before the implementation of that Act divorce and its associated issues had, in theory, to be fought out in court, although in practice most cases were undefended. The 1969 Act established the principle that, as far as possible, all aspects of divorce should be settled without the acrimony associated with fought cases. Cretney and Masson write that:

> it is now the consistent policy of the law to discourage couples from seeking what the Law Commission described as an 'unattainable catharsis' in litigation. Rather, it is thought, they should be encouraged to make their own arrangements to settle any money and property problems which flow from the breakdown of their relationship.
>
> (1990: 328)

The ethos that negotiated settlement is not only preferable but eminently possible in all but the most difficult of cases, has so permeated legal culture that for lawyers to take ancillary relief cases into court is tantamount to an admission of failure. Indeed I was told on several occasions by disgruntled registrars that the hearing I had just observed had been entirely avoidable, and that with diligent and effective lawyers it would, and should, have been settled amicably long since.

Thus in various ways the system exerts pressure on the lawyers, both solicitors and barristers, to bring about negotiated settlements. The resistance of some clients to the terms of such settlements, proffered literally at the door of the court, is interpreted by many lawyers as the clients' misguided determination to fight it out in court: to 'have their say'. Some clients did tell us that they wanted the opportunity to express their feelings about their spouse and the marriage in a formal setting. Such an opportunity is most often denied divorcing people these days because of the conciliatory emphasis of the 1969 Act mentioned above. The majority of divorcing people we spoke to, however, expressed great reluctance at having to go to court: they wanted to settle, but could not bring themselves to settle for what they regarded as less than their entitlement. If one party refuses outright to compromise, and if they are not to go to court, then the other party must accept less than her or his due. The effect in the Johnson case, as in the majority of our research cases, was that the pressure to reach negotiated settlement disadvantaged the woman.

KNOWLEDGE, CULTURE AND DISCOURSE IN THE LEGAL SETTING

Whatever the power and influence of the lawyers prior to the client's arrival at court, which is not the subject of this chapter, it becomes overwhelming once the parties are on court premises. The powerlessness of clients in the hands of their professional retainers becomes acute. The lawyers control the proceedings because it is they who possess the requisite specialist knowledge. Clients, as employers, have to accept responsibility for the actions of their employees, but their instructions are based on their employees' own advice. They are caught in the lawyers' web of power.

This web is constructed from the triadic interaction of knowledge, culture and discourse. The detailed knowledge of the law, which of course is what people engage lawyers for, is also what sets lawyers apart from other people in the legal setting; and it is the legal setting which allows the lawyer to create an aura of superiority *vis-à-vis* the legal lay person. It is not just that lawyers possess a certain know-how, but that they are also privy to the values, concepts and understandings which inform that bank of knowledge.

The statutes of law do not operate in a vacuum or in a neutral environment, but are the products of, and in their turn help to reproduce, a specific legal context. People who are not versed in this legal context and are therefore not privy to the legal culture encapsulated within it, are doubly disadvantaged in the legal setting. They are alienated from the basic facts of law and from the world-view which provides the background to those legal facts. Thus clients, even when they have been told the legal position in regard to their own case, may find it extremely difficult to see the logic or justice which their lawyers assure them is there. Equally, lawyers may feel frustrated at the apparent inability or unwillingness of their clients to accept what they regard as the even-handedness of the law.

This conflict between the lay person's view of what constitutes 'natural justice', and the legal expert's view of the same, is commonplace. One man explained to me how he felt after an interview with his solicitor, in which she advised him that the court would probably award him less than his wife: 'Well, I came out of there totally and utterly confused and bewildered, and really, justice didn't exist in this country on that day as far as I was concerned, because I couldn't see the justice in it at all.' He felt so aggrieved because it was his wife who had ended the marriage, and he felt that her 'guilt' should be reflected in the final settlement. As mentioned previously, however, the Divorce Reform Act 1969 specifically rejected the traditional notion of matrimonial offence and substituted the doctrine of irretrievable breakdown, thus moving away from the importance of the principle of 'guilty' and 'innocent' parties. This man's solicitor, imbibed in the legal perception of divorce, remained convinced that he would soon come to recognize the 'fairness' of the legal position. A registrar, discussing with me another case in which the barrister-only negotiations had almost broken down because of the intransigence of one of the parties, told me that their lawyers 'ought to be knocking some sense into them'. What must be asked, of course, is who decides exactly what makes sense?

Practical legal knowledge, and familiarity with the beliefs and practices which surround, justify and uphold that knowledge, are allied with a third powerful force: legal discourse. This is the third member of the triad from which the power of legal professionals is constructed. Legal discourse provides lawyers with a common language which facilitates mutual understanding in discussions of complex legal matters. The style of English used in law tends to be ponderous, archaic and specific. It is a style largely dictated by traditional usage, and change is inhibited by constant reference to pre-existing legal precedent.

Use of legal discourse helps to bind lawyers together as a profession and to distance them from non-professionals, exactly in the way described by Fairclough (1985) in relation to members of 'speech communities'. The complex nature of British law demands a high level of knowledge and expertise, and requires familiarity with a particular form of English. That form of the language has been developed beyond the written word in statute and envelops all that comprises legal culture. Legal discourse embraces lawyers and others involved with them in the administration of the law, and excludes all non-initiates including those to whom the law is administered.

One of the consequences of this is to cause lawyers, personality-differences aside, to empathize more with each other than with their clients. This is not necessarily recognized by the profession, which has an explicit ethic that lawyers act for, and on behalf of, their clients. As their clients' representatives lawyers are visibly in opposition to one another as, in the Johnson case, the two opposing barristers haggled for two hours to win concessions from one another. However, although they may well be in opposition in any given case, lawyers share a common understanding, not only of the legal aspects of a case, but also of the legal approach to and feelings about it. Very often in our research we noticed that the barrister's hardest job was in persuading her or his clients that the proffered settlement was acceptable, rather than in persuading the opposing barrister to accept it. Barristers frequently acknowledged to each other the problems that a 'difficult' client presented. A difficult client is one who cannot easily be controlled.

Lay people are distanced from the law by their failure to comprehend legal discourse, as well as by their ignorance of the law. Lawyers are hired both to explain the law and to interpret the legal discourse. However, lawyers are not brokers in the sense of being 'middle-people'. They act as both broker and professional. Whereas brokers in other situations usually mediate between client and patron, between suppliant and supplier, it is the lawyers' task to translate their own understanding of the legal position for the benefit of the client. As Paine (1976) points out, brokers' power stems from expertise in two forms of communication, or codification, which enables them to deal on a dyadic level with each of the other two parties. In the situation of lawyer and client, the power of the professional patron is fused with that of the broker and invested in one person, thus giving the lawyer immense power. The absence of independent brokers, and the exclusivity of the legal profession which enables it to present a united front to outsiders, helps to preserve the edifice of legal power. Lawyers are both experts, and interpreters of their expertise.

The purpose of this chapter has been to demonstrate, in the specific example of post-divorce settlement negotiation, how lawyers' legal knowledge is elevated to a higher plane by its interaction with legal culture and legal discourse. This triadic construction supports both the belief and the practice that lawyers 'know' what is best for their clients. As far as possible, decision making is taken out of the hands of clients and placed in the hands of legal professionals.

Yet this is not an explicit or overt manipulation. Legal rhetoric maintains that the client instructs the lawyer, and that the latter does as the former wishes. Superficially this is what happens, but clients act on the advice of their lawyers. The web of power in which clients are caught constricts their behaviour and limits their range of options. They may be unhappy with the law or with their lawyer but they are unable to judge for themselves if anything can be changed in their favour.

Mrs Johnson was persuaded by her barrister to accept a door of the court settlement even though it was less than she wanted; less than he had advised her to accept; and probably less than the court would have ordered. Her ex-husband was similarly dissatisfied with the agreement negotiated on his behalf by his barrister. Both clients were systematically marginalized and disempowered throughout the proceedings at the court, while at the same time being constantly assured that the final decision was theirs. How was this achieved?

The triad of legal knowledge, legal culture and legal discourse generates its own power and presupposes its own superiority. It is perceived by its initiates as placing the right construction on events, and they strive to impose this interpretation of what is correct on non-initiates. Non-initiates are not so much perceived as being disempowered for their own good, but as being empowered by being given access to the legal system. Lay people who invoke the legal system on their behalf must allow themselves to be guided by those who know best how to bring about a 'proper' conclusion. Not surprisingly, people's feelings of confusion and resentment in their dealings with the law, specifically in relation to divorce, are seldom soothed by their enforced dependence on the services of legal professionals.

NOTES

1 The Divorce Reform Act 1969 and the Matrimonial Proceedings and Property Act 1970 both came into force on 1 January 1971.
2 Matrimonial Causes Act 1973; Matrimonial Homes and Property Act 1981; Matrimonial and Family Proceedings Act 1984.
3 The research on which this chapter is based was conducted from 1988 to 1990 by a research team in the Faculty of Law at the University of Bristol. We interviewed people being divorced, their solicitors, barristers and the registrars involved in their cases. We attended clients' meetings with lawyers, observed lawyer-only negotiations and sat in on trials if the case went that far. Each of the three researchers operated from a county court, two in England and one in Wales. One of the researchers was also co-director of the team, together with a professor of law who provided the detailed legal expertise. I was the only anthropologist on the team, the other members being experienced in socio-legal research. I am indebted to my colleagues for their help, support and guidance; and we are all much indebted to the ESRC for funding the project.
4 Johnson is not the real name of this couple.

REFERENCES

Cretney, S. M. and Masson, J. M. (1990) *Principles of Family Law*, London: Sweet & Maxwell.
Fairclough, N. L. (1985) 'Critical and descriptive goals in discourse analysis', *Journal of Pragmatics* 9: 739–63.
Gumperz, J. J. (1982) *Discourse Strategies*, Cambridge: Cambridge University Press.
Paine, R. (1976) 'Two modes of exchange and mediation', in B. Kapferer (ed.) *Transaction and Meaning*, Philadelphia: Institute for the Study of Human Issues.

11 Idioms of bureaucracy and informality in a local Housing Aid Office

Jeanette Edwards

This chapter concerns the public face of Housing Aid.[1] My interest is in the way in which members of a local branch of a voluntary organization act as mediators between their clients and local authority housing departments.[2] Housing Aid workers use an opposition between 'ordinary people' and 'bureaucrats' in defining their role, and this opposition draws upon the value they place on informality. Members draw upon strategies of informality to dissolve the boundary between themselves and their clients and to distinguish themselves from members of state and local authority organizations. However, in order for Housing Aid members to be effective they need to communicate with, and rely upon, those agencies from which they explicitly distance themselves. This chapter will be concerned with the way in which their mediation entails a careful negotiation of identity; they identify and empathize with those who approach them for help and advice, and also develop and cultivate successful working relationships with those who hold the key to housing resources, despite (or hand-in-hand with) idioms of opposition.

The Housing Aid centre which is the focus of this chapter is a regional branch of a national organization. Workers at the centre describe their role as empowering people who approach them for help by providing appropriate information and advice on housing problems. In practice, members often act as mediators or advocates for their clients with local authority housing and state welfare agencies. As a young volunteer, who first made contact with the Housing Aid centre when he was aged 16 and homeless, put it: 'We're on their side trying to get a better deal'. Workers point out that those who approach the centre for help often do so as a last resort. Clients have usually been in contact with the relevant housing or social welfare departments before approaching Housing Aid and perceive the response from these agencies to have been either unhelpful or inadequate.

Rarely, if ever, is anybody explicitly refused help at the centre even though in some cases there appears little that Housing Aid can achieve.

Members place value on what they perceive to be a non-discriminatory service available to anybody with a housing problem. At the local branch of the organization only one example was given to me of an occasion when workers may legitimately withhold their services, and that is if a client makes overtly racist remarks. My impression is that such refusals occur rarely, if at all.[3]

The centre is staffed by a regional coordinator, two full-time caseworkers, a part-time administrative assistant, a number of volunteers (two of whom are generally present at any one time) and at least one student on placement from a college of further education in the region. Students are usually taking courses leading to a qualification in community work. Volunteers tend to fall into two main categories. First, there are graduates, who consider Housing Aid to be valuable work experience in helping to secure either employment in public sector housing or places on postgraduate courses to do with housing management – they generally have their own caseload and their role in the office is often indistinguishable from that of salaried caseworkers. Second, there are voluntary workers who have originally contacted Housing Aid for help or advice and have since returned to offer their services – they play an important part in the day-to-day running of the centre: making tea, answering the telephone, doing some filing or administration jobs (especially those that caseworkers profess to dislike).

The regional office serves an area which embraces the counties of Greater Manchester, Merseyside, Cumbria and Lancashire. The area is administered by thirty local authorities and the centre claims to have a working relationship with them all, although more frequent and sustained contact is maintained with housing departments in Greater Manchester. The relationship between Housing Aid and the different local authority housing departments varies considerably. One local authority has only recently resumed a dialogue, albeit minimal, with the centre after a long period of refusing to acknowledge or respond to requests.[4] With other local authorities, contact is made through named individuals and a rapport is evident in their interactions. In the course of acting on behalf of a particular client Housing Aid workers may also contact other voluntary agencies, housing associations, private landlords and building societies, as well as law centres or independent solicitors.

My work with Housing Aid spanned three years between 1986 and 1989. The main periods of fieldwork were during the first and third years of a PhD project when I spent two three-month periods in the centre. I was also able to participate in training sessions conducted by the regional coordinator and in a conference which involved Housing Aid workers from the majority of the thirty Housing Aid centres in England and Wales. During the second year of the project, I lived and conducted fieldwork in a town on the outskirts of Greater Manchester and within the region served by the centre. Interestingly, Housing Aid members viewed my fieldwork in 'the community' as an opportunity for me to 'go out' and prove 'the facts' which they were offering. Maryon McDonald (1987) makes a similar observation from her work in Brittany. She describes how members of the Breton intellectual movement were keen to present her with their version of how 'it really was' and they noted that her work in rural areas of Brittany would prove and legitimate the 'facts' of 'real' Breton life as they perceived them. I want to explore briefly what Housing Aid workers mean by 'the facts' and what they perceive to be their usefulness, before going on to describe the local Housing Aid centre and its membership.

KNOWLEDGE AND EXPERIENCE: A THEORY OF HOUSING AID?

In identifying what are useful facts, Housing Aid workers posit two different types of knowledge, in short, 'common sense' and that gained through 'education'. Such an opposition, I will argue, feeds into, and is part of, the way in which Housing Aid members categorize themselves together with their clients as distinct from members of local authority housing departments. My presence in the centre, as a researcher and sort of academic, provided additional raw material from which such creative oppositions could be made explicit.

Distilling information into a piece of writing this size involves making generalizations. Events which inform this interpretation do not, in the end, get presented in chronological order and my progressive understanding and the process of making an analysis are not discernible in the text. Events, snatches of dialogue and the way in which incidents are described or recorded by those involved are picked out and used illustratively; they are removed from the sequence in which they occurred and are placed in a different order. This process of generalization creates an order of knowledge perceived by Housing Aid members to be different to, and infinitely less useful than, the detailed, 'factual' knowledge needed in Housing Aid. For workers, the value of research lies in gathering facts which can be used to back up and strengthen campaigning issues. They would question my attempt to generalize the nature of Housing Aid and consider it to be a grave misconception on my part to play down, or indeed ignore, diversity within the field. I do not dispute the diversity within Housing Aid. The perspective I take, however, entails treating the perception of diversity as part of the data to be analysed.

The diversity in Housing Aid is perceived by members explicitly as a function of different localities and hence as a response to different needs and, implicitly, as stemming from differences between individuals providing the service. Similarly, the service they provide treats clients as individuals, acknowledging that each has a particular and unique set of circumstances. By contrast, they argue, 'bureaucratic' organizations see clients as homogeneous, treating them as 'numbers' rather than as 'human beings'.

As we shall see, however, the effectiveness of the invaluable service provided by Housing Aid workers is consistent with their own continual categorization of the social world in which they locate themselves; in short, with their own continual cultural activity of generalizing.

For Housing Aid members, poverty, housing inequality and the inaccessibility of 'bureaucratic' organizations are facts which both they (either personally or through their work) and their clients have experienced. 'Bureaucrats', on the other hand, are said to be middle class, educated, and to have experienced neither poverty nor poor quality housing. Housing Aid workers make a distinction between knowledge acquired through experience which they relate to 'reality' and knowledge gained through education which may be related to 'theory'. In the words of one worker, 'I'm not in the business of theorizing about these things. I prefer to deal with realities; and recognizing there are problems I would prefer to see it simplistically and put myself in these people's position'.

Two aspects of experience emerge from Housing Aid descriptions of their work. The first is experience gained through practice; the effective working relationships which are developed and maintained over time. As one worker commented, 'A housing advisor is only as good as his network'. The second is the experience of life shared by workers and clients. Identifying themselves, together with their clients, as working class, Housing Aid workers point to a common social background. Consequently, they argue, they are able to empathize with and understand the needs of those who approach them for help and advice and, in turn, this makes them better qualified than middle-class 'bureaucrats' to give appropriate and relevant advice.

The knowledge gained through a person's life experiences, through their particular past or 'background', and through their social and economic status may be set in opposition to, and valued above, the knowledge acquired through formal education or learning. It is in this context that the academic pursuit of knowledge is said to produce 'theory', an abstraction irrelevant to the needs of Housing Aid.

I am reminded of Judith Okely's description of her work with a bureaucratic organization. She reports that, for those with whom she worked, academic was a 'pejorative word meaning useless, obscurantist, idiosyncratic, and in binary opposition to the word "policy"' (1987: 65). It might seem, from this perspective, that bureaucratic organizations and Housing Aid are in agreement, at least on the irrelevance of the academic. However, the categories 'academic' and 'policy' are being used to assert boundaries, just as Housing Aid workers use 'experience', 'facts' and 'practice' as against 'education' and 'theory' to make explicit a boundary between themselves and bureaucrats or academics.

I should like to consider the distinction made in Housing Aid between experience and education, as well as the prescriptive rules for how it should be conducted, as part of a theory of Housing Aid. Members would disagree with this inference. In the words of the regional coordinator:

> I'm opposed to a professional body . . . because the minute you do that you introduce the theory of Housing Aid and the theory of Housing Aid and the practice of Housing Aid are two entirely different things. I hope nobody ever gets around to writing the theory of Housing Aid because the theory of Housing Aid is really a common sense and caring approach at the end of the day: and you can't be drawing lines . . . things just instinctively happen.

A 'common sense' and 'caring' approach are thought not to entail value judgements and it is this which is perceived by members to distinguish Housing Aid from other agencies. In Housing Aid the 'caring approach' which treats people as individuals is contrasted with the approach of groups such as the media who are said to be motivated by self interest – 'they're only interested in their story'. Likewise, the 'bureaucrats' are only concerned with enhancing their careers and the PhD student with getting her degree. These opposing values are set up to provide stereotypical images of what Housing Aid is not; they represent the non-equal, single-stranded, formal relationships taken to typify bureaucracy. Housing Aid workers, in this way, present themselves not only as different, but opposite to, formal and statutory organizations.

While Housing Aid workers make this distinction between themselves and bureaucrats, from the perspective of clients, workers may be seen to possess greater knowledge than themselves and have easier access to local government organizations. Indeed, local authority housing departments and Housing Aid draw on a similar pool of labour and some volunteers move into higher education or eventually get jobs with local housing authorities. How, then, do Housing Aid workers not only distinguish themselves from 'bureaucrats', but also suspend the boundary between themselves and their clients? The next section of this chapter is concerned with the way in which the public face of Housing Aid acts to diminish the boundary and play down differences between workers and clients.

A LOCAL HOUSING AID CENTRE: A PUBLIC FACE

The Manchester Housing Aid centre is situated on the second floor of a large, triangular building built as a Victorian commercial centre. The central ground floor space, where once corn and cotton were traded, is now occupied by rented stalls and shop fronts which deal in antiques and collectors' items of varying degrees of quality. Rows of anonymous-looking offices now line the corridors which circle the building and enclose the echoing, central arena. The magnificence of the Victorian architecture is recognizable in building materials and artisan skills which are not a feature of modern-day edifices. The ornate iron balustrades, marble floors and oak doors only add, however, to a general air of fortune lost.

The Housing Aid centre comprises four offices which overlook the Victorian domes and arches of the railway station. When I first made contact with the organization they were housed in the same building but in much smaller offices. The original rooms were cold and damp and faced inwards, so that the view from the cracked window was of the grimy back walls and fire escapes of another part of the building. The present offices are larger and warmer although, two years on, they are equally cluttered. The posters and charts which cover the walls give information on welfare rights, advertise the campaigns in which the organization is involved and list telephone numbers of relevant contacts.

The entrance to the centre leads into what I will call the reception room, to the right of which is a smaller administration office and to the left an inner office. The administration office houses a new computer and the orderly filing system of a part-time administrative assistant. In the reception room the new furniture which closely followed the move of premises has achieved a 'lived-in' look over the two years of occupation and it now blends in with the odd assortment of chairs, lining the room, which constituted the furniture of the former offices. A kettle and numerous mugs, no two of which match, stand on a scratched tin tray near the electric socket.

A further room, entered via the administration office, is at present made over for storage. It has been used, in turn, as an office, an interviewing room, a campaigning base and by various self-help groups to which the local centre lends its support. Examples of these organizations include Partners of Prisoners (POPS), a support group for partners of prisoners, and the Homeless Families Action Group, which was initiated by homeless and newly-housed people to support and advise people who have recently become homeless.

In the inner office a heap of collecting boxes and stickers acts as a reminder of the organization's charitable status. A photocopying machine stands in the corner and on one wall bookshelves are stacked with pertinent literature on housing legislation and welfare rights. The other walls are lined with desks piled high with unfiled leaflets and casenotes, scribbled notes, newspapers and circulars. 'The telephone never stops ringing long enough to get fully sorted', points out one of the caseworkers. Lack of time and more pressing priorities are not, however, the only factors at work in the creation of this ordered chaos. Such appearances connote informality which is valued by Housing Aid members.

Informality is made manifest in the layout of the office, in the appearance of Housing Aid workers and the language they use; in what Anthony Cohen (1987) refers to as symbols of community. The office is the place to which visitors come and as such is the public face of Housing Aid. There are no specific areas designated for waiting, or for conducting interviews. The labels 'reception', 'administration' and 'inner' offices are mine. There is no appointment system. The arrangement of desks is such that interviews cannot be conducted across them; visitors to the centre are either asked to pull up a chair to the desk, or caseworkers move and sit next to interviewees. Housing Aid workers argue that informal face-to-face interaction is more effective than a telephone conversation for collecting adequate information from those seeking help. In general the caseworker who answered the initial query continues to deal with the case and to act on behalf of the client, so that any subsequent contact that the client makes with the centre is made directly to a named member; first names are nearly always reciprocated.

Clients are sometimes offered a hot drink, particularly if their visit coincides with a member 'brewing up'. The same volunteer I quoted above told me that being offered a cup of tea when he first came to the centre made him feel relaxed and 'at home'. The layout of the office, and the offering of a drink, are self-conscious attempts at creating a particular environment. While limited financial resources make decor low on the list of priorities, and the cluttered appearance of the main offices is not deliberately contrived, these are nevertheless elements in the same studied informality.

Adherence to the trappings of informality is a means by which members conceptually include themselves within the same category as their clients, and thus a means by which the perceived boundary between the two can be collapsed. The criterion of informality is used by Housing Aid workers to incorporate clients; to locate themselves and their clients within the same category of person and to distinguish themselves from a wider category of service providers. Value is placed on disarray and conceptualized in opposition to the perceived neatness of workers in state or professional agencies. 'Bureaucrats' are typified as sitting behind their desks, thus maintaining a physical distance between themselves and clients, dressing in 'twin sets and pearls' or shiny shoes and ties, and being privy to information, some of which they disseminate in bureaucratic language designed to intimidate and confuse.

So far I have mentioned informality, first-name reciprocation, face-to-face interaction and social networks as elements on which Housing Aid members explicitly place value. I have argued that they are placed in opposition and contrasted with the values which are said to inhere in bureaucratic organizations. Yet Housing Aid workers need to interact effectively on behalf of their clients with those same 'bureaucrats' who elsewhere they castigate. And, as I have indicated, there is a rapport evident in interactions between Housing Aid members and many workers in local authority housing departments. Although written requests can be made on behalf of clients, most interactions between Housing Aid workers and significant service providers takes place on the telephone. There are some departments which are contacted more frequently than others and, without their necessarily ever having met, a relationship of rapport develops between Housing Aid workers and individuals in these agencies. This leads to a situation where contact is regularly made through a named individual and first names are reciprocated. The network of contacts developed and maintained by Housing Aid workers, as mentioned above, is explicitly valued and seen as a requisite for effective Housing Aid work. How then do Housing Aid workers make sense of their relationship with 'bureaucratic' organizations from which they explicitly distance themselves?

'BUREAUCRATS' AND 'ORDINARY PEOPLE'

We have seen how Housing Aid workers define themselves together with their clients as 'ordinary people', and in so doing, locate themselves within the same social class, making explicit what they perceive to be a similarity in lifestyle and social background. This is then used to define the type and effectiveness of the service provided by Housing Aid and to contrast it with that provided by middle-class members of bureaucracies.

The distinction between 'ordinary people' and 'bureaucrats' is also expressed through a contrast between a commitment to social change (with a more equitable distribution of resources) and maintenance of the status quo (with an emphasis on 'hierarchy' and inequality).

In their role as social critics it would be counter-productive for Housing Aid members to differentiate between themselves and their clients. To acknowledge their power in relation to clients would be to implicate themselves with state organizations and, in so doing, their credibility as fighters for social change, in opposition to 'the establishment', would be threatened. The effectiveness of their ongoing cultural critique is dependent on their uncompromising association with the working classes. At a training session for would-be housing advisors, the regional co-ordinator summed up, on behalf of those present, the reason for their interest in Housing Aid:

> Ultimately all of us really, at the end of the day, don't subscribe to the system that we're living in, and so it's about change. Our ability is limited . . . [we are] part of the working-class movement, we make a small contribution to that.

As social critics, Housing Aid members consider themselves to be part of a working-class movement. Housing Aid workers define themselves, together with their clients (who are perceived to be working class and hence axiomatically part of 'the struggle'), in opposition to 'bureaucrats' whose interest is in maintaining the status quo. However, in evoking the notion of a working-class movement, individual members of bureaucracies can, in fact, be co-opted. In this sense, all those who question 'the establishment' are located within one category which encompasses the working classes but is not exclusively so. As a member of a different Housing Aid centre explained, 'You're on one side or the other. You either want to fight for change or not. It doesn't mean you have to have dirty hands to be working class'. This comment reveals a definition of working class that suspends an association with occupation. Instead there is an identification of the working class with those who, in terms of working conditions, could be defined as middle class. A moral community of individuals is conceptualized, members of which by definition support social change – change, that is, which will result in a more equitable distribution of resources.

In the broadest categorizations made by Housing Aid members, persons are upper class, middle class, working class or referred to as 'ordinary people'. I have argued that 'ordinary' is a class label and is preferred, in certain contexts, to working class. It can include people who, in another context, would be unambiguously categorized as middle or upper class. So although this model portrays a fixed and bounded social world which contains discrete classes, the actual application of class labels is not rigid.

It has been argued, notably by Marilyn Strathern (1981, 1984, 1987), that the idea of the individual who embodies a unique set of circumstances but is nevertheless located in a collectivity with shared characteristics, is an important organizing concept of English culture. Thus, for example, members of 'the working class' can be defined as if they were a homogeneous set of persons with shared histories, experiences and perceptions of life but, at the same time, individual working-class people are thought to be socially mobile and may move up or down the social strata (made up of discrete classes).

Returning now to Housing Aid, I would argue that the same can be said of the idiom of 'bureaucracy' as Strathern has noted for the idiom of 'village'. 'Village' stands for 'class': bounded and internally homogeneous, but forever witnessing the coming and going of individuals (Strathern 1982: 273). 'Bureaucracy' also stands for class. Bureaucrats are represented as if they were a homogeneous set of persons with a shared 'background', common values and a mutual understanding of the social world. Yet individual members of 'bureaucratic' organizations are known to be helpful, empathetic and are seen to be working, like Housing Aid members, towards a more just and less discriminatory society. In this context, they are classed, together with Housing Aid workers and their clients, as 'ordinary people'.

From one Housing Aid perspective, then, members of other agencies may be categorized as 'bureaucrats' with its pejorative connotations and suggestions of power. However, from a different perspective, those same workers, as individuals, can be defined positively as 'ordinary people'. Such statements act to exclude people from, or include them within, the same moral category as the speaker. Furthermore, while the rules of Housing Aid emphasize treating people as individuals and not as numbers, the approach advocated assumes that all clients, as a class, will react in the same way to the type of practice that is prescribed.

'EMPOWERING' CLIENTS TO HELP THEMSELVES?

Housing Aid is often likened by those working in the field to a 'sticky plaster job'. The metaphor of an adhesive bandage used to cover wounds refers to the role of Housing Aid in dealing with the results of what is perceived to be bad housing policy on the part of government or housing authorities. Housing Aid members argue that, in the absence of sustained commitment by government to public housing and without the provision of adequate resources, many people continue to live in substandard accommodation without the means to move, while the malpractice of some speculative landlords continues. Although they recognize that the issues about which the organization chooses to campaign are brought into focus by the nature of the approaches made to Housing Aid centres (that is, through casework), members express frustration at what they perceive as the lack of impact they make on policy or legislation.[5]

An explicit aim of Housing Aid is to 'empower' clients by providing them with the information they need in order to 'help themselves'. The idea of working on behalf of those who are perceived to lack power means that Housing Aid workers talk about successful advocacy as a victory over the powerful. Huw Beynon (1984) describes how, for shop stewards in a Ford factory on Merseyside, service to the membership was given as the most important factor in the difficult job of mediating between management and workers.

> The idea of 'goodness', doing something 'good', is a central one. . . . While they may say that they're not interested in 'scoring points' or 'getting a dig at Ford's', they like to win a case, especially one which management think they have tied up. Victory then is doubly sweet, they get the men their due and they, as 'uneducated workers', outwit Henry Ford's graduates.
>
> (Beynon 1984: 222)

Similarly, satisfaction is expressed by Housing Aid workers in winning cases against powerful organizations. For example, there was general delight when successful action was taken to prevent the National Trust from evicting a tenant, and a strong and vociferous expression of achievement was heard when a local authority was obliged, through pressure from Housing Aid, to renovate certain of its properties.

Housing Aid members argue that officials in state agencies are more powerful than those they serve because of their privileged access to information. The equation between knowledge and power is evoked in descriptions of 'bureaucrats' who are said to make visible and obvious the inequality in their relationship with clients. Concomitant then with the idea that power inheres in the role of the 'bureaucrat' by virtue of a privileged access to information, is the notion that they make manifest that power.

On the basis of details collected during an interview and on any further information gathered from other relevant agencies, Housing Aid caseworkers advise their clients on options available. They argue that if people have access to relevant information they can not only make better and more informed decisions, but also have the tools and knowledge with which to question decisions made on their behalf. But, of course, the housing resources to which clients have access remain limited. Using their status, then, as members of a national organization, caseworkers mediate between their clients and other service providers; they arrange for appointments, make requests and disseminate information. They can sometimes, because of the information they have and their network of contacts, speed up the necessary form-filling and interviews. Housing Aid members are effective on behalf of their clients because they have information, are practised in their interactions with service providers, are knowledgeable of the effective channels through which to work and can, in some cases, draw on a pre-existing relationship with those who gatekeep housing resources. However, for Housing Aid members to acknowledge such strengths would serve to align themselves with those organizations from which a conceptual distance is maintained. Housing Aid members actively work, instead, at suspending the boundary between themselves and their clients. In so doing they draw upon the equation, noted earlier in the chapter, between knowledge and experience and suspend that between knowledge and power. Thus, while bureaucrats wield power as a result of privileged access to information, and clients can help themselves (that is, attain power) through more information, this notion is not deployed in making explicit the relationship between Housing Aid members and their clients. To evoke the equation between knowledge and power in this context would be counterproductive; it would act to distance those on whose behalf they work and to compromise their stance as social critics.

While Housing Aid workers recognize that many clients have a better chance of fulfilling their housing needs with the help of Housing Aid than they do without it, they also realize that help to individuals does not change official policy. As public housing resources shrink, housing authorities continually have to modify the criteria which need to be met before they will consider rehousing a household. In the words of one worker, 'they're always changing the goalposts'; she went on to say that the work of Housing Aid was changing substantially and it was becoming increasingly more difficult to obtain solutions. For example, criteria are laid down to judge whether a household's living conditions are acceptable with regard to overcrowding, or the level in high rise blocks at which young children should live. Standards are lowered again and again to meet an increased demand for limited affordable housing. And while priority status has to be given to homeless families compelled to live in unsuitable temporary accommodation, the chances of people being rehoused due to overcrowding or inappropriate facilities become more and more remote. Caseworkers agree that there is an inherent difficulty in imparting bad news – in giving a negative response to what appears to be a reasonable request.

Housing Aid workers know, then, that giving people information does not necessarily help them achieve what they want. And for them to act as mediators or advocates does not 'empower' clients to 'help themselves'. However, in late twentieth century Britain when poverty as a reality is increasing but poverty as an issue is hardly fashionable, and public debate on social inequality is subdued, if not bland, the fact that Housing Aid workers care, and do so passionately, renders visible the circumstances of those people who, without power, are all too easily ignored or forgotten.

CONCLUSION

This chapter has been concerned with the way in which Housing Aid workers align themselves with their clients in opposition to members of state and local authority organizations. One of the ways they do this is by drawing upon a theory of knowledge which makes a distinction between experience and education. They are then able to emphasize experiences shared by themselves and their clients and suspend, for this purpose, their educational background or aspirations. To bring 'education' to the fore would, in these terms, render visible the distinction between Housing Aid members and their clients. I have shown how the idiom 'ordinary people' acts as a class label, but at the same time it can suspend notions of occupational class or social background and instead connote physical characteristics such as dress, speech, office layout and style of working Thus, what in one context is uncompromisingly defined as a 'bureaucratic' organization, characterized by unsympathetic ears and red tape that needs to be untangled before resources are released, can, nevertheless, contain 'good workers' and, as one worker put it, 'ordinary people just like us'.

My interest in this chapter has been to show how, in different contexts, Housing Aid members include both their clients and members of state and local authority agencies within the same moral community as themselves. Specific ideas put forward by Housing Aid workers should be understood in relation to wider cultural ideas about, for example, the way in which social life is ordered and knowledge acquired. Anthony Cohen, concluding his rich and moving account of Whalsay (1987), points out that our under-standing of the organizations and institutions integral to the running of urban industrial societies can benefit from an approach which provides insights into 'complex and internally differentiated' (1987: 246) com-munities, such as Whalsay. I would add that further anthropological studies within contemporary organizations will provide rich data which will add to a cultural understanding of the societies of which these organizations are an integral part.

NOTES

1 The research on which this chapter is based was supported by an ESRC Colla-borating Award in the Social Sciences.
2 I use the term client as shorthand for those who use the services of Housing Aid. I should note however that Housing Aid workers do not commonly use this or any other collective noun, indeed many profess to dislike the label 'client'. When asked what might be a suitable alternative, one member suggested 'punter' (which, according to *Chambers Concise Dictionary* (1988), means customer (coll.) or an ordinary person (coll.)), but added that it might seem rude. In fact, 'punter', if it were not for its pejorative connotation, might be an appropriate alternative, given the Housing Aid emphasis on 'ordinary people'.
3 Black and Asian residents of the region do not generally use the service offered by Housing Aid.

4 This followed legal proceedings initiated by Housing Aid (acting as advocates on behalf of tenants) against the local authority (administering decreasing and finite housing resources).

5 I noted earlier in the chapter that Housing Aid workers perceive the 'facts' they utilize to be different from the generalizing nature of academic theory, but that the effectiveness of their work as advocates relies on their making generalizations about the needs of clients and responses of other service providers. Here Housing Aid workers point out that campaigning issues emerge from the specifics of casework in much the same way that, for example, social anthropologists would argue that theory should emerge from fieldwork.

REFERENCES

Beynon, H. (1984) *Working for Ford*, Harmondsworth: Penguin.

Cohen, A. (1987) *Whalsay: Symbol, Segment and Boundary in a Shetland Island Community*, Manchester: Manchester University Press.

McDonald, M. (1987) 'The politics of fieldwork in Brittany', in A. Jackson (ed.) *Anthropology at Home*, London: Tavistock.

Okely, J. (1987) 'Fieldwork up the MI: policy and political aspects', in A. Jackson (ed.) *Anthropology at Home*, London: Tavistock.

Strathern, M. (1981) *Kinship at the Core*, Cambridge: Cambridge University Press.

—— (1982) 'The village as an idea: constructs of village-ness in Elmdon, Essex', in A. P. Cohen (ed.) *Belonging*, Manchester: Manchester University Press.

—— (1984) 'Localism displaced: A "Vanishing Village" in rural England', *Ethnos* 49: 43–60.

—— (1987) 'The limits of auto-anthropology', in A. Jackson (ed.) *Anthropology at Home*, London: Tavistock.

Name index

Subject index

accommodation, patterns of 12–13
acrimony 190–2
activism 98–100, 107
aid, development 36
ambiguity 3–4, 59–61
analysis 10–11, 16, 23
ancillary relief 182–9, 191
appropriateness of development
  projects 35–6, 41–2, 68–9, 75, 83

behaviour 5–6, 8, 13, 18, 23, 60, 64,
  77, 130, 147, 149, 151, 153, 175,
  177, 182, 194
Better Services for the Mentally Ill
  (1975) (White Paper) 169
bitching 120–1
boundaries: bureaucracy and
  'ordinary' people 165, 200, 202,
  207; construction of 19; cultural 49;
  development project 75; indigenous
  peoples and 43; selective 14; social
  15; symbolic 145–7; work/home
  103–4
branch secretary, role of 98–100,
  102–3, 105–8
buai 80–1
bureaucracy 1, 15, 17, 19, 38; Housing
  Aid and 196–208; indigenous
  systems and 68–83; interaction of
  client and 26, 143–5, 161–6

capitalism 1, 36, 44, 59, 66, 109
care 26, 135, 200; community 162,
  166, 168–9, 171–9; welfare benefit
  services 150–1, 153–5
Care in the Community 169

case study: community care 170;
  divorce court hearing 185–9;
  Housing Aid 197–8; irrigation in
  Nepal 57–8; life insurance company
  124, 126–8; secretaries 115–22;
  wantokism 79–80; welfare benefits
  service 141–5; West Sepik
  Provincial Development Project
  (WSPDP) 69–73
change: organizational, in British
  welfare benefits service 140–56;
  social 203–4
choice, individual 170, 174–5
class, social 15, 26, 48, 116–17, 135;
  Housing Aid and diversity of 166,
  199, 203–5, 208; NUPE as working
  class union 96, 100, 109, 112;
  struggle 13–14
classification, social 21–2
coercion 118, 120
collective bargaining 97, 102–3, 108
collectivity 11–12, 58, 60, 78–80,
  204–5
colonialism 43–4, 51, 53, 68, 75
commitment 8, 38, 42, 56, 58, 63,
  80–1, 90, 105, 112, 117, 131, 138
commonweal organizations 162
community care as de-institutionalization 26, 162, 166, 168–79
compensation 70, 78–80
competence 161–2
compliance 136, 161–2
confidence 99, 101, 104
conflict 10, 12–13
consensus 3–4, 7, 19, 24, 70, 76–7,
  80–1, 83

Printed in the USA/Agawam, MA
December 23, 2013

583368.044